First Aid
in Pastoral Care

First Aid in Pastoral Care

EDITED BY

LESLIE VIRGO

T. &. T. CLARK LIMITED
59 GEORGE STREET, EDINBURGH

Copyright © T. & T. Clark Limited, 1987

Printed by Spectrum Printing Company Limited, Livingston

for

T. & T. CLARK LIMITED, EDINBURGH

First printed 1987

British Library Cataloguing in Publication Data
First aid in pastoral care.
1. Pastoral counseling
I. Virgo, Leslie
253.5   BV4012.2
ISBN 0-567-29122-7

Contents

*Previously published in *The Expository Times*

PREFACE

In 1968, T. & T. Clark published *First Aid in Counselling* edited by C. L. Mitton, at that time Editor of the *Expository Times*. Of value to many through the years, it was decided in 1983 that a new publication was needed along the same lines.

In the intervening years there has been a great increase of interest in pastoral care and counselling, and in the recognition of the need for it. Groups concerned with training and standards in care and counselling, not least the Association for Pastoral Care and Counselling, have increased in number and efficiency in this time. Training is now widely available, much more so in Theological Colleges than in the past, with a pastoral studies element included in the General Ordination Examination of the Church of England. Many Dioceses have their own training courses and counselling centres. Changes have taken place in theological and sociological perspectives over the years. The present collection of papers seeks to take account of these movements and changes.

One shift in emphasis is immediately apparent in the change of title from the earlier work. To shift from using 'counselling' in the title to the use of 'care' is to indicate a clear movement in the church and in society. Counselling is now seen to require a degree of professional skill, and therefore good training in human growth and development, counselling skills, the different models of counselling, the dynamics of the counselling interaction and so on. With all this, it is generally accepted that those who describe themselves as 'counsellors' should have submitted themselves to a reasonable period of training in self awareness, and have some form of accreditation and continuing supervision for their work.

There is a sense in which all human beings are involved in care. In fact the skills of both care and counselling can be seen to be simple extensions of everyday good-neighbourliness. Nevertheless some people will be involved in work or social groups where a particular emphasis on care is required. Certainly all priests and ministers are required to be carers, as are the members of their congregations. The distinction made between care and counselling is that care is seen to be a response of immediacy to a person or situation which may have to be contained in one brief meeting, or, at times, continued in a caring concern over a number of hours or years. Counselling implies a more formal situation in which a contract, spoken or unspoken, is entered into for the persons concerned to work together. All those engaged in care or counselling need to be as well-informed and aware as possible. It is a matter of great responsibility to enter into relationship with others at whatever level. This book is directed towards those who recognize care to be an essential element in their daily work.

The use of the term 'pastoral' in the title is to indicate that the book is directed towards those who recognize themselves to be concerned with matters of ultimate value and concern as well as with immediate problems and the need of the person before them to grow. These are representative religious persons – symbols of the gospel they represent in a way that enables others to move through relationship with them to a deeper understanding and relationship with God. The work of growth and healing is the work of the Spirit of God; pastoral carers are instruments of that Spirit, as are the persons cared for. The movement of care is one of mutual exploration and growth in that grace that is within the meeting of the 'two or three who are gathered together' to discover something more of the way of love in the particular life situation involved. Through the caring relationship prevenient grace becomes actual grace if the carer can approach the other with that degree of humility, respect, genuineness, warmth and non-possessive love that will enable the other person to respond from himself or herself, and for himself or herself rather than to satisfy the carer's need.

The book opens with an elaboration of this need to work with God in discovering the resonances of life and so entering into the Blessing. The Blessing of God is discovered in growth and development and so the first part of the book follows the stages of growth from infancy to old age and dying. The aim is to give reference points for carers in these areas of life. There are also chapters on some of the escape routes used in attempts to avoid the pressures of life – on drugs and drug abuse, on suicide. Social pressures are related to in chapters on high unemployment, delinquents and prisoners. A chapter on ethical dilemmas recognizes the problems in today's technological and rapidly changing world. A chapter on the Charismatic Movement acknowledges that even some of the best expressions of love in community can have their shadow side, and that shadow side of life continues to be taken up in a chapter on psychic disturbances.

Time is spent dealing with the skills of pastoral care, and the need for referral. The pressures under which all carers work are recognized in two chapters on care for the carers, and the book ends with a consideration of worship and pastoral care as the experience above all by which each of us may grow in ourselves, towards others and into God.

The heading of each chapter states the subject and author. Each individual title is assumed to be prefaced by the general title 'First Aid in Pastoral Care'.

Chapters marked with an asterisk in the list of contents have previously appeared in the *Expository Times* and so have been additionally edited by Dr. Rodd who, in this way, and with his patient advice, has given invaluable help. I am grateful to him and to all the contributors. Their range of expertise, experience and skill is great, and represents a wide diversity of disciplines and points of view, but with the thread of pastoral skills running through them all.

LESLIE VIRGO
[CHELSFIELD, 1986]

1. The Biblical Basis

BY CANON LESLIE VIRGO, ADVISER ON PASTORAL CARE AND COUNSELLING FOR THE DIOCESE OF ROCHESTER

NOT to juggle with words but to set a particular pattern let it be said that 'First' Aid in Pastoral Care is God's aid, ours is the privilege and possibility of secondary aid. As Bonhoeffer says, 'the ultimate word is God's, our word is always penultimate'.[1]

The fact that the 'aid' is God's is fundamental to our understanding of 'pastoral' as distinct from other forms of care. In other counselling areas the carer is regarded as an 'agent' in relationship to the client's needs. In pastoral care the carers are also recognizing themselves as agents of God.

The human race can only survive because people care. Caring is the necessary attribute which makes possible the survival of the infant, the forming of groups, the life of societies and nations. In a biblical basis for pastoral care we begin with the acceptance that the world of humanity requires a caring response for survival and that this caring response in man is part of the image of the God who so orders the creation (Gen $1^{27\ 28}$). The way will then be open to an understanding of pastoral care as an explicit involvement in the caring response of God to man, man to man, and man to God (Lk 10^{27}). The conscious acceptance of a pastoral care role is a conscious acceptance that the carers know themselves to be engaged in the responsiveness of God. Each experience of caring, however brief or inconclusive, will be recognized as part of a whole. Avoiding too high an expectation of themselves, pastoral carers will see their work in an awareness of the whole work of God, their work will be their privilege and their prayer.

Such an approach to caring avoids too high an opinion of oneself ('I am the greatest carer of them all' or, 'I always have to

[1] Dietrich Bonhoeffer: *Creation and Fall* (SCM [1959]), 19.

get it right') or too low an opinion, the sense of feeling crushed and useless when things don't go right. As Paul puts it: 'I planted, Apollos watered, but God gave the increase' (1 Cor 3^6). Here Paul uses a pastoral analogy to make plain the other side of the coin: the person cared for is potentially set free in pastoral care from attachment to the caring person for a response to the caring God. Relating 'pastoral' both to God's caring and to the care of the earth leads to a thesis for a biblical basis for pastoral care: pastoral care is acknowledged involvement in the responsiveness of God. The pastoral carer must possess and be committed to this basic framework of orientation and devotion.

Such an understanding will liberate pastoral care from over-indentification in psychology, and make clear its distinctive quality. Pastoral care will never stop at the sort of aim Seward Hiltner describes: 'the attempt by a Pastor to help people help themselves through the process of gaining understanding of their inner conflicts'.[2]

Pastoral care is care understood and experienced as our human response to grace with others and within others, so that there can be a greater freedom and experience of response for them and for ourselves. Pastoral care recognizes that 'were not grace at work, beyond all our planning or other effort, our human plight would be impossible'.[3]

Looking at the 'response of God' in our understanding of pastoral care takes us to the 'berakah' of God: God's continuous acts through blessing. The act of God in blessing creates growth: people and things responding to God's act (Gen 1, 22^{17} and so on). Within the scriptures God's responsiveness to man is made clear in continuous acting through blessing. This blessing is made complete in and through resurrection in the final and definitive blessing of peace: 'Peace I leave with you, my peace I give unto you . . . '(Jn 14^{27}, 20^{21}).

An understanding of this biblical basis for pastoral care is necessary for all who are engaged by it. First to look at blessing in the Old and New Testaments and then at resurrection as the fulfilment of blessing.

[2] Seward Hiltner: *Pastoral Counselling*, 19.
[3] Seward Hiltner: *Theological Dynamics* (Abingdon [1972]), 38.

Friedemann W. Golka[4] presents a basis of exploration into blessing as definitive of pastoral care. He sees God's continuous acting through blessing as incorporating God's acting in history –the specifically saving acts are pinnacles of blessing. Through God's blessing children are born anew from generation to generation, they grow up, herds increase, and the fields are made fertile.

Golka traces the history of blessing in Genesis 27 (Jacob gains Isaac's blessing by deceit) and in the Balaam story (Num 22-24).

The Jacob blessing is the power of life handed on at the death of the father who has only one blessing to give. The Balaam story presupposes the existence of gifted individuals who have the power to bless and curse. It is this presupposition that frequently leads people to seek out a pastoral carer. We should beware of assuming the role whilst recognizing that we are stewards of such power. Through our response people may both feel and be blessed or cursed. Such is the benefit and pain of caring.

Blessing is not limited to the people who are set apart, whether in the OT or the NT, but is given to all: 'Let us make man . . . and God blessed them' (Gen 1[26,28]); 'and God blessed Noah and his sons . . . I establish my covenant with you and your descendants' (Gen 9[1,9-11]). Especially is the blessing given and present as happiness and growth in those who respond: 'Blessed are the poor in Spirit . . (Mt 5[3]): 'Now the kingdom of heaven is like a landowner . . .' (Mt 20[1-16]); '. . .threw himself down at Jesus' feet and thanked him'(Lk 17[15-19]).

In the NT Jesus' blessing continues the OT sense in the blessing of children (growth and maturity, Mk 10[13-16]), the blessing of bread (Lk 9[16], 22[19], 24[30]), the blessing at parting (Lk 24[50-51]), which is the imparting of peace – that *shalom* which is also the greeting that carries the blessing and the goal of our pasoral care.

This view of blessing leads Golka to summarize:– 'Theological anthropology ought to be concerned with man in his entirety. It is not sufficient to say on the basis of soteriology that

[4] Friedmann W. Golka: 'God who Blesses' (*Theology* LXXXIII, March 1980, No. 692, 83-91).

in Christ man is given a new self-understanding. If consideration is given to man's growth and maturity, resulting from blessing in the Old Testament, and to the blessing of the children and the healing of the sick in the ministry of Jesus, then theological anthropology has to deal with the whole person, with man as a physical, psychic, and intellectual being. God's blessing also applies to the family, village, town, work, nation and country.'

Nehama Leibowitz draws attention to the chasm separating man from the rest of creation in the statement that he was created in the image of God. 'Both the duties, responsibilities and glory of man derive from this. *Zelem* (image) refers to the personal relationship that can only be found between "persons". The personality of man is placed *vis-a-vis* the personality of God. Only as long as man is a person·can he preserve his relationship with God. Man is a world of his own and he is not required to merge himself in nature. In other words every individual is equally significant before God, since every man was created in His image.'[5]

Whilst the blessing of the fishes carries the substance of the concept of blessing that it is God's presence in life and growth, the blessing of man involves him in the privileged position of caring for the creation of God.

'Man, as soon as he was created, received a special divine blessing. However, he was not the first creature to be blessed by God, but had been preceded by the fishes. The content of both blessings is similar but a very significant difference can be detected. Compare the blessing accorded the fishes:

And God blessed them, saying,
be fruitful and multiply

with the blessing received by man —

And God blessed them and God said unto them,
be fruitful and multiply.

The fish do not qualify for a special address to them by God.

5 Nehama Leibowitz: *Studies in Bereshit* (World Zionist Organization, Department for Torah Education and Culture in the Diaspora).

They are merely granted the power to be fruitful and multiply. This is their blessing. Man, however, besides being given the power to be fruitful and multiply, is especially told by God to be fruitful and multiply, and is conscious of his power to do so. What is merely an impersonal fact with regard to the rest of the animal creation is a conscious fact with regard to man.'

The blessing of the fishes carries the substance that it is God's presence in life and growth. The blessing of man involves him in a privilege of care in response to the grace of God. Through this response we become most fully human.

All who enter into this perspective of blessing will see themselves as pastoral carers in the broadest possible sense.

Pedersen in his classical work *Israel* describes the meaning of 'blessing' for the Israelite: 'The soul is a whole saturated with power. It is the same power which acts in the centre and far out in the periphery, as far as the soul extends. It makes the soul grow and prosper, in order that it may maintain itself and do its work in the world. This vital power, without which no living being can exist, is called by the Israelites $B^e r\bar{a}kh\bar{a}$, blessing. . . . Blessing is the inner strength of the soul and the happiness it creates. The blessing may be stronger or weaker and, according to the different peculiarities of souls, it may be of an entirely different kind. When the welter of souls is so diverse, then it is because a different blessing has been laid into the different kinds of souls. . . . All that has the vitality, also has the blessing, for the blessing is the life power.'[6]

In Isaiah 65[8] we are told of a cluster of grapes, 'Destroy it not, for a blessing is in it'. 'The blessing, it is true, originates in God, but as a power of the soul. The seat of the blessing is in the soul of the man, and it is also there that God works . . . The action of God does not fall outside man, but in the very centre of the soul; that which it gives to man is not only something external, but the energy, the power of creating it . . . Therefore the divine power within the man is his own strength, which fills him with pride and confidence'.[7] Again: 'The blessing is the power of the soul which creates all progress; it contains the strength to produce, as well as the mysterious power which really causes it to be

[6] J. Pedersen: *Israel I-II* (Oxford University Press [1926]), 182.
[7] *Ibid.*, 195.

produced, and it contains the full power to find and use the necessary means. Therefore it is related to *Wisdom* for the latter consists in the very possession of the 'insight' out of which one creates the power to make counsels that persist'.[8]

In Judges 6[12, 14] we are presented to a clear case study of blessing. Gideon involved in failure and weakness attacks God. This very strength is affirmed by God, 'Go in the strength that thou hast . . . do I not send thee?'

In this sense we can look to a biblical and theological basis of pastoral care which can undergird, inform and inspire all that we set out to do in affirming and strengthening in pastoral care. Both testaments are rich with images of growth, particularly of growth through responsiveness whether it is the responsiveness of the earth to the rain (Hos 2[20-23]), of Israel to God (Isa 62[1-5]), or of the individual and the church to Christ (Eph and Heb). Growing in grace (2 Pet 3[18]), growing through responsiveness (Lk 1[46ff]), growing in ways which overcome dryness, depression, the paralysis of guilt, the dehumanizing of exploitation, the enervation of unemployment. In the scriptures growth is presented as response to God, more specifically as response to the blessing of God to which we say Amen.

> Therefore with angels and archangels we laud and magnify Thy glorious name . . . (*BCP*).
> And I heard every created thing in heaven and on earth and under the earth and in the sea, all that is in them crying: Praise and honour, and glory and might, to him who sits upon the throne and to the Lamb for ever and ever!, and the four living creatures said, 'Amen' . . . (Rev 5[13-14]).

Pastoral care is the practical working out and involvement with and in the God who blesses. The blessing requires response: it is in our response to the person in need that the blessing is released. 'Between souls which are together there must be a covenant, and this means that a common current of blessing passes through them; this is peace, and through this men uphold each other.' In Christ, in our faith, it is not that we are simply given a new self-understanding but called into responsiveness to

[8] *Ibid.,* 198.

God's blessing with the whole person, with man as physical, psychic and intellectual being. The key parable of the sheep and the goats (Mt 25[31ff]) illustrates that the blessing is not confined to those within the faith. In fact those within the faith may not receive, or be within, the blessing if they fail to respond in caring.

If we accept blessing as the positive aspect of care we need to be aware of its opposite. 'Just as a man may utter the blessing into the soul of another, thus he can also utter the curse into it'. The curse is the dissolution that takes place in the soul, so that the soul falls to pieces and its strength is exhausted. Dt 28 sets out the deadlines of the curse. The effect on man is a rootlessness which is full of fear in an empty life. 'The whole of the soul is made empty by it, and all its fundamental values are undermined'.[9]

Pastoral care is a call to work at the interface between the blessing and the curse. Meaninglessness, loss of value, purposelessness, lack of will, drive and energy, stress, anxiety, withdrawal or aggression are endemic to mankind and in our Western society emphasized by what we call recession but might rename 'the curse'.

In pastoral care it is recognized that the blessing and the curse are always experienced together. Man experiences blessing, vitality, meaning, power always over and against experiences of lifelessness, meaninglessness and powerlessness in himself: the curse.

Every act in love and prayer is a response within ourselves and to others in the discovery of blessing, as is every aggressive movement against frustration. Yet there are particular and special ways that are pointed to in the Bible. Of these ways I would underline those that relate specifically to our human growth. In our care for people with difficulties to emphasize growth rather than in sickness or problem is to offer the possibility of release for the person into a response to blessing.

Fundamental both to theological understanding and to the understanding of depth psychology is that man lives in tension: tension theologically between the blessing and the curse; tension ontologically between being and non-being; and tension psychologically between the shadow and consciousness.

[9] *Ibid.*, 441.

The Genesis story of man (Gen 2-3) sets out the condition of humanity – caught between the blessing and the curse. The way God is shown responding to the need of man sets out the fundamental position of all caring. Adam's 'fault' is to set himself in the centre of the world; instead of responding to God, to the blessing, man is shown as usurping the place of God.

Adam acts for himself, puts himself in the centre of the world. Psychologically this is an act of inflation. Before the infant is 'aware', self-conscious, separate from mother, there is an experience of omnipotence. It is as though the child creates the breast, the world, for itself. As a child develops muscle control and self-consciousness the terms 'good child', 'bad child', begin to have meaning. Shame and guilt are the antithesis of our early discovery of autonomy.

So Adam puts himself in the centre and experiences the loss of blessing – the curse of shame and doubt. Erecting defences, hiding, trying to run from his shame, Adam becomes a symbol for a person needing pastoral care. The voice of God walking in the garden then gives to us the question which lies at the heart of caring: 'Adam, where are you?' The question invites. Adam out of the isolation of the curse and back into relationship with his Creator. There is no provision of an answer for Adam, no expression of blame or sympathy, simply an invitation into response – back into the blessing. 'Adam, where are you?' With these words the Creator calls Adam forth out of his conscience: Adam must stand before his Creator. Man is not allowed to remain in his sin alone; God speaks to him; he stops him in his flight. 'Come out of your hiding-place, from your self-reproach, your covering, your secrecy, your self-torment, from your vain remorse . . . confess to yourself, do not lose yourself in religious despair, be yourself, Adam . . . where are you? Stand before your Creator.'

In his answer, 'I was naked and I hid myself', Adam tries to excuse himself with something that accuses him, he attempts to flee further and yet he knows he has already been apprehended. 'I am sinful, I cannot stand before thee', as though sin were an excuse. Inconceivable folly of man: 'Just because you are a sinner, stand before me and do not flee'.

But still Adam holds his ground. 'the woman whom thou gavest to be with me, she gave me of the fruit of the tree, and I ate.' He confesses his sin, but as he confesses, he takes to flight again. 'You have given me the woman, not I. I am not guilty, you are guilty.' 'Adam falls back on one art learned from the serpent, that of correcting the idea of God, of appealing from God the Creator to a better, a different god. That is, he flees again . . . Adam sees grace only as hate, as wrath, and this wrath kindles his own hate, his rebellion, his will to escape from God. Adam remains in the Fall'.[10]

This is Dietrich Bonhoeffer's graphic commentary on the Fall. In it he describes our human plight and flight which leads us all to look for care and help – and he describes the Act of God – calling us out from hiding, to stand before our Creator and be accepted as we are, for whom we are. The heart of pastoral care lies in acceptance – accepting without judgment the person before us. The question, 'Where are you?', is addressed to us all. When someone comes to us for help, he is saying, 'I am here, in this particular pain or problem'. Whenever we go out to care for another we are responding to the 'Where are you?' of God:

> I am here wanting to greet the Christ in my brother, in my weakness to be ready to be exposed for his sake.

David, where are you? is the question Nathan places within his parable to the king (2 Sam 12). 'Jesus said to her, Go call your husband' (Jn 4[16]). Jesus says to the rich young man, 'Go and sell all you have and give the money to the poor' (Mt 19[21]). 'Zacchaeus, come down' (Lk 19[5]). Ways of saying, 'Where are you? Stand before God as you are – by this response come back into the blessing.'

Pastoral care described in this way has all the height and depth and length and breadth of the love of God about it (Eph 3[14-19]). The skill of pastoral care is in discovering the best response for the person before us. Job's friends were no doubt sincere and certainly were attempting to get Job back into the blessing in the way they thought right. The fault in the friends is that they assumed they knew what Job must do to respond to the 'Where are you?' and stand before his Creator. They were wrong (Job 13-14). Job's need was to say, 'I'm here – outraged, deserted, angry, let down –

[10] Bonhoeffer, *op. cit.,* 19.

why have you done this to me, God?' (Job 16⁷). How well Job's feeling may find reflection in a person who has lost a job after thirty years' loyal service. Such a man feels under the curse, cut off, depleted, wrung out. The first need is to have someone who can simply accept as anger, hurt and fear are expressed.

God blesses as he accepts, his blessing is a sign of his acceptance, and an invitation to greater response. The pastoral carer will always be endeavouring to help others to do more for themselves rather than acting on their behalf. Jesus does not live our life for us – his caring calls us into a greater responsiveness.

Jesus the carer lives out his life in responsiveness to God and man. 'When ye have lifted up the Son of man, then shall ye know that I am he, and that I am doing nothing of myself; but as the Father taught me, I speak these things, and he that sent me is with me; he hath not left me alone: for I do always the things that are pleasing to him' (Jn 8²⁸⁻²⁹). He incarnates the blessing –the vital life and power of being. At that time when he responded to the question, 'Where are you?' in Gethsemane those to whom he looked for care were sleeping (Mt 26³⁶⁻⁴⁶). He stays alone in his dread, accepting both the emptiness and meaninglessness of the curse, and the demand of the blessing which pulls him into the life of resurrection through the death on the cross.

In the end the blessing is expressed in life through death. Death is a word which collects meaning to itself as a child discovers things that don't move, react, respond. It is unresponsiveness that is at the heart of the substance given to the word 'death'.

To enter the blessing we must push against unresponsiveness. From the first breath of life we are faced with unresponsiveness – faced with little deaths. The mother who does not feed us. The legs that will not walk for us. It is as we push against these unresponsivenesses of life that we gain our true stature – we discover ourselves. As we do, we discover and are discovering responsiveness. Each movement we make in growth is a movement into the blessing of God; each time we overcome inertia we experience living through death – living through the unresponsiveness. To do this is to begin the experience of resurrection. The resurrection is the statement of Christ's overcoming unresponsiveness - in himself – in his disciples – and in the world. Inviting our following of his way he invites us to inherit the blessing, the abundant life of responsiveness. Each act in care as it struggles with those who are trapped, momentarily or chronically in unresponsiveness, is an act aimed at working with the vital force of God in his blessing as the person cared for moves forward to a new ability to think, act and speak for himself so he moves forward into resurrection.

In the blessing of his disciples Christ draws them into peace and sends them out as agents of that peace, and that is pastoral care.

2. Children and the Family

By Leslie Virgo

The daunting nature of pastoral care is that it spans the whole range of human experience. The carer will be involved at one moment with an experience of birth, at the next be at the side of someone dying of old age. In this kaleidoscopic range of experiences, which make up life itself, there is no way in which answers can be available to meet every situation of growth, development, decay and death.

In this the pastoral carer is not unlike the parents in a family. However readily people may turn to the Dr. Spocks of this world for instant remedies and guidance, the complexity of family life and human development will always escape the best endeavours to structure and order it.

To enter the adventure of parenthood is to launch out onto an unknown sea which will be both unutterably beautiful and inexpressibly fearful. To be a parent is no easy option.

Pastoral carers are in many respects parents. The carer's most helpful attitude towards another will be expressed in an absorbed and empathetic response to the person, similar to that a good mother will show to her baby.

If there are not rules and orders for parents or carers to set against life's possibilities and problems, there are attitudes and guidelines that can be of help for both parents and carers in their task.

Acknowledging that parents face a daunting task, let us go a stage further back and think first of pregnancy and then of the child.

Even before birth it is now recognized that infants react to the mother's emotional states and activities whilst within the womb. The needs of the pregnant mother for care are often overlooked. The naturalness of the event, and its private nature in spite of its public expression, may often disguise the fact that pregnancy can be both threatening and fearful for some people.

Family support is often absent today. A husband struggling to cope with work and his own uncertainties may be unable to help. It is important for carers to be aware of the possible needs of mothers in pregnancy for valuing, reassurance, and perhaps encouragement to tell the people at the clinic, or the health visitor, of their hidden fears.

For the infant, to be required to leave the secure, stable environment of the womb for the disordered, harsh and noisy world outside is perhaps the greatest trauma of all to experience. When a child is born there is a cutting of the unbilical cord: an experience of separation and shutting out. The imagery of the garden of Eden and the flaming sword must gain a lot of its power from this primary event in our lives.

The way in which an infant is received into the world can establish a pattern for the rest of life which may lead to healthy growth or difficulties in development. If we can understand the basic needs of a child who is to grow well and healthily in its emotional life, then we can be possessed of a tool that will help us in all our relationships with others – a tool which can also help parents in their care of their children.

Dr. Frank Lake, in his work on Clinical Theology[1], looks to these primary needs of the child. He describes a 'dynamic cycle' of response which needs to be built up for and by the baby. He suggest that the first and most fundamental need of the child is to be held. Simply because this work of pro-creation, this result of a shared act of creation, this child of life, child of God, is a unique and invaluable 'new world'. Every child has a right to be accepted and affirmed in a way which will say 'you are beautiful', 'you are safe with me'. Unfortunately, many children are not given this open loving. There is a sense in which the whole idea of 'non-judgmental' caring has grown from this primary need. The idea of non-judgmental caring is often mistakenly seen as a caring that encourages moral laxity – it is, in fact, a way of describing the movement of 'acceptance'. This direct and uncomplicated acceptance of the child is the first and greatest need. It is a need, moreover, not only of the child, but of every human being. Anyone who takes time to write down all that they experience when they feel 'accepted' will see

[1]Lake, Frank, Clinical Theology (London, Darton, Longman and Todd), 1966.

how basic it is at all times to help someone feel this. Just to begin such a list: valued, freed, relaxed, happy, alive, safe, and so on. It is, of course, a description of that which we all receive of the love of God without reservation or condition.

Given an experience of acceptance the infant searches for feeding. The newly born may be likened to a computer awaiting a programme. The experience of the first hours, days –even of the first few years – of life will lay the basis in the individual of bed-rock feelings which will govern the responses made to all the question which future life will contain.

The way, then, in which a mother feeds her baby will be establishing much more than feeding the body. The anxious and worried mother will be feeding-in to the child a sense of worry and anxiety – a sense that the world is an insecure and fearful place; the self-centred and preoccupied mother will make the child feel of little or no value in itself; the angry and resentful mother will be saying 'you are just a nuisance – not wanted – not loved'. The fortunate mother who responds warmly, sensuously and lovingly to her child will not only be sustaining the child but enriching its whole being.

Sustenance, then, feeding and the way of feeding, may be seen to be the next necessary stage of care for normal development. Not only for parents but for ministers and carers, the concept of giving good sustenance will be seen as essential. Here it needs to be realized that it is in the repetition of the experience that security is built up. Learning comes from reflection on experience.

This serves as a reminder of the need for care to be given consistently, not offering to do more than can be followed through and accomplished.

The way in which care is given – from positions of superiority, with a 'lady bountiful', know-it-all, demeaning attitude towards the cared for, or with a real concern to put the person in the centre and attend to their needs – will make the difference between damaging and harmful and rich and effective caring.

Given good 'acceptance' and 'sustenance', having its needs dealt with and being placed comfortably in a cot, the child may be expected to show some satisfaction with itself. A state of well-being, contentment and being at rest will be building in the child the sense of 'for me to be is good'. The *status* the child gains at these moments of richness builds up a personal pattern of 'alrightness'. Christians are told that unless they can love themselves they cannot love their neighbour (Mark 12[31]). It is at this early stage of life that we are first helped to love ourselves – or not!

One problem of parenting can be that the parents have never learnt to value themselves. In its most difficult expression this can lead to that state described as puerperal despression in the mother. A mother, lacking value in herself, will be overwhelmed by the needs of the baby. Again and again in care situations it becomes clear that a person's inability to value him or herself lies at the heart of the problem.

Christ, knowing himself accepted and sustained by the Father can say of himself: 'I am', 'I am the bread of life, the vine, the living water . . .'. So every human being needs to accept and value his or her own incarnation – each of us able to say 'I am', and at times, for someone, 'I am the bread of life . . .'.

Both mother and father are gods to the child. Our first awareness of that which is greater than ourselves upon which we must depend for life comes from the parents. In this way the face of God in later life can often be the face of the parent. Not all parents are loving and kind. Many children suffer under persecuting, dominating, judgmental parents, or weak and ineffective parents. Before helping a person to relate to God it is as well to try and discover the picture the word creates for them. For many people the process of counselling or psychotherapy will be a process within which the therapist can help the person to grow through their childhood again and so discover a new attitude towards themselves, a new sense of value in themselves; from this can spring a new way of knowing and responding to God. All of our engagements with others are doing something to model what the love of God means in act, rather than simply in sermons.

From a sense of good *status* the infant, awakening to the world from a contented sleep, can then begin to explore its own abilities and the world around it. *Achievement* for the

well cared for child will be a going out from the self in exploration and creation.

Christ's works were not for his own glory but 'to do the will
of him who sent me'. His signs pointed not to himself but
beyond himself to the Kingdom, to the Father.

Insecurity and uncertainty can lead both parents and carers
to go out in an effort to achieve in order that others will be
impressed. Works to gain applause and a pat on the back are the
root cause of many breakdowns. This happens because the
'cycle' of 'acceptance', 'sustenance', 'status' and 'achievement'
has been reversed. The person who has not been properly
accepted and so is unable to accept him or herself or feel openly
acceptable to God will set out on a proving course. The argument for this activity is 'if I do well I will be given status, if I
have status I shall feel sustained and so accepted'. Unfortunately this is a treadmill: more and better *works* must now be
produced to gain the same amount of favour. Life gets to be
increasingly frenetic until there is just not the time or the
energy to keep up with it all, and at this point the underlying
suspicion is proved to be true: 'I am useless, unacceptable'.

The understanding of this circle of acceptance, sustenance,
status and achievement can provide a valuable tool for the
ministers and carers to set, not only against the life of others,
but also, more importantly, against their own.

Erikson's[2] understanding of development is now followed
since it again provides insight and guidance for parents and
carers alike.

Given a good enough beginning the child will learn to *Trust*
. . . . Like these dots, experience must be repeated often
enough and consistently enough for a pattern to be established,
and a trust produced in a sufficient 'hope' in the continuity of
life. People who suffer from too great a disturbance to their
environment, both in infancy and later life, may well withdraw
into what others will describe as 'sickness' or even 'madness':
but for those children, those people, the world outside will
appear the 'mad' world. However, too safe an environment can
make someone too trusting. There is a need to mistrust as well

[2] Erikson, Erik H., *Childhood and Society* (New York, Norton), Revised 1963.
Identity and the Life Cycle, (New York, Norton), 1980.

as to trust, otherwise no one would cross the road safely!

Mothering can be an exhausting task; it is always demanding, but the rewards can be immeasurable. It is as well for mothers and fathers to realize that the worst sort of parenting would be doing it too well. 'A mother must fail in satisfying instinctual demands, but she may completely succeed in not "letting the infant down", in catering for ego needs, until such a time as the infant may have an introjected ego-supportive mother, and may be old enough to maintain this introjection in spite of failures of ego support in the actual environment'.[3] Children must learn to *mistrust* since an essential element in development is the coming to terms with incompleteness and failure in the self.

Should all an infant's demands and needs be met then it would remain with a sense of *omnipotence*, feeling that the world owed it a living. An adult behaving from this perspective is usually called a psychopath. The child needs to be met with some firm and clear 'no's', restrictions, un-responsiveness, in order to be brought from an 'I'm the king of the castle' state to a sense of its true potency. Parents may need help in saying no – carers often need even more help, since the Christian idea of loving availability can lead to a feeling that one must respond at all times and in all ways without counting the cost. Such an inability to say 'no' can do irreparable harm to the cared for since it fails to help them discover their own real strengths. Many ministers and carers will work unstintingly to care for others at the expense of themselves and their own homes and families. What sort of a model of valuing does this extend to the person cared for? What guilts do the cared for eventually have to carry because they have let themselves be used to enable the carer to avoid his real priority and responsibility? It is in these sorts of situations that the need for care for the carers is made so apparent.

As children learn to control their own muscles they move into *autonomy*. The ability to choose to act or not to act in certain ways brings both the chance of pleasing and of hurting mother. Toilet training is often the area of greatest learning.

[3] Winnicott, D.W., 'The Antisocial Tendency' (1956), in *Through Paediatrics to Psycho-Analysis* (London, Hogarth), 1978.

This stage of growth and the attitude of the parent can once again have long term effects for good or ill. Parents who require strict adherence to boundaries and rules, suppressing all natural responses, will be in danger of producing obsessional adults who cover their anger and rebellion under an aura of perfection and rigidity.

To be required to live to an ideal standard can only produce failure. When the church teaches 'be ye therefore perfect as your heavenly father is perfect' (Mt 5:48) she is inviting a depressive reaction in her people who, for all their striving, will remain 'miserable sinners'[4] missing the mark. When people are valued for what they can do, the response in a release of energy and well-being can be immense. Failure to value, criticism and denigration, lead to a sense of shame and doubt. Many children have to grow up in an atmosphere of constant criticism from parents who are so intent on their children 'succeeding' that they lose sight of the person in the child.

Shame and doubt need not just be negative. To accept and love ourselves does not mean that we shall never fail, nor have a sense of shame at failing as a spur to future action. Children and parents who become stricken by a sense of failure in themselves need to be helped to see that while it is human to say 'I have failed', it is blasphemy to say 'I am a failure'! For both parents and carers the most releasing and rewarding moments can come when it is possible to say to children, spouse, or the person cared for, 'I'm sorry, I made a mistake'. Children can be intensely exasperating. Parents, worried and anxious about many things, can reach the end of their tether and snap out, or slap out, in anger. At such times it can be healing and relating to tell the child that it was an over-reaction, and not all their fault. When ministers and carers are faced with violence or baby battering it is incumbent upon them to remember that we all have the seed and root of violence within ourselves and to seek to understand and accept the person, not in condoning the act but in attempting to understand the stress precipitating the action.

The growing child discovers increasing ebulliance and the

4 Litany, Book of Common Prayer.

ability to initiate activity for itself. This phase of growth is linked with infantle sexual development where sexuality is
experienced as that life-promoting, self-reproducing energy
which is both so exciting to observe in the four to six year old
and can be so exhausting to live with. This is a time of developing *initiative* in the child; a time of excitement and enquiry
when the world is full of questions and wonder; a time of
exploration and discovery. In so far as we can, all of us –
parents, ministers, carers – need to be in touch with this element of the child within ourselves, the child of whom Christ
says 'unless you become like a little child you cannot enter into
the Kingdom' (Mk 10:15).

This period is also a time when *guilt* can have real meaning
for the child. The ability to hurt others can lead to experiences
of real guilt. The inability to reach a standard can bring guilt
and a spur to action, or, when the standard set is 'ideal', can lead
to neurotic guilt.

Caring for parents may often involve helping them to relax
from impossibly high standards for themselves and their
children – a fault which is particularly noticeable in dealing
with first children. It is a recognized phenomenon that first
children tend to grow up as serious, responsible and at times
slightly depressed adults.

Many carers are first children who are simply continuing
their childhood by going on looking after the family. Such an
influence upon our lives by our primary family needs to be
looked at further.

Families provide an 'object relations' world in which the
child will grow. Before knowing the people who surround us in
our infancy as 'persons' they appear as 'objects' that are met up
with and reacted to. Mother, father, siblings, relatives all play
their part in forming the world of the infant in such a way as to
fix it indelibly as the 'assumptive' world – that is, the way that
will always be assumed to be 'the way the world is'.
Measurements of people and life are given initially in primary
family modelling. The way a person feels about men, women,
mothers, fathers, brothers, sisters; attitudes to jealousy, pain,
anger, spontaneity, rejection; all are 'given' in this initial
experience of what the world is like. However many painful

elements this view of the world may contain, however many 'lies' it incorporates – such as the feeling that you, the middle child, are not really of very much use – this is the way the adult goes on seeing the world. The more family histories are examined the clearer it becomes that the world of the child continues to be the world of the adult, even if people in that world are made to behave in ways which will fit the stereotypes of the past. 'The fathers have eaten sour grapes and children's teeth have been set on edge' (Jer 31:29; Ezek 18:2).

Breaking free from the moulding of the past is no easy thing. The greater the ability for self awareness, the greater the possibility of making one's own world and acting responsibly in it.

The time of latency in childhood, when many of the more explosive feelings of infancy are under wraps, is a time of *industry*. This is the time when the child learns to give up some part of itself in order to engage with, and share with, others. Inability to do so may spring from a deep sense of *inferiority*. Increasingly the parents may be made to feel inferior by their children. It is certainly a characteristic of many families that parents lose the ability to share in the industry of their children in adolescence.

It is also characteristic of the 'helping personality' that people who feel inferior in themselves may cover up their own sense of weakness by great activity and a need never to be seen as failing, angry or bad. Such lack of genuineness, in parents or in carers, cuts dead any real growth for and with others since it is only as we can love ourselves that we can love our neighbours.

The reminder of the way children may make parents feel inferior is an indication of the fact that the child makes the parent, as well as the parent making the child.

A family is a dynamic group, subject to all the pressures, defences, acting out, pairing and other basic assumptions of all groups. Those involved in care who would like to be more aware of the interactions of family life in order to be available to work with families should approach their local Family Therapy unit and seek training and help – such units are also an important resource for referral. Feelings have a logic of their own, and the most apparently intractable of family complexities can often be resolved when someone skilled in working with families is able to help those involved become aware of the interactions that are taking place.

One most necessary understanding of relationships within the family is that of 'boundaries'. A parent needs to respect a child, giving to it its own space in which to develop and grow whilst guarding the child from impingement. Every child has a right to be him or herself within reasonable limits – that is, each child has a boundary within which it should be free to 'be', and also clear demarcation points which limit freedom in order to enable socialization. Parents also have a right to space for themselves separate from their children and private to themselves. The most frequent disturbances in family life arise from the diffusion and breaking of clear boundaries, which should define:

1.   The child's private space.
2.   The parents' boundary for the child.
3.   The parents' own space for one another.
4.   The parent's own space for one another.
5.   Each parent's space for himself or herself separate from each other and the family.[5]

Should any of these boundaries become blurred or broken, stress and trouble arise in the family. Troubled families frequently make one family member responsible for the 'sickness' and present them as the identified 'patient' or 'problem person'. The minister and carer needs to be very aware of these possibilities particularly as they may be approached as those who will bring the authority and imprimatur of God onto the labelling.

Pastoral care often means that the carers are involved in a social, day to day meeting with others with whom they may at any time take on a more specifically caring role. This day to day acquaintance with families means that they can be particularly aware of the nature of the boundaries, and may be able to help the family gain new perspectives. However, unaware carers may well invade and destroy the family balance as they collude with one member (for example, the church-orientated) against

[5] Gibran, Kahlil, *The Prophet* (London, William Heinemann), 1980, p.16.

another, or as they align themselves with parents against children, or with one partner against another. Caring can be destructive!

The need for boundaries within the family underlines the need for all involved in care to be very careful to have clear boundaries for themselves. One of the great difficulties is the confusion that can arise when one person is required to operate in a variety of roles towards another.

Finally the example of the Holy Family may best be used to set against our understanding of children and the family. The mother who swaddles her child and makes him secure, nurtures and cares for him. Joseph, the symbol of the 'guardian' father, standing at the door of the cave, protecting the mother and child, leading them into safety in Egypt. Mary and Jospeh struggling with boundaries following the visit to Jerusalem (Lk 2:41ff); Mary, Joseph and Jesus, a family which is both trinitarian in its togetherness and in its separateness. It is a good family model.

3. Adolescence

By Tim Russ, Tutor-in-charge,
Foundation Course in Youth and Community Work
YMCA National College

The world of the adolescent often seems a mysterious one for those who view it from without. If it appears confusing and threatening, mysterious and ever-changing, this may be because that is how it appears from within. Adolescence means 'growing-up'; it is by definition a period of transition from one state to another. Inevitably, it is a period of change and therefore it is very hard to pin down those who are passing through it.

The problems associated with adolescence begin when we try to pinpoint the ages to which it refers. When does it begin and end? The usual limits are put at about 12 and 20, but this in many ways is not helpful. Adolescence begins younger in each decade, and many of the commercial exploitations of young people begin now at the ages of 9-10, with the specific marketing for this age group of pop-groups, clothes and magazines. The law marks the end of childhood with different and often confusing 'enfranchisement' at ages differing from 13 to 21. Different reponsibilities are given at very different stages and in a haphazard way. The word 'teenage' was not used widely until 1958, and then only in terms of consumer spending for the age range of 15-25. In many ways, an extended period of adolescence is a twentieth century western phenomenon, where the period of transition from child to adult is drawn out, with no clear landmarks and with no obvious links to work, family, or religious responsibility.

Given the problem of accurate definition of the age of adolescence, and the fact that it may at least be partly a commercial creation, are there identifiable attitudes and 'typical' behaviour patterns for the various stages? Probably the first stage is that of the sudden physical changes of puberty that are so often associated with clumsiness, confusion and unpredictability. Preparation for young people approaching this stage will help them be aware of what will happen, but it will still be a time of pain, embarassment and guilt that cannot really be understood at the time. Part of the confusion is about being 'the odd one out' because children develop at different rates. At a stage when group identity is so important, this only adds to the problem.

It is probably this stage of adolescence and the next where growth and change are consolidated, and where the traditional picture of adolescence as a time of moodiness and sudden anger has its foundation. Changes happen in alarming and unpredictable spurts. There is much confusion in the expectations of young people – not knowing how to treat them or what to ask. The final period, perhaps from 16 onwards, is one where sudden change ceases and maturing takes place. But it is also the time when maximum pressure is exerted from outside, by schools and colleges, by parents, by the whole issue of work and employment.

Adolescence, then, is a time of great physical and emotional changes. It is the period of transition from child to adult, usually associated with storm and stress for all concerned, as the child has to adapt to what he or she is becoming, and the parent has to learn to adapt to the changed person in the home. It is a time of confusion when neither the young person nor the adult is clear about expectations; it is the time of movement from dependence to independence; a time for moving from concern for self towards a concern for others outside the self; it is the process of becoming a sexual being from an asexual one; of moving towards having a sense of self; towards realizing a vocation; towards finding a philosophy of life; it is the time for adjustment in relationships – with parents, with peers. Above all, it is a time for experimenting, of facing the questions 'What am I?', and 'Who am I?', and 'What am I here for?'.

If that is accepted as a general view of the adolescent period of growth then it follows that adolescence is the time of a search for identity and role. This means pushing out boundaries, and with that goes a desire to shock and to challenge. The media do not make it easier, either for adolescents themselves (where the most outrageous clothes and behaviour are presented as if they were the norm) or for those responsible for bringing-up adolescents (where *all* adolescents are presented as if they are immoral and corrupt). Clothes, hairstyles, music and experiments with drugs and drink, are very traditional ways of expressing both rebellion against parental standards and, at the same time, identification with the peer group. For adolescents, this search for the ideal norm is a very important stage, because it is not *Really* safe to be different. It is important also to remember the cost of all this. Most of us, if asked to talk about our adolescence, do not remember it as a time of happiness, but as one of pain and embarrassment.

I have suggested above that adolescence is a time for establishing an identity. The traditional way to do this is by choosing a career and finding a job. We are defined by what we do – it is the next question we are asked after our names. It follows that, if we have no job, or no prospect of one, in a sense we have no identity – we become some sort of 'non-person'. We cannot be defined or categorized. We have failed. We are written-off by others either as lazy or as a 'drop-out'. This may be an exaggerated picture to paint, but in a country where the work ethic still holds good, I believe it to be a true one. We have not yet found an acceptable alternative to work. We still expect to have a job for the greater part, if not the whole, of our working lives. We do not prepare young people for a society where work for a large number of the population will not be possible. No govenment or political party has yet admitted that the unemployment rate is always likely to be in millions. Large numbers of young people, many now in their twenties, have never worked and probably never will, and this not from any choice of their own, but because of market forces in the economy. It is very hard for a young person facing that future to feel any sense of value as a person, or to have any confidence in him or herself. In addition, a job provides regular contact with fellow-workers, an income, and purposeful direction of life. All these are absent without work.

Coupled with the problems resulting from unemployment is the picture of role confusion that the media and public opinion present to young people. Marriage is still held out as the proper future for girls, despite the evidence that the younger the bride and groom, the greater the likelihood of divorce – now one in three of teenage marriages. For boys, masculinity is still identified with the role of the breadwinner. The absence of a job, therefore, will mean no sense of identity, no role, no well-being.

The legal definition of a young person's rights is a confused one, and the conferring of responsibilities happens very gradually. The National Youth Bureau, in its recent report on the process of enfranchisement of young people, points to three aspects of this process:

1. The non-formal aspect – when young people are working out their own views on issues which affect them, such as school, work, sex and alcohol.

2. The informal aspect – when young people are subject to, and coming to terms with, a complex and powerful set of pressures and expectations from other sections of society, particularly the pressure to behave in certain ways and to become certain kinds of adults.

    The formal aspect – when young people are gradually gaining the legal rights and responsibilities of adults. It includes the arbitrary and often contradictory lifting of the restrictions placed on children, in addition to the removal of immunities and safeguards. This 'arbitrary' lifting of restrictions includes the right to join the armed forces at 16 for a boy and 17 for a girl, to have an abortion at 16, to leave home without parental permission at 17, to give blood at 18, to buy on HP at 18, to be tried in court at 10, to be sent to prison at 17. Although young people may work full-time at 16, and leave home at 17, they may not have a bank cheque guarantee card until 18. No contract for money entered into before 18 is a valid one. Marriage at 16, with parental consent, is.

The reaction of young people to all this confusion has led sociologists to be divided over whether a separate youth culture exists or not. Talcott Parsons asks if there is a coherent challenge on the part of young people to the 'socialisation process' of the family, the school and the media. Certainly it often looks as if young people have a network to spread the

latest ideas in clothes and hairstyles. The past thirty years have
seen a succession of trends that the media have seized on and
used to point to the 'decadence' of the younger generation.
Stan Cohen, in his study *Folk Devils and Moral Panic* sees this as
the response of the establishment to various manifestations of
young people's sub-culture, as skinheads and punks succeed
mods and rockers. But any theory of deviancy depends on a
concept of normality that is often hard to identify in the twentieth century. Certainly there is a feeling of desperation and
alienation in much of the music and even in the dress of young
people in the eighties. The alarming growth of glue-sniffing as
a cheap and easily available escape for young people who cannot afford the alcohol that their elders use in ever increasing
quantities; the violence and denial of life that is the usual
theme of most pop music at present; the increase in urban
violence and football 'hooliganism'; there are amongst the factors that point to an increasing gap between parents and young
people. *The Times*, in a series of articles (February 28th, March
1st and 2nd, 1983), identifies the growing feeling of desperation that many children from ten years old and upwards feel in
the face of the nuclear threat. If that is added to the likelihood
of unemployment, then it is often hard to be positive about
the future.

What, then, can be the response of anyone with any involvement with young people or responsibility for them? It is
necessary to separate the response of individuals from that of
the community.

1.   Seeing the world through the eyes of others is as necessary
     for those working with young people as it would be with
     fellow adults. It may be more difficult – or, at least, the
     idea of it may be more difficult – but it is an essential part
     of any general pastoral or specific counselling ministry
     that the other person be respected and accepted. In Chris-
     tian terms, all are children of God even if they have a
     Mohican haircut, dyed green, and are wearing studded
     leather clothes whilst on the dole! Any approach that
     assumes *less* than equality before God, that appears to be
     approaching from judgment or superiority, is doomed to
     fail, and ought not to succeed.

2.   As preparation for approaching, or being approached by, the other person, it is always necessary to be aware of one's own feelings and prejudices, and especially those at our own roots. Just as anyone working with black or Asian people must be aware of their feelings of racism and our use of racist concepts and language, so working across the barriers of age and sex will also produce reactions in ourselves that will colour and distort our approach. Our own unworked-out and unresolved feelings will act as barriers between us and the other person. The assumption that each one (even I) is prejudiced, is judgmental, is condemnatory, is almost certainly a true assumption. One's own prejudices can be worked on too. Awareness of them diminishes their impact.

3.   The person before you is an individual, she or he may have gone to great lengths to proclaim that to you. She or he is distinct from all the other young people that the popular press and popular opinion have lumped together. She or he has to be *seen* for her or himself, and listened to as that.

4.   Anyone working with young people has a responsibility to be aware of the trends and influences on the young, and an overview of their concerns and enthusiasms. This means time must be taken to listen to and explore the views of young people; not in a desperate attempt to be trendy, but as part of the responsibility we each have to be aware of the enthusiasms and concerns of others around us. This will also enable the worker to be an interpreter to others of young people's ideals, trends and fashions, and to be able to work effectively across the gaps between generations. What may be alarming if it is happening to your child becomes somewhat less so if it is seen against a background of change and questioning and experimentation.

5.   Working with young people also includes working with their parents and other responsible adults, and the role may then be that of supporter to anxious people. It is notoriously hard to be objective about your own family, and if what you read *generally* about young people is that they are at risk, then this problem increases. The media

picture of young people as violent, glue or drug addicts with over-developed sexual appetites may be an exaggerated one, but if it is *your* child who is late home or behaving unnaturally it may be a real source to feed anxiety. Helping parents to see that rebellion against their standards is a natural part of growing-up (and something they did to their parents!) is a valuable service both to parent and child. The pressure on the latter, which will almost certainly be increasing any problems there are, will be relieved, and it allows the former to be more free in their responses. Helping a person to see that there is another point of view may be difficult, but it is essential.

6. An anxiety for anyone working with young people is that real signs of something wrong may be missed. When does an adolescent mood become a sign of depression, or erratic behaviour indicate drug abuse? Clearly there are no easy answers, and much of an individual's ability to distinguish warning signs from usual behaviour will depend on the quality of the relationship that exists between the people concerned. It is, however, the responsibility of anyone working with young people to make sure that they do some background reading of the issues affecting young people so that tell-tale signs can be picked up. Many agencies publish material that is suitable to give to young people, as well as giving clear information to parents, teachers and clergymen. A list of possible material and its sources follows at the end of this chapter.

If these are some of the responses an individual can make, what of the community? The partnership that exists between the statutory and the voluntary sectors of the youth service in England and Wales means that young people are usually well-served in leisure provision, particularly in the big cities. In rural areas the service is patchy, and cuts in the youth service budget have meant that in some areas statutory provision is minimal. There may be a role, therefore, for the voluntary sector to look afresh at the service it can offer, both in leisure provision and in specific service provision. Many areas, for instance, lack a counselling service for young people. Real questions need to be asked about the appropriateness of offering counselling in a formal setting to them. It may well be that the structure and theoretical bases for counselling make it unsuitable for young people, who do not share its preconceptions. However, these counselling services perform a valuable role, not only in offering formal, skilled couselling facilities, but also in providing advice centres, and training in specific skills for those who work with young people.

Another possibility for community sponsorship is the use of MSC monies for employment projects and for life-skills training. Many churches and Christian organizations have been pioneers in setting-up well-thought-out local and national schemes to eliminate some of the hardships caused to young people by unemployment. In areas of high unemployment one of the main problems that faces the unemployed is the lack of cheap, warm places in which to meet friends, to study, to play games, or simply to get out of homes. Drop-in centres perform a useful function and meet many of these needs.

The other task which can be taken on by those working with young people is that of informing public opinion and moving attitudes away from prejudicial responses (both generally to young people, and specifically to unemployed young people) to a more enlightened understanding of their needs. Professor Ralph Dahrendorff, in his recent addresses on the state of Britain, has pointed to the need to engage in debates about alternatives to work – he suggested 'activity' as a reasonable substitute. All of us need to think about, and help others to think about, what sort of society we want and can help create. The growth of microchip technology points to the possibility of us all enjoying more leisure. Those of us with work have to make sure that proper provision is made for leisure to be enjoyed by all, and not force it upon a few, willy-nilly.

Inevitably, much of this chapter about the specific needs of young people and possible responses to those needs, has been generalized. It has also pointed to young people as if they were a race apart, which they are not. They are people passing through a particular phase in development on the way to adulthood and shared responsibility with us. The experience they have now will colour their attitudes in the future. That should be sufficient reason for working with them to enable them to use their experience positively. Failure to do that blights the future for all.

GLUE SNIFFING Useful pamphlets:
  Siniffing Glue & Other Solvents, Release Publications, 1 Elgin Avenue, London W9.
  Teaching about a Volatile Situation, Institute for the Study of Drug Dependence, Kingsbury House, 3 Blackburn Road, London NW6.
DRUGS *Young People and Drugs*, National Association of Boys' Clubs, 24 Highbury Grove, London N5.
HEALTH MATTERS Including alcohol, smoking, glue-sniffing and drugs.
  Publications, films, etc. from The Health Education Council, 78 New Oxford Street, London WC1.
YOUNG PEOPLE GENERALLY Two monthly magazines, *Youth in Society* and *Scene*, plus numerous other publications on all aspects of young people and their needs, are published by The National Youth Bureau, 17-23 Albion Street, Leicester. They also have an efficient library and document loan service.
YOUNG PEOPLE AND SEXUALITY Free facts sheets on all aspects of sexuality, including homosexuality. Both of the following organizations have a good bookshop for all aspects of young people's sexuality and personal relationships: The Family Planning Information Service, 27-35 Mortimer Street, London W1. The National Marriage Guidance Association, Little Church Street, Rugby, Warks.
SOCIOLOGICAL STUDIES of YOUNG PEOPLE. Cohen, *Folk Devils and Moral Panic* H & P Williamson, *Five Years*.
YOUNG PEOPLE & THE LAW *Enfranchisement: Young People and the Law*, (NYB, 1981).
WHERE TO GO FOR ADVICE
  The National Association of Young People's Counselling & Advisory Service, 17-23 Albion Street, Leicester, Tel. 0533 554775 will put you in touch with local agencies that specialize in counselling young people.
  Most of the major Christian denominations in Great Britain have youth officers who will know about local statutory and voluntary services. A phone call to your headquarters building will put you in touch with your local representative.

4. Drug Abuse

BY THE REVEREND KENNETH LEECH,
BOARD FOR SOCIAL RESPONSIBILITY, CHURCH OF ENGLAND.

THE field of drug use and abuse is one which is marked by an abundance of misinformation. Much of this is promoted by sections of the media, and it leads to a combination of fear, panic and paralysis in many people. Fear, because 'drugs' seems to represent an unknown and strange world; panic, because the sensational accounts of drug action in many papers often produce a panic reaction in parents and friends which can be as harmful as the effects of the drugs themselves – and sometimes more so; and paralysis because, at the end of the day, it seems that there is really nothing that can be done. So it is necessary to begin by urging a process of unlearning: unlearning much of the misinformation, and learning not to rely on media versions of reality in this area. Often the facts about a drug are worrying enough without being over-dramatized; and in many cases, 'respectable' drugs are more dangerous than they are believed to be. So it is important to stay as calm as possible, and to try to leave behind for the present most of the mythology of drug abuse.

The world of drug abuse is not as strange and alien as people think, nor is it a world which only, or mainly, the young inhabit. The bulk of drug users, and the bulk of drug abuse problems, are in the middle-aged and elderly range. The drugs may be different, though that is not always the case. As the *Glasgow Daily Record*, commenting on a research study, noted on 3 March 1976: 'The major Scottish addiction problems are alcoholism and barbiturate dependence among the middle-aged and elderly'. And that could be repeated for the rest of Britain, though the problems of the minor tranquillizers would need to be added. Drugs are an integral part of adult society. Most of the drugs which are abused, whether by adults or young people, are legal drugs, legally manufactured, and legally distributed.

Most drugs are open to misuse (occasional wrong use) and abuse (prolonged wrong use), and some produce what is called addiction or dependence, in which there is an overpowering compulsion to obtain the drug by any means, combined with physical symptoms (abstinence syndrome) when the drug is withdrawn. The most widespread drug of dependence in our society is, of course, alcohol. In recent years there is considerable evidence of an increase in alcoholism, not least among young people. Because alcohol is so acceptable, its potential for harm is often underestimated and its ability to produce physical and psychological dependence in a small but sifnificant percentage of its users is ignored. While this chapter will be concerned with drugs other than alcohol, it is essential to emphasize at the outset that alcohol is itself a drug of addiction, that alcohol addicts heavily outnumber addicts of all other drugs, and that the detrimental effects both on the individual and on society which result from alcohol abuse are far more serious than those of most other drugs. One third of Britain's alcoholics are women, and research in recent years has shown an increase in heavy drinking among housewives. A study in 1976 suggested that there were around 150,000 female alcoholics in Britain. There is also evidence of alcoholism among the young. A study in Scotland in 1978 claimed that possibly up to 40 per cent of young people in some areas may be on the way to alcoholism. However, only a small proportion of drinkers become addicted. Due to the economic situation as well as to other factors, alcohol consumption has actually declined in Britain, and, while over 90 per cent of the population drink alcohol, most do so moderately. However, the problem of heavy drinking has become worse in the same period.

Alcohol is a sedative and, in higher quantities, a hypnotic (sleep-inducing) drug. Other such drugs include the barbiturates and such preparations as Mogadon and Mandrax, commonly referred to as sleeping tablets. The addictive potential of barbiturates has been known for many years, and the frequency of their use in overdose and suicide is well documented. Between 1966 and 1975, prescriptions for these drugs fell from

16 million to under 7 million. However, abuse of barbiturates remains a serious problem. The spread of non-barbiturate hypnotics has added to, rather than replaced, the problems created by barbiturates. By 1970 over two and a half million prescriptions were being issued for Mandrax and for Mogadon; together they formed a quarter of all hypnotic drugs prescribed in England and Wales. In addition there has continued to be massive consumption of the minor tranquillizers, particularly Librium and Valium, probably the most widely prescribed drugs in the world.

Opposite in effect to the sedative-hypnotic range of drugs are the stimulants. As sedatives reduce activity, stimulants increase it. Some preparations (such as the Drinamyl pill which became famous in the early 1960s under the nickname 'purple hearts') combine an amphetamine with a barbiturate or sedative drug. The amphetamine range of drugs have been the most commonly abused stimulants in Britain. Early forms of the drug included Benzedrine (including the Benzedrine inhaler), Dexedrine, and Durophet. Throughout the 1960s high dose amphetamine use became a serious problem in the United States, Scandinavia, Britain and elsewhere. Later there were epidemics of intravenous amphetamine use, first in the form of Methedrine (methylamphetamine) and later in the form of injected amphetamine sulphate powder. Since the early 1970s the illicit manufacture of amphetamine has increased as has the use of other cerebral stimulants such as Ritalin (methylphenidate).

Amphetamine is known in the drug culture as ˙speed˙, and 'speed kills' was a popular graffiti from the late 60s when the dangers of the drug became widely accepted. One of the most worrying aspects of amphetamine abuse is its ability to produce a chronic psychosis, a condition marked by paranoid delusions and often by vivid, frightening hallucinations, confusion and general excitement. This amphetamine psychosis is particularly acute when the drug is injected intravenously. High dose amphetamine users – in drug slang 'pillhead' or 'speed freaks' – take the drug in massive doses to obtain the maximum effect, and will then stay awake and highly active for days. But this period of excitement and hyper-activity will be followed by a 'crash' or 'come down' with exhaustion, depression, and sleep.

Another powerful and dangerous stimulant is cocaine, previously used in conjunction with heroin, but increasingly used in recent years as a drug of the upper middle class fashionable groups (though by no means restricted to them). Whereas in the 1960s and earlier, cocaine was used intravenously with heroin, it is now often used by people who are not part of a needle culture.

A third category of drugs is that of heroin and the opiates, that is, drugs derived from opium. Opium has been used as a drug of intoxication for centuries, and preparations containing opium (such as laudanum and 'Dover's Powder') were used in Britain from the seventeenth century. Morphine was extracted from opium in the nineteenth century, followed by codeine, and later heroin (diamorphine, produced by heating morphine over acetic anhydride) was synthesized. Heroin and other opiates have been used in medicine in Britain for many years, and until recently medical sources constituted the major source. Illicit heroin, adulterated and marketed by criminal syndicates is relatively new to Britain, and its increase is directly related to the cut down of medical sources of supply since the setting up of the out-patient clinics. Today it is still possible to obtain heroin from medical practitioners, but it is increasingly difficult, and so the black market has grown. Illicit heroin comes into Britain from Hong Kong, Iran, and Pakistan. During 1982-83 observers of the heroin scene noted that the price was down and the purity was up. There has been a marked increase in heroin use, a geographical spread and a spread to younger age groups after several years during which the addict population seemed to be getting older. In 1982, 76 per cent of new addicts gave heroin as their drug of first use. In a recent case in Liverpool, an 11-year old was given heroin by his 13 year old sister. A recent study in Ireland suggests that there are some 1,500 heroin addicts in Dublin, and around 3,000 experimenters, while 270 new heroin addicts were identified in Scotland in 1982. Recent Home Office figures show a total of nearly 4,400 known narcotic addicts in the UK, but estimates of all users of opiate drugs are around 20,000.

A very different class of drugs is the so-called 'psychedelics' or mind-expanding drugs of the LSD type. These are drugs which are believed to expand the mind and enlarge the vision, enabling people to see reality in different and deeper ways. The use of such drugs is very ancient, and many describe their use in religious terms. LSD is a drug derived from ergot, a fungus which grows on rye. Previously used in psychiatry, it became a popular drug in the youth counter-culture at the time of the hippy movement of 1966-67.

Cannabis, known by such names as marijuana, hashish, pot, grass, and so on, is a mild intoxicant which is used in many parts of the world. It is not strictly a drug at all but a herb which produces drug effects of varying potency. It was once used in the medical preparation cannabis tincture, and, while some physicians would claim that it still has valuable medical properties, its use in Western medicaine is virtually obsolete. Cannabis can be smoked, eaten (as in cannabis fudge or in cake) or drunk. Its active principle, a chemical called tetrahydrocannabinol (THC), is highly potent, and preparations alleged to be synthetic THC appear from time to time on the street drug scene, though they are usually shown on analysis to be something else.

Finally, a range of glues and solvents have increasingly become subject to abuse by young people. Technically the problem is wider than 'glue sniffing': what it involves is the use of vapours from a variety of products. Both sniffing and inhaling by mouth are used. Broadly there are three categories of products which are used in this way: volatile solvents, aerosols, and anaesthetics. Solvents include toluene (found in Evostick, Araldite, and so on), benzene (as in petrol and rubber solution), acetone, and the fluorocarbon propellants in aerosols. Products used include plastic model cements, nail polish remover, paint thinners, and cleaning fluids. Aerosols such as hair sprays, deodorants and insecticides are also used, though they are less common. Anaesthetics such as ether and chloroform also figure from time to time. But it is solvents which have recently caused the greatest concern. Most of those involved with solvent abuse are young males, and on the whole the phase does not last beyond adolescence. However, while it does last, there are serious health dangers, and an increasing number of deaths are linked with solvent abuse.

These are simply some of the drugs commonly abused in Britain at the present time. For more detailed accounts, readers should refer to the sources listed in the appendix.

Because ours is a drug-using culture, the use of drugs to meet a variety of needs is likely to continue. We have been encouraged over many years to seek chemical solutions to internal problems: from headaches to depression, from anxiety to severe emotional pain, drugs are offered as 'treatment'. Those people, not all of them young, who have turned to drugs to help them find meaning in life are simply taking a logical next step from the 'better living through chemistry' ethos of the mainstream culture. It is important to recognize how central to the dominant culture is the use of centrally acting drugs: it is the people who use no drugs at all who are the 'deviants'. For the most part, therefore, first aid in the field of drug abuse will be concerned with the reduction of drug-related harm, and with response to the crises and accidents which occur from time to time. The long-term response will have to concern itself with the creation of alternative approaches to health and problem-solving, and with removing the economic, spiritual and social causes in our society which lead a growing section of the population to seek refuge in drugs. We know that most of the killer diseases have been reduced more by changes in the environment than by the use of medicines. However, there are some basic principles of first aid which are important.

The commonest type of drug crisis is overdose. While the treatment of overdose and other forms of poisoning is a medical matter, it is important to remember some elementary guidelines. The patient should not be moved unless it is absolutely necessary, but should be placed face downwards with the head turned to one side. He or she should not be propped up in a chair, or allowed to lie on his or her back. Tight clothing should be loosened, and airways be kept clear. Breathing should be checked, and the chin raised. If the person is unconscious, artificial respiration should be tried. But an ambulance should be called, or, particularly in London and in cases of mild overdose, it may be quicker to take the patient to hospital in a taxi. It is always important in overdose cases to try to identify the drugs taken: these drugs, or any labels, packets or vomited material, should be taken to the hospital. If the overdose involves glue or vapours, the person should be removed from the contaminated area. Verbal reassurance is always valuable even when the person seems to be unconscious.

Verbal reassurance is particularly important in dealing with adverse reactions ('bad trips') from LSD. This is known as the 'talk down' method, and is preferable to medication with drugs such as Largactil which will simply cut the trip dead. The person who has had a bad trip needs to be brought down gently, in a quiet room, with subdued lights. The people present need to remain very calm, avoid sudden movements, and quietly reassure the person that she is still herself. However, the amphetamine psychosis ('the horrors') cannot be dealt with in the same way, and will need medication, but verbal reassurance can help to control the person in the meantime. It is very important that people without medical knowledge do not use drugs in treating overdose. However, in most cases, inactivity and excretion are the most sure methods of restoring normal functioning.

Individuals who are involved with drug users need to go to some trouble to find out what facilities exist in their locality, such as treatment centres, out-patient clinics, professional agencies, clubs, after-care centres, and so on. These vary enormously from one area to another. Many out-patient clinics only cater for addicts of heroin and other intravenous drugs. It may be difficult to find treatment and help for the much larger numbers of users of amphetamine, or for the young experimenter seeking to resolve his or her problems through drug use. SCODA (see Appendix) will give advice on facilities in particular areas. For the intravenous addict, the out-patient clinic can be the first stage of treatment. However, most drug users need different kinds of help and support, and it is wrong to see addiction as purely a 'medical problem'. Often an unattached youth worker who is in touch with the street culture is a key person. Some areas have liaison groups in which people from various disciplines who are involved with drug users meet together. The non-professional caring person is very important within this network of care, and should not be made to feel inferior or out of her depth. Of course, it is vital to be as well-informed and as up to date as possible, but the view that drug abuse is only a matter for 'experts' should be rejected.

A major area for pastoral care lies in the support of the family and friends of the drug user. These are often grossly neglected, yet it is vital to recognize the severe pressures on them, and to try to provide adequate support and strength for them. Mistaken reactions of parents to their children's drug use can raise as many problems as the drugs themselves. It is essential not to panic, or to imagine that we can create an entirely drug-free zone. Drugs are part of the world in which children are growing up, and it is absurd to imagine that we can keep children away from them altogether. We can try to ensure that they are well-informed, aware of dangers and risks, and sufficiently well integrated and 'together' that they will not seek to make drugs a substitute for living.

One aspect of adult over-reaction is the growth of a kind of vigilance which can be oppressive to the young. Too much vigilance can produce a suspicious spirit which communicates to our children a basic lack of trust. Indications of drug abuse are often difficult to distinguish from the normal mood chages of adolescence. Parents often speak of 'odd behaviour' in their children. But all adolescent behaviour is odd! So, while it is possible to look for indications of drug use, it is necessary to warn against becoming obsessed with drugs. So drugs become the parents' obsession, *their* problem rather than their children's, while to the children they may not be all that important.

The word 'problem' is so associated with drugs that we need to remember that not all drug use raises problems, and that people take drugs for a variety of different reasons. Understanding the reasons is more necessary in some cases than in others. For example, the original reason why a drug was taken may relate to an event in the past which is no longer relevant: what matters is the motivation for drug use now. However, many people use drugs in order to cope with deep-rooted emotional problems, or with apparently unalterable social conditions. It was with the latter that Marx was concerned when he made his famous remark that religion was the opium of the people: that is, it was a pain-killing drug which made intolerable conditions bearable for a time. It is important then to consider some of the possible reasons why people choose the drug response. Not that 'choice' is always the main factor, since in many communities and subcultures drug use may be endemic, that is, it may be the norm rather than the exception. A more appropriate question then would be, 'Why do some people *not* take drugs?' Cultures and subcultures however can also discourage drug use, or at least discourage the use of particular drugs. Pastoral care must involve feeling the pulse of the local culture so that one is aware of the points of leverage, the potential for change, the pressures working in favour of, or against, particular forms of drug use.

It is impossible here to examine all the possible reasons why drugs are used, but three main reasons may be mentioned: intoxication and relaxation; coping with pain, both physical and emotional; and seeking meaning in life. Most people use alcohol, and many people use cannabis, for the first of these reasons, and it is essential not to view all such recreational drug use as intrinsically problematic. Again, many people use analgesic drugs (such as aspirin, paracetamol, and so on) to kill pain. Those suffering exteme emotional or mental pain may turn to more powerful pain killers. Drugs of the LSD type are often used by people who are seeking some deeper meaning in their lives, trying to discover who they are, and to explore 'inner space'. There are many other reasons, and it is important to try to understand the motives and the factors which lie behind the drug use in each case.

The Christian pastor may find herself or himself confronted with issues of drug abuse in a number of settings: in hospital chaplaincy, in school or college campus, or in the context of parish and family. It is vital not to try to minimise the medical role but to recognize the need for spiritual struggle and a ministry of compassion (in the most literal sense of the word). The pastor must see the drug-using person as a person of value, made in God's image, and must assert this and manifest it in a context where increasingly he or she is a client, addict, patient, and problem. The pastor must represent hope in an apparently hopeless situation, recognizing, in the words of an American account of work with heroin users, that 'the church must suffer and be crucified with those it seeks to serve: and that it must keep on being crucified even though the nails bite deep and the hope of resurrection is obscure' (Bruce Kenrick, *Come Out the Wilderness*, Fontana [1967], 155).

Resources

For further elaboration of the points made above see Kenneth Leech, *What Everyone Should Know About Drugs* (Sheldon Press 1983.)

The following are important sources for information and help:

Institute for the Study of Drug Dependence (ISDD), 3 Blackburn Road, London NW6 (01-328-5541).

Standing Conference on Drug Abuse, same address (01-328-6556).

Release, 1 Elgin Avenue, London W9 3PR (01-289 1123; 24-hour emergency service 01-603 8654).

5. Marriage

BY MRS JOY THOMPSON, B.A. (OXON), M.INST. G.A.,
WILLISDEN, LONDON

MARRIAGE was never more popular, never more risky than it is today. The popularity extends to second and third marriages, the risk arises from a combination of high expectations and of tough social pressures. In consequence, breakdown, one-parent families and complicated step-relationships are now part of our normal social fabric.

Clergy, responsible for pastoral care amongst their congregations, and concerned about the quality of life in society as a whole, are more and more questioning how best to support both marriage and the casualties of marriage. Our public image portrays the church as more concerned with condemning divorce than with sustaining marriage. Our inherited patterns of both spirituality and pastoral care tend to be concerned more with individuals than with couples or families. However, it is my belief that the local church has great opportunities for realistic education and support for marriages and family life, and that we need to put more energy and thought into this positive pastoral action, alongside the problem-centred pastoral care for the casualties which can so easily consume our attention.

Before looking at this task, however, we need to think about the assumptions we make about marriage. Each of us has been shaped by a particular experience of marriage, whether our own, or our parents', and this makes it impossible to be objective. We need also to look at what God is saying to us through the trends of our times. For we believe that God has always made himself known through the events of history.

A historical perspective

I see two facts which have a far reaching impact on people.

First is the arrival in our time of safe contraception. This must be one of the major revolutions in man's history, yet it seems to have come upon us unawares. For the first time, sex for pleasure and sex for procreation can be separated. This means that what was in the past the main reason for chastity has disappeared. Fear of pregnancy was always the strongest reason for not sleeping with your boyfriend – and suddenly it's all changed.

One result of safe contraception is the complete change in the life-style of women. For centuries most women spent most of their lives in childbearing and nurture of the family and home – often a rich and rewarding life. Now they can choose. This is a great freedom, but also means we can be at sea and confused; men's and women's roles change in relation to each other, and there are no guiding norms.

The second crucial fact is the great increase in mobility and the break-up of neighbourhood and kinship groups. The old village or street provided reasonable support in time of hardship and loss, as well as considerable restraint on behaviour. Even now, what passes in the anonymity of the city would not be so easily tolerated in a village community. Young people have always rebelled, but where do they look today for the norms and rules to rebel against?

Both contraception and mobility are part of the centuries long process by which the individual has emerged from the tribe and family. The industrial revolution, bringing the weekly wage and the separation of home and work gave the individual a sudden new freedom. Before, most households formed an interdependent economic unit, in which each member played a part, even the children. They depended on each other for survival in a harsh world. So the moral codes surrounding marriage were designed to safeguard property and to protect this basic economic team. In such a world, unsupported mothers and children stood little chance of survival and the wife was essential and intrinsic to the success of the household economy.[1]

Marriage is of course still an economic convenience. But today survival is not at stake and so we can afford also to hope

[1] See *Society of the Family*, Michael Anderson (Penguin Education)

for and expect personal fulfilment and enrichment. Today's big cities, with their impersonal housing developments and their privatized suburbs breed appalling loneliness. Much of what we call permissive behaviour is simply an attempt to alleviate this loneliness and find some human comfort. The family and kinship group has shrunk to the small nuclear family, often living in alien surroundings and so looking to each other for the fulfilment of all their needs for affection, emotional support and companionship. The idealised images of the TV screen fan our fantasies and our disillusion.

However it is also exciting and challenging, that freed fron the harsher economic necessities surrounding marriage we can now look at the relationship of a man and a woman and value it for itself. In Dr Dominian's words, 'In marriage, God has put into our hands one of the principal means of developing relationships which prepare us for our eternal state'.[2] Marriage is hard, just because it is the place of personal growth.

The Christian Viewpoint

What has the Christian tradition to say about this relationship? In such a short space it is only possible to point to some essentials of our faith.

Our scriptures give us one supreme model for all relationships, and that is the relationship of God and his people, revealed through the love-story that unfolds in the OT and in the person of Jesus. Marriage is seen as a reflection of this relationship both by the prophets and then by St Paul. A relationship is not an idea, but something alive, and therefore growing and developing. This is seen to be so in God's relationship with his people and also in marriage. So the result in both is a growing maturity of the persons involved.

What are the characteristics of this model we are given, this covenant of grace? First, we see God's faithfulness. Again and again the assurance is given that, however we let him down, he will never forsake us or betray us. We know that this security, this reliability is necessary for any person to grow, whether it is a child in a home or a pair of lovers. The child must know that his parents will never forsake or abandon him however bad he

[2] *Marriage, Faith and Love*, J. Dominian (Darton, Longman and Todd).

is. A lover must be able to risk displeasing the loved one some-times, if he is to be true to himself. Threats of abandonment are the worst kind of cruelty.

Secondly, we see the primacy of grace over law. Sinners res-pond to Christ, while those who keep the rules are blind to their need of him. The prodigal returns hungry, not penitent, and is met in the way by the Father. Yet laws and rules remain necessary to any social group. All of us must live with the ten-sion between maintaining standards and rules, and welcoming with compassion the human nature (our own included) which fails to reach them.

Thirdly, we see that the relationship involves the whole of a person, body, mind and heart. God reveals himself through the flesh and blood of a man; the body is spoken of as the temple of the Spirit. The physical is always a vehicle for communication and meaning; sexuality is always sacramental. By contrast, the Greek notion that the body is inferior to the mind can be seen as responsible for the deeply split consciousness which despises the body and leads both to Victorian prudery and to por-nography. A rediscovery of the holiness of the body is the best antidote to pornography.

Fourthly, if the relationship is like a growing plant, the com-munication, the way we connect with each other, is like the sap. We nurture our prayer, the sap of our relationship with God. Learning to speak to one another is almost as difficult. Often the way we understand and misunderstand each other is coloured by assumptions from the past. For instance, my own mother was a doctor; my mother-in-law was always at home with a ready cup of coffee. It took my husband and me years to see the unspoken effect of our different assumptions on our behaviour to each other. Each person brings to a marriage unquestioned assumptions about money, sex, bringing-up-children, parental roles, and we have to work hard to find ways to talk about these things and also to say the difficult and hurt-ful things, to 'speak the truth in love'. The fear of hurting is often a major but mistaken block to speaking the truth. Some-times the problem is simply not knowing each other's language; she wants him to *see* her, to notice her new dress or hairdo, he finds a quick hug an easier way than words to say he loves her, and the two can so easily end up each feeling rejected and hurt. Learning to express our deepest selves to another human being is a life-time's work, a discipline of listening and risking.

And so we are given the symbol of the Trinity. The Trinity is made up of three distinct and different persons whose nature is one. What unites them is love, the love of absolute equals in relationship with one another. Thus 'The key to the Trinity is persons in relationships of love. Each person is totally differentiated from the other and possesses themselves fully and affirmatively. The love of spouses is similarly one of complementary relationships in which spouses become gradually differentiated and acquire possession of themselves . . . They become fully available to themselves and thus can donate themselves fully to and for others, their children and ultimately the whole world.'[3]

Our pastoral work is rooted in these truths. Whatever we may proclaim in words, it will be by our actions that God is either recognized or obscured. So it is that the first pastoral task is to enable the local Christian community to be what it proclaims.

The life of the Christian Community

It follows then that every Christian group is called to exhibit God's faithfulness by our commitment to people, whoever they are and however they may let us down. We show his grace and forgiveness by accepting people as they are, even when they are far from agreeing with us or behaving as we would like. We show his wholeness by an involvement in all aspects of life, not just in the 'spiritual'. And a Christian group or community must be developing a quality of open and truthful communication which sets people free to be their true selves.

A parish church can become a modern, redeemed, version of the extended family. In it everyone has something to give and to receive, there can be proxy grannies, uncles, cousins and in-laws, and a chance for three or four generations to be together, a modern *tribe* in which a whole variety of relationships flourish.

Within the framework of its liturgy a parish church may also

[3] See *Families and How to Survive Them*, R. Skynner & J. Cleese (Methuen).

make connections between the words of theology or scripture and the daily events of family live. More occasions like Mothering Sunday and All Souls tide might be used to focus on specific aspects of life, so that the Sunday Worship begins to breathe the atmosphere of marriage and family life, and the split between sacred and secular is lessened. Also, if we believe the Holy Trinity is the model for our married life, clergy will be careful not to make demands which strain people's marriages, and laity will expect clergy to put their own marriage first, as the place where true humanity is most deeply learnt.

Beyond this basic commitment to making room for the Spirit to work in our own relationships of family and church, there are some special pastoral opportunities.

Marriage Preparation

The present high divorce rate has caused a good deal of crea-.tive new work to be tried, including schemes resourced by Family Life Education workers in some fourteen dioceses and by the Catholic Marriage Advisory Council. There have long been clergy who made this work a priority and others who used Marriage Guidance Counsellors to run preparation courses.

Whoever else is involved, the interviews with the priest who takes the wedding service are central. It is the relationship he makes which will help the couple feel relaxed and enjoy their wedding. Most couples come to marriage with high hopes and little knowledge of how their hopes will work out in practice. Even those who have already been living together do not know how the marriage bond will affect their relationship. (It often produces quite new difficulties.) The promises and commitments are serious matters for them. But what they most need from the priest is intelligent interest in themselves as people. Where they are hoping to live, how they will cope with each other's parents at the wedding and afterwards are the kind of concerns which may be occupying them. But to break through the expectation that the Vicar will give them a talk, and to instil enough trust to talk openly of these things is not easy. It involves the priest in letting go of his own egocentric desire for people to be interested in the things he believes matter, and making the costly leap of trying to stand where they stand, and to see the world as they see it. This is the essence of what we call 'love'.

This letting go is easier if we give this work realistic aims. If our aims are to *embody* the truths of the gospel and to help the couple talk to each other about what the marriage means, starting where they are is the only place to start. This may enable them to ask the questions they really want to ask. Married clergy may naturally be able to refer to some of the difficult times in their own marriage, and suggest that hiccups are normal, and seeking support and help a sign of maturity. Perhaps the most important information we can give them is that marriage is never easy. Male and female think and feel differently, family backgrounds are different, and just because of this coming together of differences, each couple has a chance to create something quite new. I often use the image of two flints rubbing against each other, and through the *friction* creating a spark of new fire. As Dr Robin Skynner puts it, 'It takes two to create something new.'

Using Lay People in Marriage Preparation

Marriage preparation is a ministry which some clergy are now sharing with lay people. It is a sharing of ministry, not a delegating, for nothing should detract from the time spent by the priest with the couple. The lay pastors, usually working in pairs, (not necessarily married pairs) should themselves receive good training from some specialist agency. They have the advantage that many couples will relax more quickly with them, because they see them as more like themselves.

Grouping parishes together for such a scheme makes sense when the number of weddings is small. This provides a more interesting mix of lay pastors and makes it more likely that the couples can meet in small groups. Grouped together, couples will spark each other off, someone may be given courage to say something difficult because someone else's partner has said it, they see for themselves the variety of possible approaches, which helps to break down the illusion that there is one 'right' way.

Such lay pastors are not sophisticated counsellors or trained group leaders and so it has proved helpful to provide them with structured activities to get the group going. Two particularly helpful aids have been a set of cassettes prepared by the Redemptorists, each of which gives short dialogues in a range of subjects. These raise many discussion points. The second is a set of questionnaires prepared by CMAC. Each person fills in answers privately and then compares notes with his partner. Different sheets cover: The meaning of Marriage, Roles in the Home, Work, Money, Sex, etc. Typical questions could be:

> What is your partner's favourite meal?
> Do you want your marriage to be like your parents' marriage?
> How will you celebrate your first Christmas?

They are fun to do, produce some laughter and surprises, and stimulate discussion of difficult subjects, either in the meeting or afterwards in private.

Flexibility must be the key in such a project. It is never easy to get the couples together and sometimes impossible to fit in even three sessions. Some interviews have taken place in a pub, most in the lay pastors' own homes. It has been rewarding that they have often been asked to the wedding, sometimes invited to read a lesson, and cards have been sent from the honeymoon.

Babies and Baptism

The arrival of the first baby propels a young couple into profound changes and can be a time of high stress for them.[3] Through the work of psychiatrists such as Bowlby and Winnicott we now know more of the basic importance of the child's first months and years. The parent is the first person through whom the baby learns that he or she is of value, is worth loving, and whom he or she will learn to love in return. The mother is 'the Vice-regent of God', loving the baby just for being himself. Without the trust created by this first relationship human personality is stunted from the start, and the concept of a loving God can mean nothing. Support for young parents in this most important of all callings is needed more than ever before.

[3] See *Families and How to Survive Them*, R. Skynner & J. Cleese (Methuen).

Where a church can provide a structure of pastoral care for the parents, theological scruples over baptism feel less difficult. Such care can come through a 'coffee set' or a 'parents and babies' group. These can be an opportunity for clergy and lay Christians to make friends with the young parents, discovering what their lives are like, and what their needs are, and above all enabling them to support and help each other through group discussion of a relaxed and informal kind. Such provision translates our theological words into action, and makes the church a *sign* of God's love.

Either preparation or follow-up groups for baptism could explicitly connect theology and life. Take for instance three aspects of baptism: 'Joining a Family' – What happens when the twosome becomes a threesome? How does each partner cope with the new demands and still make time for each other? What does joining the church family mean for the baby, and for them? 'Dying to Sin and Rising to New Life' – What are the parents' hopes for the baby's life, and how, in practical ways, can they cope with what stands in the way? 'Naming, a new Identity, a Child of God' – What does the name chosen say about the kind of person they want the child to become? How can they best help the child grow into his own unique self and at his own pace? How do they cope with worries about what mother-in-law expects, or which clinic baby is doing best?

Support for Parents and Couples

Another important transition comes when the child begins school. Through the schools, the churches could do much to meet the parents. In the cities the school is often almost the only local meeting place, and provides an opportunity to build up a network of support. The school gate is one of the most fruitful places to do pastoral work!

From meetings for parents of children starting school, through to parents of adolescents and to couples facing retirement, the needs, and therefore the opportunities, are endless. The resources are also there, if we see our part as enabling the people with needs to help each other. Leaders for such groups need the confidence given by a short training scheme focusing on group management and listening skills and practice. The mutual support the members can give each other will in time reduce the pressures on their marriage partners.

Marital Problems

It is distressing to become involved in someone else's unhappy marriage, and especially when the couple are friends, or members of the same church. This makes it very hard to stand back and not project our own wishes for them. Sometimes a listening ear will resolve the tension. Sometimes the clergy can provide a vital bridge, helping the couple reach the point where they will seek expert professional help.

So when a parishioner pours out her distress at her husband's infidelities or drinking problems, how do we react? A few simple guidelines may help.

The first is to remember that most people, most of the time, are doing the best they can manage given their circumstances. We should not condemn – and especially not without extensive knowledge of the past. The second is to remember that in every marriage there is a *Fit*. There are unconscious reasons why they chose each other. The husband of the depressed, suicidal wife may need her weakness to make him feel strong. What unmet need drove the alcoholic husband to drink? Is his wife frigid and grudging with her affections? Is the drinking a punishing substitute for unexpressed resentment? The wife who is obsessed by her husbands' infidelities will be unaware that she gets some secret voyeuristic pleasure from his behaviour while retaining her own virtuous self image. This means that, even if we can only talk with one partner, we must always in our minds see both and try to understand how each is contributing to the problem.

This has several consequences. One is never to get involved as a go-between, acting for one or the other 'side'. The task is always to help each see that neither you nor they can bring about changes in their partner. A person can only change himself or herself. However, if he or she does that, the other will have to change in response. So for instance, if I stop blaming you, you will have to take the consequences of your own actions. The image I use is a see-saw. If one end is down and the other up, movement at either end will shift the balance. Often the one with the complaint can be helped to work out what he or she can do to produce the reaction they desire in the other. This very activity restores some feeling of potency.

Thirdly we usually need to help each to express the way he or she feels to the other, both the positives and negatives, and to check all the time whether the message has been received and understood. Taking trouble to say the positive things sometimes works wonders. And many difficulties arise from not accepting nor understanding the way the other feels and from the wish for someone who naturally thinks and feels as I do. This is to wish for a mother/baby relationship rather than the adult and painful discovery of the otherness of the other.

Following this way of working, it often emerges that at some crucial stage in the marriage, one partner felt unsupported. It could have been the birth of a baby, a bereavement, an abortion, a move. The resentment at having to cope alone with the distress can build up over the years into a wall of silent anger. Sometimes it is possible to go back over this incident, helping each one to express how they felt and to understand the other.

Resentment over unsatisfactory sex is common too, and often not openly talked about. With Christians especially there may be guilt involved and uncertainty about what sexual practices are 'acceptable'. Again the profound differences between men and women need to be brought into the open. People may need permission to enjoy sex, and to give up some of the illusions and sexual goals which make love-making into work instead of play. In play there are no rights and wrongs but only what is enjoyed. Many people have to learn to be explicit about what they enjoy and so help their partner provide it.

Another illusion to give up is that marriage should work 'naturally'. Marriage is difficult, simply because in marriage we discover our true selves in relation to someone *different* to whom in our nakedness we are immensely vulnerable. The covenant we make means continually risking our presence, not withdrawing into safe isolation. It is helpful to think of the image of being angry while we hold one another. This is true fidelity, staying with each other in the moments of worst anger, distress and shame, when the parts of ourselves we least like are exposed to the other. Often this only becomes possible through the presence of a third-party – through that person's fidelity.

Learning to express vulnerable and painful emotions to each other takes time. The first step towards improving many marriages is to make time to be together. The intrusion of the TV set into our living rooms is reducing the space for families to talk to each other and so impoverishing our powers of self-expression.

Care of the Divorced

For some people divorce is the only possible answer. For some it may take more courage than just carrying on in the old patterns. For others it may be an avoidance of facing painful realities. The pastor has the task of respecting the decisions once they are made, and of conveying by his or her actions full acceptance of the people involved. There will be an especial need to reduce the immense feeling of failure and shame which many people feel after a divorce, and help may be needed in the complicated relationships of step parents and step children.

The Wounded Healer

Of all pastoral activities, marital counselling is possibly the most difficult. It takes courage to stay alongside the pain in an unhappy and destructive marriage, and to hold on to the hope for the partners in a realistic way. That hope must be that they can take one step more towards mature humanity, whatever the cost, and that is something we cannot do for them. True hope arises from having gone through our own confrontations and marital difficulties, from having learnt that the wounds of truth are more fruitful than the unruffled waters of collusion, from knowing in our experience that love and hate are closely woven together, and that their opposit is indifference. Our greatest resources lie in our own wounds and the confidence which grows from embracing them. If marriage is a route to maturity, it will involve us in all the ordeals of John Bunyan's Christian on his way to the Celestial City. And the purpose of the journey is to risk giving ourselves in the present moment to another human being.

In T. S. Eliot's words, this is

The awful daring of a moment's surrender
which an age of prudence can never retract.

('The Waste Land')

6. Sexual Problems

By Deaconess Mary Anne Coate,
Maida Vale, London

This chapter is intended to focus on the situation when a person comes to a pastor because he is having difficulty in handling his sexuality. It will not include a detailed discussion of homosexuality or marital problems. Neither will it consider at depth the more uncommon sexual deviations which may indeed be presented to a pastor, but which he may feel he can respond to with the offer of a referral for more specialized help. This is not because this area is unimportant – far from it – but because people experiencing such difficulties are not, except perhaps in certain inner-city areas, likely to be a large percentage of those who come for help. What follows is for the pastor in his more general ministry.

Why is sexuality likely to be a problem for religious people?

I am writing here with Christianity mainly in mind, and am not sure how far it will apply to other faiths. There is that strain in theological teaching and church practice that has tended to over-exalt the virtues of celibacy and continence, from Paul via Augustine through to the former preface to the marriage service of the Church of England! The latter is regrettably lacking in celebration of sexual love in itself, but focuses on the aspects of pro-creation, mutual support and the containment of that which could become disordered.

Furthermore, some of the harshest of church discipline has been concentrated on this and allied issues; the teaching on homosexuality, the indissolubility of marriage and even the position of women's ministry. We have also to add to this the dictum – found in the Gospels – that the thought is as bad as the deed (Mt 5²⁷,²⁸).

Why should this be – that this most fundamental and powerful part of us should have become so fenced around with

strictures, penalties and even myths – such as that of the destructive physical effects of masturbation? Perhaps just *because* of
the power and essential uncontrolledness of sexual love which,
allied to the power itself inherent in worship, ritual and
relationship with God, cannot but help becoming a force to be
reckoned with – for good or ill. It is this alliance which found
expression in pagan rites and excesses and has played a dark part
in what is known of satanic worship through the ages. Yet it is
also the chosen language of some of the greatest mystics for an
individual's personal relationship with God, as in the poems of
St John of the Cross. They saw the language of sexual love as
the best medium for expressing the passion and intimacy of
prayer.

So we are left with an ambivalence –a sense of power yet
danger –and in the institutional life of the church it is the sense
of fear and danger that seems to have prevailed in a 'safety first'
policy. This of course has its great attraction, for the structures
of religion are then available to us, either to help us subdue
what feels unruly or even to keep us in unawareness of some of
our deepest feelings and desires. The extent to which this
defence may be helpful we shall look at later, but here I want to
make the opposite point; that which is pushed under and not
allowed to exist may burst through into consciousness in a way
that is exceedingly uncomfortable to the person and can cause
considerable emotional pain mingled with guilt.

Thus it is that sexuality may be more rather than less of a
problem to religious people than might, on the surface, have
been expected.

*The first need – the Pastor's understanding and acceptance of his sex-
uality, and of his role as a minister or priest.*

I put this first because I think it comes first. Yet paradoxically it can easily be glossed over or even ignored altogether.
The pastor is himself the product of his religious tradition and
so shares, both consciously and unconsciously, in the heritage
suggested in the previous section. And so a primary need for us
as pastors must surely be to work on our own sexuality – do we
accept that part of ourselves for what it is, how far have we
managed to work through our own feelings in this area?

Without such selfunderstanding and awareness two opposite things are likely to happen.

First we can respond harshly towards people's sexual problems if they touch, too nearly, unacknowledged parts of ourselves. In such a stance we may feel we have the 'support' of the institutional church since many of its pronouncements tend in this direction. We can even invoke the 'will of God' as the ultimate law-giver and agent of punishment.

At the other extreme we may see ourselves as the agents of liberation who feel that 'anything goes', who are predictably 'agin' the institution and can sometimes discount a sense of remorse having its basis in actions which a person may, in maturity, regret. This can happen when we have *half* worked through the implications of our sexuality and perhaps reached an 'adolescent' stage of experimentation and quasi-freedom, *without* the discernment of what it is a person is actually asking of us.

This applies of course to all who work in counselling but there are other difficulties for a pastor inherent in his role and in himself in so far as his personal development has colluded with or been stunted by this role. For example he may himself have some fear of his sexuality or of other people and feel 'safe' in his position as a minister and yet in reality be very vulnerable. Many pastors could describe, often with a sense of failure and shame, occasions when pastoral relationships have gone wrong because members of their congregation have become attached to them, either in an overtly sexual way, or in a dependence in which the idea of there being a sexual involvement would shock and be hotly denied by one and probably both parties. Furthermore, this someties seems to happen to pastors of high calibre, and if, as sometimes unfortunately happens, scandal erupts in the parish or a clergy marriage breaks up, everybody is shocked and surprised and asks in bewilderment, 'but how could this happen?'

What then can a pastor do, for such situations are likely to arise, given the nature of sexuality and the religious congregation's shared myths about it. Two things stand out, first the minister's need for mutual support. This is more difficult than it sounds because we are often reluctant to admit that we

have got into a muddle. But the growing awareness of the need
for support groups and the chance to talk things through outside the hierarchical structure is a hopeful sign. Secondly we
need to grow in the ability to keep our personal boundaries and
to set limits for ourselves and others, preferably before a situation deteriorates to the point where rejection has set in.

Why has this person come to a Pastor?
   It seems that there are two kinds of people who are likely to
turn to a priest or minister for help with sexual (or other) problems. The members of his regular congregation may come,
and the complete stranger, particularly in inner-city areas, who
decides to take the church at its word that pastoral care is for
any who seek it. Obviously the sorts of encounter that ensue
are different, but there is one underlying question that is the
same: 'Why a pastor with this problem?'
   It may be that the person knows nowhere else to go, the pastor is the obvious and only source of help. In this case the pastor
will have to discern whether he feels he can deal with what is
being presented to him, or whether he is really being asked to
be the channel towards a more appropriate source of help.
   But it may be, and indeed most usually is, that somebody
who wants to see a pastor about sexual difficulties has come
precisely because he is a minister. Some of the reasons for this
he may be aware of, others he may not. He is likely to have
expectations of the minister, that he or she will take a certain
line and uphold certain values. He may come, with or without
a sense of sin and guilt, fearing a harsh response, or perhaps, at
some level of his being, seeking one. He may come seeking
support and strength in his upholding of his principles, or he
may come in confusion, caught between these very principles
and his instictive desires. He may come seeking absolution or
he may come seeking permission. He may come, in effect, asking the pastor to help him put back his defences, or he may
come wanting to explore these defences and what lies
behind them.
   As pastors we may feel that we both cannot and do not want
necessarily to meet our congregant's expectations. But this is no
licence for a crude violation of another's defences and value

system even when they may be in sharp conflict with our own. Faced with a person's discomfort with their sexuality we need to take time with them to explore their values and beliefs. There is likely to be a particular difficulty for both pastor and parishioner here since the ideals of the church and its official pronouncements are in potentially sharp conflict with the norms of present day society where cohabitation, sex before marriage, etc., are all acceptable and becoming more general. What is a pastor to respond if he is faced with the question, 'I'm sleeping with someone I'm not married to – is it all right?'

A possible response might be:

> I think we both know what the church has taught about this. So it may be important if we could look a bit at the sort of feelings you have about doing something that seems against that teaching, and what has brought you to want to talk to me about it . . . You ask, 'Is it all right?' I wonder what your yourself are thinking . . . or fearing.

To condemn out of hand will not be caring. To set the boundaries of the church's position as you geuinely understand them will be.

This sort of response can clarify the question that is being asked and can be made independently of the *personal* position, on these issues, of the pastor. But the pastor *will* have a personal position, and having a more general 'caring' rather than an explicitly counselling role, there is the danger that he will 'unload' this on his parishioner to the latter's disease and detriment. For example it will not help for a person to be told by a 'liberal' pastor that sex before or outside marriage is acceptable, if his firmly held religious belief is that it is not. The only way, it seems to me, is to explore first the sense of guilt and its possible origin so that the person has a chance to re-evaluate it and the pastor and client together can clarify the goal of pastoral care in a particular instance. Is it to help the person come to terms with a *conscious* conflict between his principles and desires, probably involving some continued personal suffering? Or is it to try and help him sort out whether this suffering is really required by his religious beliefs or is self-imposed through a misunderstanding and distortion of them? In either case the beliefs and values matter to the person and need to be explored as central to the experience; it is for this dimension that he has perhaps come to a pastor.

What sort of difficulties are likely to be presented?

The first important point here is that a person worried by sexual problems who goes to a minister may not start by talking about them at all; he may fear that they will not be acceptable in this setting and start with something like difficulties with faith which he feels is the 'right' thing to take to a minister. It is difficult to give guildelines as to how we may know that there is something else which is not being said, but as in all counselling, a sense of being heard and given time without premature conclusions and advice-giving may allow the person to go on and say more. There are sometimes hints in the initial material – often loosely connected to the idea of relationships or to doing or thinking things which 'seem wrong' which can be gently picked up.

A sense of conflict between desires for thought or action and present principles or past upbringing is the most likely difficulty to be revealed. A person may experience unbidden sexual feelings towards other people, often those people who are in some sense 'forbidden' to him. It may be that sexual feeling and arousal obtrude into prayer or the sacraments. In all these guilt at the inability to subdue sexual feeling and arousal is likely to be a major source of discomfort and the person is unlikely to be able to celebrate his sense of creativity and being alive. Basically he is experiencing what he thinks his religion says he should not experience; he may also be afraid that his feelings will go over, without control, into action which the rest of him does not want and which he fears may have disastrous consequences.

These difficulties stem from a sense of an excess of sexual feeling. Yet though there does seem to be a taboo on the celebration of sexuality, there is also quite a pressure, in church circles, to conform to the norms of marriage and family. So there may be another group of people who come, not from fear of their own excesses, but becuase they feel they do not have it in them to be adequate in the field of relationships, marriage and family. There are people who come afraid of sex and with fears of their own essential unattractiveness; men who feel impotent as partners, husbands and fathers, and women who are frigid and never really enjoy that side of marriage and so never live the whole of it. Somehow their religion, whilst not favouring sexual celebration makes them also feel guilty if they don't get by *well enough* within the structure – both spoken and unspoken. Or again there are those who enjoy a sexual relationship outside marriage but realize that in this they have gone beyond the norms of the congregation; though it must be said that such 'norms' vary between congregations and geographical areas. These people may not feel that their sexual feelings are either excessive or inadequate but that they do not fit rightly into the model of a 'good' religious married and family life.

Then there are those – usually in a minority – whose sexual tastes deviate from the norm either in fantasy or in actuality. People can be very worried and upset by sado-masochistic fantasies which are not uncommon and, like anger, can be taboo for Christians. If this occurs in someone who is a regular member of a congregation and they have come to the pastor they may well be in considerable distress about it and find it very hard to express.

How can the Pastor help?

I want to avoid the 'cook-book' approach here for the essence of good pastoral care and couselling lies not in our administration of 'recipes' and solutions but in our sensitivity to the unique story the person tells us and the relationship we can make with him. Nevertheless there are some points we may have in our mind as we listen. *First* we can listen, and so help the person say what he needs and wants to say. This may sound simple but of course it is not so for several reasons that we have touched on already, and the following 'dialogues' between pastor (P) and congregant (C) will, I hope, point them up. The parishoner may go round and round before he comes to the point.

C. Sometimes I just don't feel adequate . . . You know, when you think you ought to be able to do something and can't.

P. Something very important to you?

C. Yes . . . and its awful to let someone else down and I end up feeling terrible and ashamed and its not easy to talk about.

P. Very personal things are sometimes very hard to talk about.

C. Yes, it is personal, so personal that I'm not sure you'll understand, or perhaps you'll think its awful for a man to have this difficulty.

P. Perhaps that I might write you off as a man because of it?

C. Yes, that's it . . . I feel useless as a man when I most want to be one and to make other people feel good with me.

P. You sound as if you're talking about not feeling a man in close relationships.

C. Yes, very close and private . . . you know the sort.

P. The sort I'm thinking of are marriage and other partnerships where the whole of us is involved – emotionally and sexually – is that perhaps what you're meaning?

C. (with a sigh of relief) Yes, I was, and its the sexual bit I can't manage (and then goes on to talk about his impotence).

Or the pastor may find what he hears uncomfortable and distasteful to him:

C. (woman in mid-twenties) Well, I'm sleeping around – I know the church disapproves, but I do it. I've slept with four different men in the last three weeks; I find after a while I can't resist them when they try so hard.

P. You said something about the church disapproving, but perhaps the more important thing is what you feel about it.

C. Oh! I don't feel much either way – it's just what happens.

P. So I wonder what's brought you to talk to me about it.

C. I'm not sure really; I thought you'd go on about the church and me being a bad member of the congregation – I wasn't expecting you to care about how I felt.

P. Is that what you usually find – that people don't care about how you feel?

C. (angrily) No, that's the trouble, they don't and I don't. I don't have any feelings about it and I'm all dead inside. I'd rather even feel bad.

In the first example the pastor might have been tempted to give reassuring responses particularly at the point when his parishioner felt he wouldn't understand and would think him awful. Yet had he done so the person might well have been inhibited from going on; 'how can I accept this reassurance feeling the shame I do; if he *really* knew what I was meaning he wouldn't be able to say that'. In fact the pastor stayed with the content of the parishioner's fear, using it to go a little further along the path until the awful thing was nearly said between them. At that point the pastor ventured a guess; if he hadn't but continued the dialogue as it was going the parishioner might have come to it himself. This is always a point of judgment – whether or not to help out. To do so too early can seem like an intrusion or prevent the person from owning or experiencing for himself his distress and difficulty, and of course the pastor may be on the wrong track. Yet to withhold it in the interest of a counselling model that says it must come from the client can be uncaring and even torturing when the other person is desperately struggling.

In the second instance the pastor could well have felt that his parishioner was flaunting her sexuality at him, in a sort of bravado and making much of the sense that the men all wanted her. It would have been easy to have responded from a hidden anger in the disapproving church role that the client was asking for rather than make it possible for her to recognize and begin to express some of her discomfort and distress.

In both these examples listening, and trying to pick up the 'music' rather than just the notes of the communication, was to enable the parishioner to go beneath what he or she was able to come out with initially. Giving in to the need or the desire to reassure or chastise –perhaps the occupational hazard of being a pastor – would probably have brought the telling to a full stop. It is the telling and *being heard* that can begin to bring relief.

There may occasionally be an exception to this guideline of listening. The pastor may become seduced into wanting to hear more of this sort of material –for himself and not for the other person – or there may arise that instance when the pastor comes to feel that he is being almost 'used' as an audience in a way that gives a perverse sexual satisfaction to the teller. Difficult as it is to discern when this is happening or when the material is touching something difficult for us, if it seems to become clear that it is happening then it probably belongs to true pastoral care to say so. This may in fact help the other person more than if we feel the need to be the passive recipient of anything and everything.

Secondly we need to remember that our sexuality is only part of us, but a part that is sensitive to the whole of us. Our sexual problem may be an expression not so much only of that part of us, but perhaps of a basic lack of self-confidence or self-esteem. Just as the person may conceal his sexual difficulties under religious ones so the sexual problem itself may be the symptom and not the whole.

Thirdly the pastor can try to help get things into perspective. It is easy for sexual sins to assume complete pride of place and for guilt for them to reach colossal proportions, backed up often by childhood memories and half-digested snippets of teaching. Do we expect such perfection in other areas of our religious life? What makes sexual failings so unforgiveable? Are we likely to be the only people experiencing them? All these questions are pertinent, and even without their being raised directly the parishioner may come to be more realistic and compassionate towards himself without violating principles. It may well be how comfortable the pastor is with his own sexuality that can facilitate this process. Nothing may be *said*, but much may be *communicated*.

Fourthly there can be specific points of exploration and education, involving perhaps the disabusing of certain myths. Again I will attempt to illustrate this with an example. Suppose someone comes to us and says, 'I wanted to come and talk to you because I have some questions about masturbation. I do it quite a lot and enjoy it at the time, but it bothers me a bit afterwards. There are two things really: I've read somewhere that it can do you physical harm and the church calls it self-abuse, and also that you shouldn't have or give way to fantasies whilst you're doing it, and that these fantasies can be harmful'.

On the first part a helpful response for the pastor might well be actually to answer the question, explaining that masturbation is not detrimental to physical health, and putting the misconceptions that have been current in both the church and the secular world into historical perspective. This sort of education may be all that is wanted and needed; though if the parishioner finds his doubts and questions persisting irrationally then it becomes important to look at how he learnt them and whether they reflect a deeper layer of personal guilt or something left over unresolved from childhood and the way in which he was brought up.

The second question raises the issue of the relationship between thought and act, fantasy and reality. The educational role of the pastor lies here in helping clarify the *difference* between thoughts, feelings and fantasies which in themselves are not good, bad or sinful – they are simply what we have and which we deny at our emotional peril – and it is their going over into consciously planned action which may be inappropriate, undesirable and even harmful to ourselves and others, but over which we have, potentially, control. This is a separate issue from whether the *content* of our fantasies – as distinct from the fact of our having them – is frightening or unpleasant to us. For this reason it is usually helpful to encourage someone to be specific on what he fantasizes and how the fantasies affect him to see if exploration of them, rather than education on the difference between them and reality, is more appropriate.

Fifthly there can be mutual recognition of conscious conflicts and the offering of continued support in facing and exploring them.

These all belong in the area of pastoral care and may be all that is necessary or wanted. If it emerges that the sexual problem is more serious, resistant and crippling or that it seems to be the visible expression of a more deep-seated emotional difficulty then the pastor has to decide whether to enter into a more specific counselling contract, or whether to work towards referring the person to somebody else for help. The pastor who feels he wants to refer needs pastoral skill to do this so that the person does not feel pushed off or rejected by the person from whom he chose to seek help.

To whom can he refer?

I find this a difficult question. Sex therapies and therapists have abounded in recent years, but they have had mixed results, have often confined their work to couples and have tended to focus on the presenting sexual problem rather than on difficulties of relationship or personal life that may underly it. It is also impossible to generalize on how acceptable they would be to those with strong belief and value systems. There are central psychotherapeutic resources, some specializing in sexual difficulties as does the Portman Clinic in London, some, such as Westminster Pastoral Foundation and its affiliated centres, offering a more general service, but all considering the symptom against the total emotional life of the person. Yet an individual pastor will probably do best to get to know the resources in his area to learn whom he feels he can trust and those to whom he can make a personal referral. The Association for Pastoral Care and Counselling or the Personal, Sexual, Marital and Family division of the British Association for Counselling are there to help in this process of building up a network.

Either decision – to refer or not to refer – raises the issues of confusion of roles, and boundaries and limits.

Personal intimacy

There has been and is a widespread myth that personal and sexual intimacy are identical; difficulties in the latter have sometimes made people feel that they are somehow less than 'proper' people. Yet sexual intimacy is only one part of close personal relationships and maybe what the pastoral dimension can especially offer is this insight. Sexuality and sexual relationships need to be seen in the wider perspective of meaning and the valuing of each individual person.

Finally, perhaps the most most important point in this kind of pastoral encounter is that he who comes for help with a difficulty that perhaps he finds very hard and shameful to acknowledge should go away feeling that he has been heard and *respected* as a human being.

7. Homosexuality

By Jim Cotter, Priest and Counsellor
working in the Anglican diocese of St. Albans

'Homosexuality is much more complicated than I thought – and much less frightening . . . The more you study it the more you discover that it is really about people and their relationships and their happiness and the ability to live their lives creatively.' (The Bishop of Gloucester)
'(To be homosexual is a) fundamental and ordinary way of being a human being.' (Axel, a character in Iris Murdoch's novel *A Fairly Honourable Defeat*)
'The Church could make no more important contribution to the public understanding of homosexual relationships than to provide a model of how one may look carefully and clearsightedly at the issues – and having done that (and before doing that and while doing that) to listen to homosexuals.' (The Editor of *Crucible*, the journal of the Church of England Board of Social Responsibility)

'That's not easy,' most pastors would say. We cannot *of ourselves* be all things to all folk. Our 'in-Christ-ness', or Christlikeness, is incomplete. People come our way whose stories, if we are honest, provoke strong feelings in us, not least where the unfamiliar is concerned. Fear and hostility can compound our ignorance, so that we communicate rejection, however reasonable and kind we try to be on the surface, however much we say to ourselves, 'This too is a fellow human being for whom Christ died'. We may hide our feelings with a statement of authority, 'The Bible says . . . ', or 'The church teaches . . . ', but we thus avoid any real encounter with the person in front of us.

Does this response need to be changed in the light of a more considered examination of what is, from any point of view, an emotive issue? How *do* pastors give 'first aid' to the folk who are troubled by some aspect of their relationships with others of the same sex or of their overwhelmingly or predominantly homosexual orientation? Attitudes *have* been changing over the last generation, both in the church and in the wider world: according to a poll published in *The Observer* on 23 September 1984, between half and two-thirds of the population now think that homosexual people should have the same civil rights as heterosexual people, and Christians are not noticeably less tolerant than anybody else. But this puts the pastor in a dilemma who approaches the issue in a traditional way.

Here is a minefield which can be personally very disturbing. We need St Paul's prayer in Philippians 1.9: '. . . it is my prayer that your love will abound more and more, with knowledge and all discernment . . . ' (RSV). I take it that, as pastors, we do *pray* that the self-giving *agape-love* may abound in our helping and may increase in those whom we seek to help. But what in this minefield is *knowledge* and *discernment*? What are the facts? How do we discern the will of God in the dispensations of the Spirit?

The facts are complex, disputed, and nearly always bound up with feelings. Hardly any word we use is neutral. As far as I am aware the basic statistical facts discovered by Kinsey in the 1930s in America (the survey was published after the Second World War) have never been successfully challenged. He measured the incidence of sexual activity and found that, among men, 5% were sexually active *only* with others of their own sex, and a further 5% *almost* exclusively so. The figures for women were slightly lower. Those facts perhaps don't surprise us as much as they did Kinsey and his colleagues, although we may still very much not want to believe them. But they have alerted a new generation to a phenomenon widespread enough for concern, for much thought, and increasingly for a new awareness to grow among the members of this minority. Quite simply, we are talking about a great many people. What has also become clear is that we are talking about a phenomenon that is by no means as simple as the mere figures about behaviour might suggest. The variety of lifestyles adopted by homosexual people is quite bewildering, as is the plethora of theories as to the 'origins' of homosexual orientation. These are sometimes illuminating, but always unproven and often very selective in the kind of people they have observed, usually those who have come the way of researchers in the medical world because they are the ones who are ill at ease with their sexuality. Michael Schofield in a book called *Sociological Aspects of Homosexuality* (Longmans, 1965) showed how he had surveyed certain groups of people according to criteria of emotional maturity. He drew comparisons between homosexual people who had been convicted of a crime, those who had been patients, and a random sample of others, together with samples of heterosexual people in each of those categories. He concluded that the random sample of homosexual people (the third category) were more like the random sample of heterosexual people than they were like the samples drawn from homosexual people who had been convicted of a crime or been patients. Having said that, I need to add that there is as yet no book that has presented all the main theories, with their strengths and weaknesses, and come to a conclusion acceptable to those people concerned about the issue. No doubt the quest will continue: meanwhile, feelings and facts will continue to mingle, and we have to look elsewhere for pastoral guidance.

Further, nearly all the words used to describe homosexual activity and persons have pejorative associations. Scriptural language gives us 'sin', 'sodomy', and 'abomination'; legal language gives us 'a crime against nature' and 'buggery'; medical language gives us 'homosexuality, a pathological condition of perversion or inversion', or, in more recent and sympathetic accounts, 'a state of emotional immaturity'. This has produced the reaction among homosexual people themselves of taking over words and phrases that were once thought appropriate only to marriage, in turn provoking the disagreement of most heterosexual people. It is worth asking, 'Can I think of "making love" as desirable in both homosexual and heterosexual contexts?'.

Again, it may matter a great deal to the troubled person in the study whether or not the pastor uses the word 'abnormal'. It *may* have a dictionary definition of 'not according to the statistical norm', but in common usage when talking of homosexual activity it has emotional and moral overtones which the more carefully chosen, neutral, and rarely used 'unusual' does not have.

Another complication arises when the pastor relates to people with this attitude of 'Hate the sin' but 'Love the sinner'. No doubt what is intended is a sincere effort to help the person in trouble, to give that person a true sense of being accepted as he or she is. The 'sin', in this case a homosexual act, is thus made into an object, condemned, and expelled. The difficulty in this approach is that our sexuality, whatever its orientation, is bound up so closely with how we express ourselves as bodily beings, that an outright rejection of a particular act, whatever the circumstances, motives, and consequences might be, is inevitably experienced as a rejection of the whole person. So it may be more honest to say, 'I cannot cope with the fact of your being a 'practising homosexual', and the only way I can relate to you is by excluding that fact from our relationship'. Whether or not that is a pastorally effective statement is another matter. It does seem hard for us to bear ambivalence, to say, 'I have to hold together my concern for you and for your growth in the love of God and of others, as well as my dislike of you as the person who is a "practising homosexual"'. This 'you' is a 'person-including-activity', not the person somehow detachable from deeds done. After all, Jesus himself *enjoyed* the company of 'sinners' at meals *before* he challenged them to face deeper questions about the springs of their behaviour. The problem is that most homosexual people find it hard to trust that this approach will be followed by the representatives of the church. Their experience is usually of a kindness that smiles but is really a mask for hostility: clear and comfortable and reasoned opposition is rare.

Moreover, the very term 'practising homosexual' distances the pastor from the person. It seems to turn the person into a phenomenon to be investigated rather than a person to be recognized. It is much like the by-passing of the disabled man referred to in the third person, 'Does he take sugar?' If you sense that your sexuality is interwoven with the rest of your life, it makes *no sense* to you to be treated as if that sexuality were isolable, examinable, and replaceable. The homosexually orientated person in the pastor's study is a human sexual being who needs help in enabling that sexuality to serve the ends of a wide and deep loving, and help in making enough space within to be able to make responsible moral choices for him or herself. The first pastoral task is to see and listen to such a human being steadily and whole.

The church as a whole, through its representatives, has until very recently, and at least since the thirteenth century, tended to reject *people* with same-sex relationships, not just the sexual activity of those people. So the invitation to the pastor is to meet and recognize the one who is different, to be involved, not in a debate in which one side has to win, but in a dialogue in which both parties may reach a deeper understanding of each other, both changing in the process.

In the hope that this dialogue might increase, I want to mention three organizations which can be contacted if any reader wants to meet gay people who have at least partially thought and lived their way through rejection and apathy to dignity and liberty. These are: Gay Switchboard (01-837 7324) which operates a 24-hour information service and has the numbers of all the regional Switchboards: Campaign for Homosexual Equality, 274 Upper St., London N1 (01-359 2973); and Gay Christian Movement, (BM Box 6914, London WC1N 3XX (01-283 5165). Also of relevance are the Scottish Homosexual Rights Group, 60 Broughton St., Edinburgh, EH1 3SA, and other Christian groups; Quest, for homosexual Catholics, and Friends' Homosexual Fellowship, information about both of which can be gleaned via the Gay Christian Movement. If I had to choose one novel to recommend it would be *Consenting Adult* by Laura Z. Hobson (Heinemann), not least because it is told from the point of view of a mother coming to terms with her son's 'difference'.

I turn now to some of the other issues on which pastors will have strong feelings and opinions. One is the use and authority of the Bible. We may be genuinely accepting of people different from ourselves, recognize them, have talked long with them, and still take a different stance about the morality of particular sexual activity. And this can be based on a thorough analysis of the biblical record on the broader concerns of sexuality and marriage as a whole, not least on the matter of the complementarity of men and women, sometimes supported by a theory of 'natural law', and coming to the conclusion that sexual activity is intended by God to be restricted to a lifelong exclusive partnership between two people of opposite sexes. There will be argument as to how far such activity should *always* be open to the possibility of conception, but there is a strong argument for marriage as the place where most people will find the greatest happiness, will heal each other's emotional wounds, and enable each other to grow into a more mature loving. Most people probably need that kind of security and commitment, guarded by a promise of sexual exclusiveness, if they are to flourish as adults.

Now it is clear that the biblical writers are against any kind of sexual activity between those of the same sex. The specific references are Genesis 19 (with its parallel in Judges 19), Leviticus 18.22 and 21.13, Romans 1.24 – 27, 1 Corinthians 6.9-10, and 1 Timothy, 1.9-10. Even if the context is taken into account and it is argued that what is being condemned is group rape or prostitution or idolatry or violence, I think that such a writer as St. Paul would still want to say that even in the context of a loving relationship, genital activity between members of the same sex would be wrong (even if his specific example in Romans is of heterosexual people who switch to homosexual activity). It would offend against the natural order, against God's blueprint of creation: it would be one example among many of the fallenness of humanity and of the whole creation. (The same argument would be used about certain kinds of food – there is an 'Unnatural', 'disordered' incompleteness about some fish and mammals.) If you agree with this approach (a typical charitable exponent is David Field in *The Homosexual Way: a Christian Option?*, published by Grove Booklets), then you are bound to want to help your troubled person either to explore any possible latent heterosexual feelings (and some may be bisexual in their attraction emotionally and sexually), or, if these are non-existent, to be totally abstinent sexually, and to seek to put sexual energy into other creative channels. Some do follow this way and find, like the celibate who has chosen such a vocation, that their sexuality can become diffused throughout their being and can bring zest and sparkle to all their loving. Harry Williams in his autobiography, *Someday I'll Find You* (Mitchell Beazley), writes movingly of how he has reached that place in his own life, though it is after experience of actual sexual relationships, both satisfying and not. Another personal story from an evangelical point of view is that of Alex Davidson, in *The Returns of Love*, published by the Inter-Varsity Press.

The question remains, 'Is this the only Christian option?' It can be argued, for example, that the biblical writers were condemning a turning away from heterosexual acts to homosexual acts, and that was a going 'against nature' *for heterosexual people*. They (the writers) couldn't have been *aware of* – their whole history and background anyway wouldn't have allowed them to *see* – that minority of people whose homosexual orientation and experience of falling in love and making love with another of their own sex is *to them* natural indeed. To try to force or persuade such people to change may be as cruel as the witch hunts and inquisitions of old which used the argument still heard today in the homosexual context: 'We are hurting your body so that there may still be a chance that your soul will be saved'. There are too many stories of people known personally to the writer who have been 'exorcised' or 'excommunicated' from Christian groups and congregations for there to be a too easy insistence that all homosexually orientated people *must* be abstinent in all circumstances. 'Homophobia' is a relatively new word to describe those who have an irrational fear of homosexual behaviour, and the sad fact is that it is not uncommon among pastors who claim to be motivated by Christian love.

A different approach is possible. It begins with the plea to take natural justice seriously, and would point to those passages of Scripture which are concerned with God's particular love of the outcast and the rejected, a love which found its focus in the Incarnation. That compassionate note is occasionally found amidst the more usual exclusions and condemnations: even eunuchs and foreigners will one day have a more favoured place in God's realm than those who see themselves at the centre of the life of God's chosen people (Isaiah 56. 1 – 8). In the

New Testament it is significant that the first non-Jewish Christians spoken of in the Acts of the Apostles are represented by two who were conventionally suspect – the Ethiopian eunuch and the Samaritan. (And the eunuch was rejected on the grounds of his infertility, as were any whose sexual organs were imperfect.)

Further it can be argued that the biblical record does not see creation as something that God did at the beginning in such a finished way that Adam was handed a blueprint complete with the Maker's full instructions. Rather God *is creating* the universe. So the Bible makes us to help towards the fulfilment of God's purposes as he seeks to bring us through our sin and pain and muddle to the wholeness and love that will reflect his glory?

We need to take into account as well some detailed historical research (communicated by John Boswell in *Christianity, Social Tolerance, and Homosexuality*, University of Chicago Press, 1980), which shows that for most of its history before the thirteenth century the church was usually tolerant and sometimes accepting of homosexual relationships, which it hardly could have been if the biblical evidence had been unequivocal and the experiences it was reflecting accorded exactly with their own.

If we are thus open to the possibility of re-thinking, there will still be the task of establishing some criteria by which to discern the morality of sexual behaviour, criteria which need firmly to be in the mind of the pastor who seeks to bring clarity to the confused person who has come for help.

It is clear at the beginning that certain kinds of behaviour can always be regarded as sinful, on the grounds of their violence rather than because the behaviour is sexual. It seems to me that there are three clear No's: (1) Do not force your attention on anyone; (2) Do not trivialize another human being as a disposable object; (3) Do not take advantage of another's ignorance or immaturity.

Beyond this, it is fair to point out various Christian opinions and approaches, from the abstinence mentioned above to one or other of the following, outlined in the Report of the Working Party of the Board of Social Responsiblility of the Church of England, 'Homosexual Relationships' (1979).

One view is reported as saying that 'so long as a sexual relationship is minimally personal, it is at least to be accepted, even if a more completely loving relationship would be better' (para. 139).

Another would disagree with that: 'Sexual intercourse . . . is thought of as the uniquely appropriate expression of profound erotic love and as such, therefore, not to be engaged in where genuine love is absent . . . Some would hold that genuine love involves a life-long exclusive commitment . . . (others) that the relationship should be exclusive but need not be permanent; it would last as long as love lasts and no longer' (para. 138).

Infusing such relationships for the Christian will be values of commitment, creativity, mutuality, unselfishness, gentleness, passion, sensitivity, trust, truth, responsibility, and generosity. Time is needed for such values to be expressed fully and maturely, and a loyalty and faithfulness needed if there is to be that space between two people which takes them from possessiveness to freedom to love. The logic therefore is towards the higher valuing of the more permanent and exclusive relationship, while realizing that in the social climate of the day this may be very hard to achieve for many homosexual people, and other relationships may be 'good', if not 'best'.

It may be a useful exercise for the pastor now to ask if sexual activity is akin more to killing or to eating. In the former case, the approach will be, 'Do not do this except under certain very restricted circumstances', and in the latter, 'Apart from certain limited circumstances, this is a good thing to do, and occasionally it will be marvellous'.

How far do we consistently think, feel, believe, and act on the belief that our sexuality is *good*? Do we believe that it truly is a God-given means of our drawing closer to one another? A theological and ethical approach which gives a resounding *Yes* to these questions can be found in James Nelson's *Embodiment* (published in America in 1978 and by SPCK in this country). A book by Joan Ohanneson charts the progress of recent Roman Catholic thinking, especially in America, and is significantly entitled, *And They Felt No Shame: Christians Reclaim Their*

Sexuality. On the front of the book is a quotation by Jean Houston: ' . . . the coming end of the dark ages of the body in the Church'.

Pressed further, the question becomes the profound theological one of the goodness of creation. Christian answers have varied from 'completely corrupt' to 'mildly warped'. To think long and hard about homosexual relationships is a touchstone of our own approach. Further, in the context of the Incarnation, how much do we talk of the goodness of the flesh in proportion to our talk of the weakness of the flesh? Many troubled people have at the heart of that trouble such a hatred of themselves that they find it hard to accept themselves as bodily beings with sexual desires, regarding themselves as unworthy of any caring and healing touch.

When a person has begun to recover a measure of self-worth, it may be possible to open up the question of Why? Why was I born – or made – like this? It is a different question form that of *origins* (the latter being fruitless in terms of any convincing answers). If there is a God-given *purpose* in being sexually orientated towards your own sex, then you may be able to give up blame-throwing for your condition – either at self or parents or institutions or God. There is no obvious answer to this question either, but it may be suggestive to explore the value to a society of those who are at its edges, the explorers, the ones at the frontiers, the ones most alert to the changes that are coming in the future. If the majority of human beings are needed to spend a significant part of their lives in marriage and bringing up a family, the minority is needed to quest into the future, to be the 'prophets' who alert the majority to impending danger. They may very well be without honour in their own country, and they have to seek affirmation from the few who perceive, but they will be doing something essential for the well-being of the many. I am not saying that there are not heterosexual prophets, nor that all homosexually orientated people *are* prophets, but it is a stance that can give to the person who has always felt 'different' an increased sense of value and worth and vocation.

When this stage has been reached in the pastoral guidance of an individual, there will be a degree of maturity realized that can enable that individual, with conscience educated, to be at last free to make a *choice* of lifestyle, a choice that may be celibacy or may be some kind of sexually loving special friendship. In the end, the goal for all of us is that our lives should be totally enGodded, and that means that all our relationships should become increasingly Christlike: that needs all the prayer, love knowledge, and discernement of which we are capable.

A Note on AIDS

Up-to-date information can be obtained from the Terrence Higgins Trust, BM AIDS, London WC1N 3XX (01-278 8745). There is also a helpline (01-833 2971). The virus (HTLV–3) is hard to catch, although it should be recognized that it is a blood-borne disease. The great majority of those exposed to AIDS may never develop symptoms, but are capable of transmitting the virus. AIDS may be similar to latent cancers, a hazard we all probably have to come to terms with.

The most necessary and essential pastoral response is a warmth that really comes close and makes it clear in word and act that the sufferer is not seen as a leper. Both AIDS sufferers and their families, friends and partners need a great deal of warm support, and help to understand that neither their disease nor any other is a punishment for sin.

8. Race and Racism

BY THE REVEREND KENNETH LEECH,
BOARD FOR SOCIAL RESPONSIBILITY, CHURCH OF ENGLAND

I HAVE assumed that the readership of this chapter will consist for the most part of white pastors, some of whom work with multi-racial church and neighbourhood communitites, many of whom work with churches and communities which are entirely white. That is a reasonable assumption, for most pastors in Britain are white, most churches and neighbourhoods are predominantly or wholly white. For many pastors in multi-racial communities, much of the following will be superfluous and elementary: indeed, I have learnt much from many friends who have shared their experiences with me. [1] I have tried to bear in mind specifically two kinds of pastoral needs: the needs of those who find themselves working within a multi-racial church, or a church seeking to serve a multi-racial neighbourhood but uncertain of the way forward; and the needs of churches in all-white neighbourhoods, whether in city, suburb or countryside. First however, it is necessary to grasp the situation.

1. Race and racial minorities in Britain

If we are to minister effectively our ministry must be rooted in truth, and this calls for a true awareness of the situation and a refusal to accept the multitude of falsehoods and false sterotypes which dominate so much of the media coverage of this area. In the area of immigration data, for example, when facts contradict fiction, it is often the facts which are regarded as dubious. Of course, the mere dissemination of accurate information will not bring about a commitment to racial justice: in fact, the more people know, the more their attitudes may harden. The relationship between information and change is not a simple one. On the other hand, it is not possible to build a programme of pastoral or social action on false premises.

[1] In particular I wish to thank Bernard Ball, Pat Dearnley, Ann Dummett, Michael Hollings, Bob Kenway, Jean Mayland, Bob Nind, Harry Potter, David Randall, Judith Roberts and Phyllis Thompson for their ideas.

So a primary requirement is access to accurate information. Some resource points are given at the end of this chapter. It is important to recognize that many of the assumptions made by sections of the media, and promoted by certain politicians, are quite false. Thus it is widely held that most immigrants to Britain are black, and that most black people are immigrants. In fact, most immigrants to Britain are white, and this has always been the case. Since the controls introduced by the Commonwealth Immigrants Act 1962, primary immigration from the 'New Commonwealth' (that is, the non-white parts of the Commonwealth) was virtually halted. It follows that most black people here have either lived here for many years or were born here. A high percentage are British-born black people and should not be referred to as immigrants. Nor is it correct to speak of the black community as the 'immigrant community' as if these were synonymous terms.

Again it is important to remember that the black community,[2] or cluster of communities, is a small section of the total population. One reason for this is that almost as soon as there was evidence of organized racial violence (in 1958), the agitation for control spread. The controls were introduced within four years of the 1958 disturbances. Earlier immigration from the Caribbean, as from parts of Europe, had been recruited at a time of labour shortage. The motive for the encouragement of West Indian immigration was economic, not altruistic: it was a demand for cheap labour. The same people who promoted this campaign for cheap labour later campaigned for control, and sometimes for repatriation, when other sources of labour became available.

According to the Office of Population Censuses and Surveys in 1982, 3 per cent of the population originated in the Caribbean, Africa and the Indian subcontinent. This population, like the British population as a whole, is unevenly distributed. Thus in Greater London in 1982, some 14 per cent of the population lived in households headed by a person of New Commonwealth or Pakistani origin. However, a survey of young

[2] I use the term 'black' to include both people of Afro-Carribbean and of Asian origin, although it should be noted that some Asians, particularly of older generation, do not accept the word as an accurate description.

people's attitudes in 1981 showed that the belief that the black population in Britain was over 10 million was widespread, and a survey of theological students in 1982 showed that ignorance was widespread among them also.

According to Government figures, the highest percentages of ethnic minorities are in London boroughs, in particular Brent, Harringay, Hackney, Newham, and Ealing. However, the definition used is 'resident living in household where the head of the household was born in the New Commonwealth or Pakistan'. This gives information therefore about recent immigrants and their children, but not about long-established black communities. Thus the figure for Liverpool, where the black community goes back two hundred years, is 1.7 per cnet! The Runnymede Trust produces regular and up to date information on the facts and figures relating to ethnic minorities.

2. *Ministering in multi-racial churches and communities.*

As in the case of the national scene, accurate knowledge is vital. The pastor needs to know his or her neighbourhood. Who lives there? Where do they live? From what backgrounds do they come? What is their experience of living in Britain? It is important not to rely on established myths about the local population, for serious research often shows them to be incorrect. Equally, it is important to avoid repeating, thoughtlessly, generalized accounts of the parish. One London priest a few years ago often used to say, 'there are more coloured people than white in my parish'. In fact, the figure was around 6 per cent. Often clergy do not know the origin of the immigrants in their locality. If they are Asian, are they fron India, Pakistan or Bangladesh? Are they Muslim, Sikh, Hindu? What is their pattern of religious life? Who are their religious leaders? If people are from the Caribbean, from which islands do they come? There are enormous differences between islands, and it is not helpful simply to see people as 'West Indian'. The pastor needs to learn something of the history of the countries from which people have come, or from which parents or grand-parents have come. There is not substitute for an accurate knowledge of the neighbourhood and its population. The local history library often has material which is of great value and can refer clergy to other sources of knowledge.

However, systematic visiting of the neighbourhood is the best way of acquiring a detailed, street by street knowledge. When visiting, one should be aware of the fear of proselytizing. On the other hand, a sensitivity to cultural expectations is essential. To refuse an offered cup of tea, or food, can be seen as an insult. English clergy, who often are prone to rush around, sit on the edge of a chair, and stay only a few minutes, need to learn from people from overseas the value of relaxation and a more relaxed approach to time. Again, many African and West Indian Christians will expect a visiting pastor to pray with them. A pastor who is obviously embarrassed and ill and ease in spontaneous prayer needs to learn from his or her fellow Christians. On the other hand, there are many areas with large Asian communities who are almost entirely neglected by the churches, perhaps because they are not potential 'pew fodder'.

One purpose of visiting is to learn and listen. Listening to the experiences of black people is something which can be prevented by the kind of liberal conscience which feels it knows what should be done. The film strip *The Enemy Within* and the Zebra Project's worksheet 'Listening' (both referred to at the end of the chapter) will be helpful. The listening process will involve receiving a good deal of anger and pain. One priest in a parish with a large black population has commented: 'I am continually impressed by the generosity of so many black people and their graciousness to white people in spite of their experience of rejection, their experience of prejudice, an experience which they may successfully hide from you. But the hurt is there, and you have to know that it is there if you are to be of any pastoral use.' It is vital that the white pastor seeks to understand and recognize the pain which the persistent, day by day experience of racism has caused over years and centuries, and this requires an intensity of feeling and a willingness to try and enter into the experience of others.

Racism manifests itself at many levels: international, national, local, personal. The pastor needs to face the racism within himself or herself, needs in fact to 'take racism personally'. The personal awareness approach to racism has become know in recent years as Racism Awareness Training, and there are now a number of groups promoting such training. One such group, the Ecumenical Unit for Race Awareness Programmes (EURAP), established in 1983, seeks to work within the churches. There are two dangers in such programmes. One is that, as with other forms of experiential group work, race awareness training can become yet another form of self-indulgence by which middle-class whites contemplate their racist navels. The second is that, by focusing exclusively or mainly on the personal dimension, such training may actually hinder the struggle against racism in the structures of society. Nevertheless, programmes of this type can be valuable, and pastors need to be helped.

Again, knowledge of cultural practices among people from overseas is essential to good pastoral care. The pastor needs to become familiar with marriage and funeral customs. The English practice of getting a funeral service over in ten minutes is seen as disrespectful and cold by many Christians from other countries. Church functions and social gatherings need to take account of the preferences in food and drink of members of their congregations. One Roman Catholic church with a large Maltese and West Indian membership was dominated by Irish culture, and so the music at all parish functions was provided by a ceilidh band. An Anglican parish found that its West Indian members never stayed behind for coffee after the service; it took a while for them to think of providing tea as an alternative. Music is very important not only in worship but also in parties, youth clubs, and so on. Many British churches would be greatly enlivened by insights from Afro-Caribbean worship and music. At the social level, the type of music often determines the composition of social functions. Too much Reggae can quickly produce an all black youth club.

The pastor from one of the mainstream white-led churches will probably find that there are black-led churches in the neighbourhood. These will usually be Adventist or Pentecostal in ethos. Many West Indians in the mainstream churches are suspicious of or hostile towards these 'sideways churches'. Nevertheless they represent a vital and growing spiritual force among black Christians. The work of such groups as the Zebra Project has shown how dialogue and shared fellowship between the older established churches and these new churches can be developed and have very beneficial results. As well as the black-led churches, the Rastafarian movement will be a significant presence among Afro-Caribbean young people. There is much ignorance and misrepresentation of Rasta, and pastors should seek to study this movement and its spiritual meaning for increasing numbers of black people.

Many black people regard the Rastafarian movement as a form of illusion, a way of evading the necessary conflict with a racist society. Increasingly, black Christians are moving from a spirituality of comfort to one of combat. White pastors need to be ready to learn from their black brothers and sisters as they seek to rediscover the good news of salvation in the context of racial oppression and liberation.

3. *Ministering to the white community.*

'We don't have a race problem around here' is one of the most frequently encountered comments by suburban Christians. Invariably 'race-problem' means the presence of black people. No black people, no race problem. Black people are seen as intrinsically problematic. One of the most difficult, yet most urgent, of pastoral needs is to help white Christians to recognize the racism which is so deep within us and within our culture. Those pastors who have honestly faced the reality of racism in themselves will be best equipped to help others face racism in their own lives.

Racist attitudes and prejudice are often found within Christian communities. 'Whiteness' and 'Britishness' are seen as the norm, blacks are 'them', an alien presence. History and religion are seen through British eyes. Fears, often promoted or reinforced by the media, go deep, as do false stereotypes of other cultures. Sadly the church often not only fails to correct such ideas but helps to reinforce them. Religion and intolerance are often found together.

Pastoral care is often identified with the provision of comfort and the preservation of peace. Challenge and conflict are not welcomed by those who see the prime purpose of religion to be the dissemination of comfort and calm. Combating racism therefore will raise hostility and dissension within the local church, and pastors need to be prepared for such hostility. For example, in areas where racist and fascist movements are active in organizing racial fears and hatred, it will be necessary both to speak and act against them. This will certainly result in intimidation, abuse, anonymous racist letters, and perhaps physical threats or attacks. Here again the English fear of politics will surface, and the pastor who seeks to stand firm on gospel principles will be accused of 'dabbling in politics'.

In the struggle against organized racism, pastors would do well to find kindred spirits, comrades both inside and outside the Christian community. Support groups for prayer, fellowship and study will be helpful. A national organization such as CARAF (Christians Against Racism and Fascism) can be a valuable way of linking up Christians involved in combating racism and it also produces a good deal of popular literature.

Suburban Christians often say that there is nothing they can do. The pastor needs to help them to see the interconnections between the suburb and city. Many of those who live in suburbia occupy positions of power and influence over what happens in the inner city. They will often be readers of newspapers such as the *Daily Telegraph* which day by day help to reinforce false stereotypes of black people. They can be encouraged to write letters, to use their power and influence, and to identify the points of leverage in their lives and work. It is also important to help suburban Christians to recognize the links between racial and other forms of oppression. The racial conflict can thus become a spring-board, leading people to look more closely at oppressed and disadvantaged groups within their own districts. More than anything, it is important that white Christians in white neighbourhoods should begin to set their own houses in order. Why *are* they so wholly white? What are the social and economic factors which make this so? And what can be done about them?

Contacts between parishes of different ethnic compostion can be very useful in destroying false ideas. But such links must not be seen as a patronizing act of charity by which the affluent and comfortable minister to the deprived. White congregations can be helped to see how deprived *they* are by their isolation from a multi-racial community and the cultural impoverishment of their lives. Through well thought out links between parishes, some of the misunderstanding between city and suburb, town and countryside, black and white, can be overcome. This also applies at the international level. The Roman Catholic communion, with its strong international links, is at a great advantage here. Anglicans need to be helped to see that the Church of England is a small part of a worldwide and multi-racial church. In two respects it is very untypical of world Anglicanism: it is established, and most of its members are lapsed. On the other hand, Anglicanism is growing and flourishing in Africa. The Church Missionary Society (CMS) and the United Society for the Propagation of the Gospel (USPG), through their local groups and their journals, can do a great deal to get across the international aspects of being a Christian. The USPG runs 'Christians Aware', a network of young people, which promotes links of understanding between nations and races. Racism and nationalism are closely linked: the church as an essentially non-racial and international community needs to communicate to its members what in reality it is. Its response to black people and the reality of racism can therefore be seen as a diagnostic test of ecclesial faithfulness.

Some guidelines for further resources

For up to date and accurate data on race, immigration and related issues the following organizations are important:

Institute for Race Relations, 247 Pentonville Road, London N1 9NG (01-837 0041). The Institute publishes a journal *Race and Class* and has an excellent library. Runnymede Trust, 37A Grays Inn Road, London WC1 (01-404 5266).

Commission for Racial Equality, Eliot House, 11-12 Allington Street, London SW1 (01-828 7022).

For practical help and literature on immigration and nationality questions:

Joint Council for the Welfare of Immigrants, 44 Theobald Road, London WC1X 8SP (01-405 5527).

Much valuable educational material can be obtained from:

Community and Race Relations Unit (CRRU), British Council of Churches, 2 Eaton Gate, London SW1 (01-730 9611).

At the same address is the Committee for Relations with People of Other Faiths.

The Zebra Project, Bow Mission, 1 Merchant Street, London E1 (01-980 3745).

AFFOR, 173 Lozells Road, Lozells, Birmingham B19 1RN.

Evangelical Race Relations Group, 12 Bell Barn Shopping Centre, Cregoe Street, Birmingham B16 2DZ (021-622 6807).

Harmony, Harmony Centre, 22 St. Mary's Road, Meare, Glastonbury, Somerset BA6 9SP (04586-311).

The following, some of which are mentioned in the text, are of particular importance:

The Enemy Within (filmstrip and cassette) (CRRU). *Race Relations Teaching Pack.* For schools (AFFOR, £4.99).

Zebra Worksheets: education for racial justice (Zebra Project £1).

Issues and Resouces: a handbook for teachers in the multi-cultural society (AFFOR).

Roots of Racism (£1) and *Patterns of Racism* (£1.50). Illustrated books for use in schools (Institute of Race Relations).

Resources for a Plural Society (CRRU, Free).

Education and Racial Justice. (Board for Social Responsibility, Church House, Dean's Yard, London SW1P 3NZ, 20p).

The Ecumenical Unit for Race Awareness Programmes can provide courses on personal racism. Its address is:

56 Camberwell Road, London SE5 (01-703 4136).

On the philosophy of race awareness training, the basic text is Judy Katz, *White Awareness: a handbook for anti-racism training* (University of Oklahoma Press [1978]).

Material on the black-led churches includes:

Dialogue between Black and White Christians (Zebra Project, 50p).

Exodus. Bi-monthly magazine produced by black Christians, 75 Norlington Road, London E11 6LA (01-539 3900). (£8 p.a. by post).

Black Christians Speaking (Zebra Project).

Paul Charman, *Reflections: Black and White Christians in the City* (Zebra Project, 50p).

Ira V. Brooks. *Where do we go from here?* The history of the New Testament Church of God in Britain (Obtainable from Zebra Project).

On Rastafarianism, the following will be useful:

Joseph Owens, *Dread: the Rastafarians of Jamaica* (Sangster, Kingston [1976]).

Rastafarians in Jamaica and Britain (Catholic Commission for Racial Justice, 1 Amwell Street, London EC1R 1UL [1982]).

For suburban churches:

Understanding Race: a study pack for local churches (Board for Social Rsponsibility, Church House, Dean's Yard, London SW1P 3NZ).

There is important documentation on racist movements and their activities in:

Searchlight (monthly) 37B New Cavendish Street, London W1M 8JR (01-607 2648). (Postal subscription £6 p.a.)

CARAF, (Christians Against Racism and Fascism) is at 1 Brock Place, Devons Road, London E3. Its publications include:

Derrick Knight. *Beyond the Pale*. £3.50. A detailed study of the various 'Christian Right' groups who campaign against Christian Aid, World Council of Churches, etc., and numerous leaflets.

The missionary societies mentioned are:

Church Missionary Society, 175 Waterloo Road, London SE1 8UU (01-928 8681).

United Society for the Propagation of the Gospel, 15 Tufton Street, London SW1 (01-222 7222).

9. High Unemployment

By the Reverend R. P. Taylor, M.A.,
Newport and Gwent Industrial Mission

There is little need to take space in this book to show how serious a social problem unemployment is; it has aroused the concern of the churches in a way that no other public issue has done for many year, as is evidenced, for example, by the very high response to the initiatives taken by 'Church Action With the Unemployed' (CATWTU). At the same time it has become clear that while many churches *want* to do something about it, they do not always know *what* to do or how to go about it.

Church centres

On the principle of starting where we are we can point to two assets which the churches can bring to bear. Between them they have premises in all the places where people are unemployed, and they have skills in counselling which go beyond the simple giving of information and advice. With regard to the first of these, a number of churches have been disappointed that they have opened a room, tried to make it reasonably comfortable and pleasant, provided for coffee-making and so on – and then nobody has come!

If it's any consolation, it is not only *church* centres for the unemployed that have found this. The problem comes from trying to start halfway through the process instead of at the beginning. A great deal of work needs to be done, making contact and building relationships, and possibly forming some sort of cohesive group, before the stage is reached where it is appropriate to think in terms of a regular place to meet and the kind of organizing that has to go with it. Even then it is usually better to respond to a request.

None of this is easy, of course. The proportion of unemployed people in most churches is much smaller than that in the population as a whole, and many churches consequently know very few of them. They are not easy to find; they look just like other people, and lists of names in Jobcentres and DHSS offices are confidential, while many of them, if they are actively looking for work, do not actually think of themselves as unemployed at all, much less identify themselves with a category labelled 'the unemployed'. To use a word now becoming familiar in other contexts, the experience of unemployment has become *privatized*, individuals and families coming to terms and coping with it on their own as best they can, and tending not to look elsewhere for help or mutual support among others in the same situation. For these and other reasons there is more to setting up a centre for the unemployed than simply unlocking a vestry door.

It should also be said that the churches are not alone in seeking to help the unemployed. Trades unions and community groups of various kinds are very active in this field, and churches should think carefully about the opportunities for cooperating with others before deciding to go it alone.

In turning to consider pastoral counselling for the unemployed, we do well to remind ourselves first that while this function has great and, as we shall see, sometimes critical importance, its location in the range of Christian responses to economic change is that of a casualty service, seeking to repair damage already inflicted. Within the ministry of the local church there is clearly a high priority for healing the wounds, binding up the broken hearted and encouraging new resolution and hope. But we need at least to register here that this cannot be the only way in which the churches respond to the basic changes going on around us of which high unemployment is only one of the symptoms.

Background

A survey of just over 300 houses in Newport, undertaken three years ago, revealed some important information about the impact of high levels of unemployment which the pastor or counsellor may find helpful as he approaches his task.

1. It was found, for example, that the experience of unemployment is very much more widely shared than the monthly statistics might lead us to think. At a time when the

unemployment level in Newport was standing at 14.9 per cent, 30 per cent of those interviewed said that they had been unemployed at some time during the preceding two years. A further question provided the rather startling statistic that 45 per cent of those *households* had directly experienced unemployment in the same period. This is the effect of the turnover; but we also know that an increase in the total number of unemployed really means that the average waiting time 'between jobs' is longer, and that the proportion of long-term unemployed is rising faster than the overall figure.

2. This leads to the second of our observations: many people admitted to feeling helpless. Their unemployment had resulted from decisions and events over which they had had no control and there was nothing that they, or any other local body, could do to change things for the better now. The Americans use the non-judgmental term 'the discouraged' of those who have simply given up looking for work, and more than a quarter of the unemployed in our survey belonged to this group; and though many of the rest regarded themselves as actively 'looking for work', they included a large number who did not think that they would find it. Whether they were right or not may be another matter, but this is what they thought and their hopelessness is another factor that the counsellor will encounter.

3. A year before the survey, when Llanwern steelworks was shedding a fruther 4,300 employees, the Industrial Mission had set up an 'Information and Counselling Network' in the area, linking all the advisory and counselling agencies, voluntary and statutory. As the months went by we were rather surprised that none of them reported any dramatic increase in casework. Now we see this as another aspect of the 'privatization' referred to above, because when we knocked on doors we found much more distress than is indicated by presentations to the caring agencies. It also underlinded the interrelatedness of economic, psychological, physiological, domestic and social factors.

4. To draw attention to one more element, we found a great deal of evidence that distress is experienced not only by the unemployed themselves but much more widely in the

community, including many who are still working. Thus counsellors may well find themselves counselling people whose anxieties stem not from actually being out of work but less directly from the uncertainties and insecurity of so much employment today. High levels of unemployment have raised the general level of strain and worry about the future, and any who had thought themselves to be safe now face the realization that it could happen to them. Without in any way wishing to diminish the problems of the unemployed, compared with many others now it can be said of them that once the blow has fallen they know the worst and know where they stand. One great area of uncertainty has been removed, even if new and daunting problems take its place.

There is no single homogeneous group of the unemployed who share the same characteristics. They do not even share the same circumstances; some are young people who have never worked, others have a large mortgage and children in college, yet others have received substantial severance payments and qualify for an early pension, and so on. What they *Do* share is the knowledge that at present, and for who knows how long, society does not need them for their skills or their labour. Instead of being able to make a contribution, and to be valued for it, the relationship is reversed and they are dependent on the rest of us, either completely or to a greater or lesser extent.

We appear to be at a point in history when a number of things have come together which make it unlikely that we will ever return to what we used to call full employment. If 'work' as we have known it is going to become less dominant, it will also play a smaller part in giving people a meaning for their lives and in determining purpose and status. Changes in the structures of our economic relationships will lead to changes in social relationships; and in all this the churches have an important part to play.

But meanwhile, though some of the things that herald a different kind of future are already beginning to happen, most of us still live within the categories, criteria and language appropriate to the immediate past, and the person who has just been made redundant is not likely to be given to much speculation about the course of history because the bottom has just been knocked out of his world.

Psychological effects

The psychological consequences of this experience are not dissimilar to those following a bereavement or any other major crisis. Though they may vary in intensity and length, these may be divided into four phases, though they need not more than summarizing here.

1. *Shock*. Whether this takes the form of immobilization (inability to plan or perform even the simplest tasks) or aimless pottering and pointless activity, it provides a period when the mind can be making necessary adjustments – though it can be accompanied by inexplicable pains, headaches, sleeplessness and tension.

2. *Defensive retreat*. Here the harsh realities of the situation are rationalized away to the point where they appear trivial and unimportant, as if nothing has really changed. It brings a feeling of relief or even of euphoria; but it cannot last because the real world does not go away and the attitudes of other people do not fit the fantasy. Thus a process of learning begins.

3. *Acknowledgement*. Small decisions and actions may be tentative at first, but they represent the first steps in regaining normal control, and as they meet with some success confidence grows and bolder moves can be made. The subject discovers resources both within himself and around him which enable him to tackle the situation in a realistic way and this can lead to a lessening of anxiety and depression. It is still the real world, however, and the subject's imporved state is not a reflection of any objective change in the circumstances. These may remain intractable and bring further disappointments and setbacks which throw the subject back into one of the earlier phases. If this should happen the concern and patient support of others can be a major factor in resuming progress and re-establishing control.

There is, of course, no claim to orginality in this analysis. The progression was set down by Fink in 1967, and it was subsequently taken up and used by Harrison in his writings on redundancy and retirement. But it may not be out of place to mention that it occupied one-and-a-half pages out of sixty in a book aimed at those made redundant which has been given wide circulation over the last eight years [*Redundant! A Personal Survival Kit* – see 'Resources' at end], and that we have received more thanks for that one section than for all the rest of the book put together. Many had clearly been perplexed and worried by the strange reactions they had experienced, and it came as a great relief to learn that they were not the only ones to have suffered them and that it was quite normal. In fact we could go further and say that to be aware of the sequence actually helps to reduce both the duration and the intensity of the first three stages. This does not mean that knowing about it is a way of getting off scot-free, however. I have known some who have helped as many as hundreds of others through the crisis of redundancy and who have then been dismayed by the intensity with which they have experienced what they had told others to expect when their own turn came.

The family

References above to the importance of family support and understanding should not lead us to underestimate the extent to which redundancy is a *family crisis*, especially, though not only, when it is the main breadwinner whose job had disappeared. It is almost too easy to overlook the fact that some of the most pressing problems are the obvious ones like not having as much money or having someone around the house all the time. The self-image of some families can be severly disturbed when it becomes impossible to maintain family obligations and commitments, eat as well, or sustain social contacts, let alone go on holiday. Uncertainty over how long it will last presents many difficult decisions affecting the whole family: the mortgage, whether to sell or change the car, what to do with a lump sum, what is best for the children.

There are many permutations. It is not uncommon nowadays, for example, for the 'breadwinner' to be the only member of the family not working! Or he may be left at home with the children while their mother goes out to work. The secondary place in the labour market assigned to most working women is almost sure to mean a less adequate family income;

but as a cause of family tension and disagreement that could well be less potent than confusion over roles and the division of labour in the home. Unhappily to this must often be added the interaction between blame, guilt, resentment, impatience, disappointment, frustration and impotence which undermines relationships, lowers the emotional threshold and makes everyone more difficult to live with.

When the loving support of the family is strong, and sometimes even when it is not, there is a risk that the symptoms of strain will appear first not in the member whose job has been lost but in other members of the family. The emotional cost of sympathy and encouragement, the discipline of restraint and of care not to provoke, or the strain of living in a highly charged atmosphere can sometimes prove too much. It is by no means impossible for the pastoral counsellor to be greatly impressed by the resilience and optimism of someone made redundant, only to discover that his wife is having his nervous breakdown for him, or that their teenage children have suddenly kicked over the traces and gone wild.

All this serves to underline the need for the pastoral relationship, wherever possible, to be with the *Home*. It also points to the importance of encouraging the family to talk both about the practical adjustments they must make in their changed circumstances and about their feelings.

Wider consequences

There have been innumerable attempts to measure the effects of unemployment in other ways. One of the best known is that of Dr Harvey Brenner of John Hopkins University. Using sophisticated techniques he made a correlation between certain economic indicators, of which unemployment was the most important, and indicators of disturbance relating to life span, mental and physical health, and criminal activity. He concluded that a 1 per cent increase in unemployment in the United States, sustained over six years, had resulted in 36,887 *extra* deaths (including 20,240 from heart and kidney diseases, 495 from cirrhosis of the liver, 920 suicides and 648 murders), 4,277 extra admissions to state mental hospitals and 3,340 extra admissions to state prisons.

Dr Brenner's methods, and the accuracy of his analysis, have been questioned; but there can be no doubt that some such link between economic and pathological factors exists, and I mention it here to alert the pastoral cousellor to these dimensions of the problem presented by unemployment. I might add, reinforcing the point made above, that this study does not say that these consequences affect only the unemployed themselves, but that they take place *in the community* where rising levels of unemployment occur.

The longer term

It is easier to find another job if you already have one; and those who fail to find new employment in the first few weeks on the dole (some would say in the first fortnight) discover that it becomes increasingly difficult as time goes on, partly because employers are more reluctant to take on people who have not worked for a while, and partly because the motivation to go on looking for work after many disppointments tends to evaporate. But since the number of long-term unemployed is growing, both absolutely and as a proportion of the total, the balance of pastoral need is tending to move away from the immediate crisis of redundancy to the bleak prospect faced by those who do not quickly find alternative work. The myth that there are still jobs for those who really want one dies hard; but there are some who are unlikely ever to work again, and whether they will or not depends to a large extent on where they live and who they are. Those who for reasons of age, sex, race, education, skills or geography are already marginalized will find the same disadvantage operating against them in their search for work as well – and they are most likely to be among those who have yielded to despondency and hopelessness.

It is not the counsellor's task to pull comprehensive solutions to intractable problems out of the hat. He is there to help the subject to clarify his own thinking and to deal constructively with the problems confronting him. Even so it may sometimes be an advantage for the counsellor to have some familiarity with the workings of the employment and social security services, as well as with the options open to the unemployed, and to be able to suggest practical steps that should or might be taken. A reference book of some kind could be useful.

The theological task

On a deeper level, however, the subject is likely to be struggling with problems of identity, rejection and the anomie that comes from the removal of familiar boundaries and the break-up of patterns that onece regulated his life.

The churches cannot be entirely absolved from responsibility for the distress with which unemployment is experienced by some, usually older, people. They were brought up at a time and when the churches were still providing a fairly uncritical theological undergirding to the 'work ethic'. But when guilt is added to the frustrations, uncertainties and economic stress of unemployment, or when people speak of its stigma or of 'being thrown on the scrap heap', then the pastoral task demands a theological re-evaluation of 'work' more appropriate to a time when full employment is no longer the norm.

The opportunity should not be unwelcome; for much of the work through which people have found dignity, status and prupose has also been dangerous, unhealthy, degrading and dehumanizing, generating new forms of poverty, injustice and exploitation. It is not over yet, and in some parts of the world it is only just beginning. But in the changes taking place around us there are signs that we are starting to emerge from an economy dominated by what the industrial revolution taught us to call 'work'. A high level of unemployment is one of those signs, and those who are suffering it are bearing the brunt of the cost of the transition. Insofar as that cost is economic, given the political will it is not beyond the wit of man to share it more equitably. But since we are living through a kind of overlap, the cost is also expressed in loss of identity, anxiety, strained relationships and meaninglessness. Here the caring role of the pastoral counsellor clearly has a prime importance.

The pastoral relationship may sometimes yield something more, however; for among the unemployed there are those who are discovering how to survive, without a job, but with their human dignity intact and their lives becoming integrated around different values and purposes. The counsellor will, of course, welcome and encourage such positive responses, not only for their own sake but because they have a wider significance as signs of hope. Set free from the constraints of 'work', some are discovering that they have been released to become more fully human, not less; and as we talk with them we should listen very carefully to hear what they affirm and how they choose their goals. What is happening among them could have great importance for the future. This may not be a disaster but a *kairos* – that is, a time of opportunity.

Resources

Newport and Gwent Industrial Mission: *Redundant! A Personal Survival Kit* (£2.00 + 25p postage); *Redundancy: The Last Option* (£1.00 + 25p postage). Both books together post free. From Mr F Newman, 22 Harrow Road, Newport, Gwent NP1 8BY.

Industrial Committee, BSR, Church House, Deans Yard, Westminster, London SW1P 3NZ: *Unemployment and the Future of Work* (A Study Pack [1982]).

Paul Ballard: *Towards a Contemporary Theology of Work* (from the author, Faculty of Theology, University College, Cathays Park, Cardiff, £2.40).

Roger Clarke: *Work in Crisis* (St Andrew Press [1982], £4.95).

Guy Dauncey: *The Unemployment Handbook* (NEC [1982], £2.25, from 18 Brooklands Avenue, Cambridge CB2 2HN).

Sarah Lloyd Jones: *Women and Work in Gwent* ([1983], £1.25, from People and Work Unit, 34-38 Stow Hill, Newport, Gwent NP1 1JE).

The address of *Church Action with the Unemployed* (Director: Mr Norman Oliver) is 146 Queen Victoria Street, London EC4V 4BX.

10. Midlife

By the Rt Reverend James Thompson,
Bishop of Stepney

My qualifications for writing this chapter are not academic or clerical, but rather those of a balding 46-year-old whose shrinking trouser waistbands insidiously confirm he's middle-aged. My ideas are based more on shared experience than research, and on the insights of theology rather than other equally important and appropriate disciplines.

I am taking the title 'Midlife' to refer more to the time which we feel to be midlife – 45 onwards – rather than the average calendar mid-point which would be 35. In each of our lives there are rather difficult in-between periods when we pass through times of transition – adolescence, between being a child and becoming an adult; marriage, between being an adult and becoming a parent; midlife, between being young and becoming middle-aged; retirement and then the shaky path towards greatly increased physical dependence. It is my belief that these in-between periods require considerable skill and flexibility if we are to go on growing and developing in a way which is fulfilling and creative – not only for ourselves, but also for other people. They are times which are most fertile for crises because not only do our physical capacities change, but our relationships and our roles in life usually also need to be modified.

In each of these areas – our body, our relationships and our role in life –midlife can provide complications. Although youth has its pitfalls, it is often a beautiful time – especially in retrospect – and it is difficult to let go. For women, the menopause is, in some ways, the most powerful symbol of this change – perhaps we could almost call it a bereavement. It involves the loss of capacity to bear children which still for some is the essence of womanhood, and will be accompanied by all the tell-tale physical signs. Even with the most expensive techniques, the signs can only be momentarily delayed. For the male, there is no such clear physical landmark and the change is more external, but can be equally dispiriting. Perhaps if you have been a sportsman, your performance begins to wane – and you have to rely more on cunning and less on physique. Both men and women may try to compensate with smarter clothes and sundry skilful devices, but none of us can put the clock back. We can, of course, put the clock forward by the misuse of our bodies and by failing to prevent disease. Over-eating, lack of exercise, smoking, heavy drinking, all can contribute to premature decay or even, in many cases, to midlife becoming endlife.

This physical decline can lead us into all sorts of unstable behaviour. It can feel like the last chance – 'soon I'll no longer be attractive' – 'I'm losing my powers' – the sad comeback boxers – the love affair with someone much younger – the deep introspection as we ask ourselves about the nature of our sexual fulfilment or deprivation – the anxiety which only makes things worse by comfort eating or escapist drinking. It is a vulnerable time when in one sense we are grieving for lost youth.

The Bible has some fairly abrasive words to say to us – and, in this area of our physical decline, they may be just what is needed. There is such a passage in Ecclesiastes – the rather melancholy Preacher – and in his message I believe there is both wisdom and encouragement. We are part of nature and we ignore this beautiful and brute fact at our peril. One of the important clues to each stage of life is to recognize and accept it as a stage with different opportunities and changing capacities. The Hebrew word for spirit means 'breath' and from the moment of the inbreathing of Adam, who comes from the earth, to the giving up of breath when we return to the earth, we are earthly, natural creatures. As Ps 103 in the funeral service reminds us:

> The Lord knows of what we are made;
> he remembers that we are but dust.
> The days of man are but as grass,
> he flourishes like a flower of the field;
> when the wind goes over it, it is gone
> and its place will know it no more.

This may be a solemn reminder of our transience, but there can also be a deep comfort in the recognition that we are all part of the natural order, and we do best to recognize and adept to its rythms, to breathe its time scale. So the Preacher says

> For everything its season, and for every activity under heaven its time:
> a time to be born and a time to die
> a time to plant and a time to uproot . . .

The acceptance of the time is important and is essential to deal with the anxiety caused by the fear of losing youth. Our Lord also had some strong words to shake us into the reality of natural being and to accept our limitations:

> Is there a man among you who by anxious thought can add a foot to his height? If, then, you cannot do even a very little thing, why are you anxious about the rest? (Lk 12[25-26])

This in no way suggests that we should not care for our body, take all the steps we can to prevent flab and stress, to keep as fit as we can, but rather that we will be happier if we accept the natural characteristics and limitations of the stages through which our bodies pass.

But the 'midlife' body is not just a matter of physical health and capacity, but through sexual experience it is also a focus of our most intimate relationships. It is clear that questioning about sexual experience and opportunity is one of the key midlife issues. This can take many forms. It may be that as children grow up leave home, husband and wife are faced more sharply by the nature and scope of their own relationship. Indadequate sexual experience, discontent with a lack of warm physical affection, a feeling that responsiblity for staying together just for the children's sake is finished, the desire to experience life more richly, the sense of boredom and apathy through the decline of attraction and romance, all can lead to experience of inner loneliness and the seeking for satisfaction outside the marriage relationship. For those who have never married or never had a more permanent relationship, it can be a time of inner panic that life is passing them by, and the spectre of a lonely old age can lead to an inner despair. There may be some married people for whom even the positive upgrading in their own self-image through new work opportunities can rock a marriage – for example, a mother might discover herself to be a person of far greater potential than she previously imagined and this could lead to discontentment with a relationship built upon a protective father-figure type husband. She may look for a lover and equal partner if she and her husband can't find the flexibility to change the nature of their relationship accordingly. Or it may be that a man or woman may discover, or become more aware of, the homosexual side of their nature which perhaps during the time of child-rearing they have had to repress or hide. They may have missed out on sexual fulfilment altogether. Midlife may be a time when such people want a chance to become who they truly are and opt for a different life style.

So it is that many people break their relationships at this time –looking for some greater fulfilment, discovering what they believe is a new, true romance which sets their adrenalin racing, makes them feel young again – opening up vistas of satisfaction, intimacy and affection which have become very much things of the past in their marriage – just fond memories in a deadened relationship which only survived through meeting the needs of the children, or in which the romance between partners died because all the energy went into building external assets, security, and status.

These difficulties are serious and failure to cope with them is widespread. This is not only demonstrable in the frightening divorce rate, but perhaps even more sadly in the way people drift into coexistence and simply remain together because it's too difficult to part, and spend much of their time sniping, scoring small victories over each other, only making the gulf between them wider and more despairing.

So the sexual needs become strong as the person sees youth receding and faces the downhill journey in the fear of sexual frustration, boredom and loneliness. The person who has coped with all this and become more loving and more human is always a pleasure to meet, and it is a delight to be in the compnay of a couple who have gone on developing their own relationship – enriching their physical intimacy and going deeper and deeper into the marvellous capacity human beings have for physical affection.

To those in midlife the Christian faith has some important things to say about sexual satisfaction. Whenever the Christian talks about 'love' he or she is under the light of the Cross. Many have made the distinction between *agapē* – self-giving love – and *erōs* – the more natural love based on attraction. I would hate to have to make such a distinction in my own life. They intertwine – the one giving rise to the other. Someone who begins a relationship in self-giving love may well end feeling natural as well as supernatural love. Someone who experiences natural attractive love may end up having to face desperately difficult self-giving love. A self-giving love in marriage can be a way to deep down resentment if one partner is always the giver. It may do neither much good. There is a proper place for both to have needs and fulfilment. But if the relationships are rocky in the changes of midlife, it becomes especially important that love – whichever kind it is – for the Christian is bathed in the light of the Cross. This love of Christ shows that our own are only one set of needs within a whole series of others. It may seem to a wife or a husband that her or his own fulfilment is the ultimate good and therefore sufficient reason to abandon other relationships, but the Christian has also to consider the ultimate good of the other people involved – wife or husband, grown children, wife or husband of the possible new partner and their children. There are a lot of people involved in this pursuit of personal satisfaction. Before making the decision to make changes which can have such wide and maybe damaging effects, we ought to do everything in our power to enrich, restore, reinvigorate, recreate the relationship we have. So there needs to be a rediscovery of the fun, the physical relaxation, the wonder in the affection we once knew. I am not advocating an impossible ideal, and I realize that for some the breach is so severe that there can be no going back, but I believe that for many, a new look at the relationship, a new honesty about hidden resentments, a new sharing of what gives pleasure, a new set of shared interests, a new way of looking both at the individual and the partnership can work miracles. It has been suggested that at fifty, every married couple and every individual should have a time of evaluation of where they've got to and where they're heading. Love demands that we look not just at our own fulfilment –our own self-realization – but also take into account the fulfilment and self-realization of those closest to us.

The fear of losing youth and potency can also be alleviated by another aspect of our faith. At several times in our lives, sexual drive and needs become so important that we can think of little else. In adolescence it is difficult to concentrate because of this claim upon our attention. Midlife has a lot in common with a second adolescence and for a time again sexual fulfilment can loom very large in our thoughts. If it's been very satisfying we can fear to lose it, if it's been very frigid and unfulfilling then we can fear that we may never experience the bliss which is part fact and part fantasy. Our faith can put this side of our lives sharply in perspective. It's important to us –yes – but it is only one part of life – maybe the most fulfilled sexual athlete has left a large part of the rest of his life untapped and undeveloped. There is so much to do, to understand, ot be interested in, ot study, to enjoy, to contribute, to give, to fight for, that sexual satisfaction can fall back into a more realistic place in the priorities for the midlife. In the OT when the people of God worshipped false gods everything else was distorted. When they worshipped God everything fell into place, hence the strength of Jesus' statement 'You *cannot serve* God and mammon'. Faith in God – investment in the spirit – should help to keep in proportion the valuation and investment in sexual fulfilment. it is as misguided to rush away from sexual intimacy into work, creative interests, service in society as it is to undervalue them and believe that all satisfaction is for some reason based upon sexual fulfilment.

So in the marriage relationship or in single life, the love we seek is not just of our own self-realization, but also for those about us – and the full variety of life should help put the sexual fulfilment in perspective – to open up the way for greater friendship both within marriage and for the unmarried, which can bring the affection, the fun and the loving which we all need.

Even if in midlife we have our relationships, our sexual life and our physical well-being under control, we still have to face considerably changing roles. If we are married and have children, they will be growing up and taking on a new freedom and responsibility. It may be that our best friend or husband or wife dies, and our parents walk into the valley of the shadow of death. These changes all present us with a new phase in our relationships. Our children are no longer children, so we lose authority and control over them. We have to let them go in order that they can come to full maturity and learn the costly way of standing on their own feet. In that change they and we may make mistakes which we feel are painful, and sores can be aggravated in a way we could never have thought possible just two or three years before. This may be especially difficult for the mother who has invested her whole self in her children and suddenly finds herself without her main reason for living. It can be as traumatic as retirement can be to a man, and more especially because it comes at a time when she may be feeling rather worthless and inadequate due to physical changes. She must at this stage find other ways of self-expression and service, otherwise she will be tempted to continue to try to enclose her grown-up children, or manage her children's new partners, or transfer all her energy into her husband. Yet although she may feel bereft at this point, she should see that it is a time of great possibility. She may be able to turn her maternal gifts to wider use, or develop a new role in life by starting work, or concentrate her efforts on some much needed social contribution. She may have time to develop her own identity. It may be that in bringing up the children she has been reduced to a very poor idea of herself – a sort of dogsbody who has totally forgotten what it is like to think what she wants to do or to be. If she manages to find herself, to develop the experiences and gifts she has acquired in being a mother, or to start some new activity and interest, she will be enriched and be able to enrich others. It can be a generous outgoing time of life and there are myriad ways of developing a new self and making a new contribution.

The relationship with the children can also deepen, because on a new and much more equal basis, they can become friends.

Parents too can present one of the tests of midlife. They will be becoming old and having to cope with all the problems that old age can bring. There may be illness, dependence and anxiety in the place of the rock-like strength and security they have provided in the past. Suddenly people find themselves parents of their parents –having to help them in very basic ways which can be a source of shame and inadequacy for those who have been very independent all their days. There will be all sorts of serious questions to be faced about the future – many of which will invoke the painful giving up of driving, of gardening, of holidays and even of home. There may be serious loneliness because one of the parents has died, or depression and reducing capacity for life. Our old people's homes are full of people who have not coped with this very difficult stage in life. Many of them are there as a result of their children in midlife not coping with their parents, not able to take responsibility for them or perhaps choosing the greater personal freedom glimpsed when their own children left home. In our modern society it is good that more parents, as they grow elderly, are able to keep a real degree of independence – by the pension and with the greater availability of flats and bungalows which can be situated near to their family. This can help the parent to have their independence and yet to be near enough for the mutual affection and support which most of us need throughout our lives – parents of children, and children of parents. But such accommodation is frequently not possible and people live in confined space so that it is difficult to take an elderly parent into their home – and, more important, the total mobility of our society means that jobs and family demands separate parents from their children so that both are deprived. This is one of the responsibilities of midlife, and I believe that our society suffers greatly because people do not find ways of giving proper priority to their ageing parents. On the other hand, it has to be remembered that parents can make matters almost impossible by failing to cross that other difficult in-between period of our life from retirement to old age, and making impossible demands.

The teaching of the faith is that we are bound to honour our father and mother. What this 'honouring' entails often leads to great conflicts of loyalty and obligation for the midlife children. It is something which both parents and children should try to work out together. By careful planning it may be possible to get the physical environment and situation right – by selling the family home or getting a new and more appropriate council flat, to enable someone to pop in every day and give regular support and yet not deny independence. But it is not only the external situation which has to be right, the attitudes and relationships have to be right as well. We all know of situations where the elderly parent has the perfect situation and environment and support from his or her children, but is still trapped by his or her own attitude. It is important to accept the natural rhythm of our lives and not to fight and strain against its proper limitations. Rather we have to travel inwards and grow in the spirit of being. It's important that not only the midlife children but also the elderly parents have to achieve adjustment. It's so easy to be bowed down by the guilt when the problem is the failure of the elderly parent to accept the ageing process. Faith and acceptance can help enormously, as can the cheerful motto 'no-one owes me anything'. There are debts between children and parents, but an insistence on such obligations can be a hindrance and a source of hidden resentment. In dealing with this a marriage can prove its worth because together the task becomes more possible and it is hoped the joys will be found. It can sometimes be a temptation to treat elderly parents like children – sometimes their behaviour may seem to deserve it, but it is wise to remember that it will only be a brief twenty years before our children may be worried by our own awkwardness and refusal to accept how much help we need.

It is not only the body which changes, not only the relationships which change, but also our role in life. For some people midlife brings success in their field of work with greatly increased reponsibility and new and wider horizons. For others it brings the sad realization that ambitions are not going to be fulfilled. It may be that a hoped-for promotion has gone to someone else – or we feel in a rut. Maybe the job has not brought the satisfaction we hoped for. There are many in some parts of the country who face the foreseeable future without the work which has been, in our society, the most important source of personal identity. For those who thrive and succeed and enter the fifties still with a great deal of promise and expectation of even greater responsibility and status – not to mention wealth – there are many dangers in the midlife period. It is a time when personalities can change and become corrupted. Power itself is seductive in whatever walk of life. Suddenly you become addicted to it – you enjoy having power over people's lives – it's amazing what people will do to hold on to power even though the accompanying responsibility looks a killer – and sometimes is. It is also a time when most people begin to enjoy comfort, and food, and have higher material expectations, settling into a higher standard of living and becoming dependent on it. For the Christian these facets of success can be a trap. They are the subject of many of the Lord's warnings and, surprisingly such people are in great 'soul' danger. The picture of holiness given by Jesus – who never reached midlife – is the strongest corrective to midlife 'success'. If it's power or status we seek we should listen to this:

> You know that in the world, rulers lord it over their subjects and their great men make them feel the weight of authority; but it shall not be so with you. Among you, whoever wants to be great must be your servant, and whoever wants to be first must be the willing slave of all.
>
> (Mt 20$^{25-27}$)

an unusual recommendation for managing directors, professors, barristers, brigadiers, members of Parliament, bishops, etc. Feetwashing is hardly the top management model. So whilst it is proper to pursue such responsibilities, the seduction involved in them needs to be continually recognized and set before the *eikōn* of Christ.

If it's wealth and security, there are equally tough words.

> There was a rich man whose land yielded heavy crops. He debated with himself 'What am I to do? I have not the space to store my produce. This is what I will do – I will pull down my storehouses and build bigger. I

will collect in them all my corn and other goods and then say to myself, "Man, you have plenty of good things laid by, enough for many years; take life easy, eat, drink, and enjoy yourself"'. But God said to him 'You fool, this very night you must surrender your life –your soul'.

(Lk 12$^{16-20}$)

Jesus seemed to have warned over and over again that wealth flattered to decieve. It promised to bring comfort and satisfaction, but it was always subject to moth and rust, it was worthless in the face of death, and its attractions tended to separate people from God.

Even if it's something as exalted as wisdom or knowledge or skill which we pursue, it all looks frail, transient and paltry before the wisdom, love and knowledge of God. So midlife for the comparatively successful becomes a key period when they are either taken in by their rewards and achievements in the world in material success, in power, in wealth and in status – or they recognize more and more their true status vis-à-vis God and their neighbour – namely as a servant, as a child, as not knowing.

For those who believe they are a failure – who feel in a rut, or useless, or rejected, or wasting their lives, there is a very different answer. They are not in the danger of the self-righteous, the prosperous or the powerful. It may be their role in life is going to be fairly imconspicuous and humble; perhaps they're out of work, or doing a job that brings no satisfaction, or doing a job they can't do. It is often the case that feelings of failure in work also reflect upon people's role in the rest of their lives. Because there is no confidence in the outside world, this can be translated into life in marriage and other relationships. It can involve a retreat from belief in the value of the self. In midlife this can become extra painful. This is where it is so important to see ourselves both as we are and as we can be. Our faith is of great assistance because Christ affirms and asserts individual value. It is possible to wallow in self-pity – but that achieves nothing – it only makes matters worse. The important thing to remember is that to each of us the lasting values and ambitions are on offer. These are honesty, kindness, truthfulness, patience, tolerance – the list goes on.

It is also true that many opportunities exist to widen experience, to develop creative gifts. The person who is good at carpentry, or gardening, or drawing, or being friendly, or listening . . . all this enriching of the human experience is available, and midlife can be a time when such interests can be developed. The world is offering us all its own majesty and beauty for our study, enjoyment and wonder.

So we have seen that midlife is a period of great change – in relationships, in physical make-up and in the roles we play. I have suggested that it is a time for taking stock – doing an inventory or assessment of where we are and where we're going. It is a time when it is possible either to retreat into self-pity, anxiety, or lethargy, or alternatively an opportunity to discover a new freedom and develop the possibility of an increased generosity of life. We have, with good luck and good health, more than a third of our life left to live and we face it with the benefit of our experience – its victories and defeats. So it's a time when we should ask, who have I become? Who do I want to be? Who can I be? At such a stage we should give more time and energy and affection to relationships and friendship and learn flexibility to become friends of our children and retain respect for the desire for independence of ageing parents. It is a time to question success and the effects that power and responsibility may be having on us in the light of Christ. It is a time to take steps to develop creative and communal interests and to see that all of us can be 'employed' in the good use of the time the Lord has lent us.

This leads me to my last and perhaps most important point. The journey in the Spirit is one which does not require the gifts of youth. It is an ageless pilgrimage. It is interesting how many people come to faith again in midlife –they begin to find in prayer and meditation, in reflecting upon nature and experience and opening the mind to God, that there can be a profound flowering of themselves in taking steps towards holiness. There is not the same irresistible impatience of youth, and the scriptures, the mystical writings, and philosophy can mean so much more. Ideas which were dismissed in youth can seem to have a stunning relevance to the ultimate questions which seem more urgent. What's the meaning of my life? My mother and father have died – are they lost to me forever? I have seen so much suffering – where is God in it all? The world seems to be in a terrible mess –how can I make my own contribution, however small and insignificant it may seem to me? I'm living in a way which brings me no satisfaction and I'm a misery to myself and those around me. All these very basic questions have a spiritual dimension – they can all be found in the prayers and psalms of the religions of mankind. The whole world is still there –the whole ocean of the spirit is there to be explored and developed. So much that was only glanced at in the pace of youth can be studied and reflected upon, and we can begin the next chapter with an eye towards the epilogue, even though still in the middle of the story and the heat of the plot.

11. Ageing

By Dr Zoe Slattery, F.R.C.Psych.,
West Suffolk Hospital, Bury St Edmunds

A RECENT article in *The Lancet*[1] states that awareness of the implications of the projected increase in the proportion of the population who are elderly is now very general. While I realize that most people know that there is such an increase, I am not sure that the implications are appreciated. If they are, the appreciation is not reflected in the provision made for old people who become dependent by reason of mental or physical fraility.

Attitudes

We hear about 'the Greying of Nations', 'the Granny Boom' and 'the Rising Tide' – the last being the title of a recent Health Advisory Service report on mental illness in old age.

Opposing views of age and the aged are expressed: on the one hand we hear of 'crumblies, wrinklies and geriatrics'; on the other, of 'Senior Citizens'. Some see old age as necessarily portrayed in the senile toothless inhabitant of a long stay ward. Others maintain that the elderly are the repositories of tribal wisdom.

Such sharply divided views are not new. In 2500 BC the Egyptian philosopher Pta Hotep wrote:

How hard and painful are the last days of an aged man. He grows weaker every day, his eyes become dim, his ears deaf; his strength fades; his heart knows peace no longer; his mouth falls silent as he speaks not word. The power of his mind lessens and today he cannot remember what yesterday was like; all his bones hurt. Those things which not long ago were done with pleasure are painful now; and taste vanishes. Old age is the worst of misfortunes that can affect a man. His nose is blocked and he can smell nothing any more.

[1] Editorial, *The Lancet* (18th August 1984), 385.

Contrast this passage with the words of Confucius:

> At 15, I applied myself to the study of wisdom; at 30 I grew stronger at it; at 40 I no longer had doubts; at 60 there was nothing on earth that could shake me; at 70 I could follow the dictates of my heart without disobeying the moral law.

Both these passages are quoted by Simone de Beauvoir in her book *Old Age*. It was Simone de Beauvoir herself who said that the aims and aspirations of a society could be judged by its treatment of the elderly.[2]

It would be interesting to know if the attitudes of our own society will be seen to be reflected by the improvement in services for the welfare of the old or by the rise in mugging of old age pensioners.

Who are the Elderly?

We all number among our friends and relatives people who seem young at 80 and others who seem prematurely aged at 65 or even 55. For administrative purposes, old age begins at the time when the majority of citizens recieve the state pension. This has some validity since the acceptance of a pension brings with it changes in status and lifestyle which tend to separate the elderly from other groups. Even for the well to do, retirement reduces income, but for those who have 'just managed' it may bring real hardship. The elderly form a sizeable proportion of the 'new poor' in our relatively affluent society.

In 1901 there were 1½ million people over 65 years old in the UK.[3] In 1971 the figure had risen to 7.1 million. This represented a rise of from 4% to 13.3%. Present projections suggest that the numbers of those over 65 will continue to rise until the 1990s. Though the rise in the number in the group as a whole will level off at that time, the numbers of those aged over 80 will continue to increase well into the 21st century. At present the over 80s represent 35% of the over 65s, in the year 2000 they will represent 45%.

This has quite dismaying implications for those involved in

[2] Simone de Beauvoir, *Old Age* (Weidenfeld & Nicolson).
[3] Margot Jefferies in *Care of the Elderly*, eds., Exton Smith and Grimley Evans (Academic Press).

providing hospital and social services since it is those over 75 years of age who are at the greatest risk of succumbing to mental and physical illness of the kind which produces total dependence.

Where are the Elderly

It may seem to the hard pressed hospital doctor or the warden of an Old Peoples' Home that the aged are all 'in care'. This is not so; only 6% of over 65 year olds are in any form of residential establishment. The rest live in what is fashionably called 'The Community'. In real terms what does this mean? A recent publication by the Office of Health Economics[4] identified 41% of old people as living with a spouse in a two person household, 12% as living with children, 28% as living alone and 13% in other types of household'. Only 6% were in residential care.

The majority of those over 65 are women – that is to say two out of every three over 65s and three out of four over 80s. Men and women differ not only in their survival rates, but in their marital status. Women are more than twice as likely as men to be single, widowed, divorced or separated.

As shown above, the elderly are poorer than the young. Their social conditions may also be adverse. Mark Abrams[5] in a survey for Age Concern showed that old people were more likely to be living in substandard, privately rented accommodation than in owner-occupied or council housing. Where they were owner-occupier, they might have lived in the same house for a long time without being able to afford upkeep and inprovements. Many lacked such basic amenities as adequate heating and indoor lavatories. Curiously the majority of the elderly interviewed were satisfied with their lot. Perhaps this is not so surprising when one thinks most men and women born at the turn of the century were familiar with the concept of the poor house and have lived through two major wars and the intervening period of depression.

[4] *Dementia in Old Age* (Office of Health Economics [1979])
[5] Mark Evans, *Beyond Three Score Years and Ten* (Age Concern Research Publication [1978])

What is Ageing

Before discussing the ills which may afflict the old, it may be helpful to look at the nature of the ageing process.

Ageing takes place at different rates in both individuals and systems. We are not made like Oliver Wendell Holmes 'Wonderful One Hoss Shay' whose components were designed so as to decay simultaneously.

Writing in *Recent Advances in Medicine*, John Grimley Evans[6] points out that the central concept of ageing is loss of adaptability of individual organisms with time, so that on average the old are more vulnerable to environmental challenge than the young. In twentieth-century Britain, age specific mortality rates fall from birth to a nadir round the age of 12. After perturbation in adolescence and early adult life, due to accident and complications of reproduction, rates rise as an exponential function of age. On a statistical definition therefore, human ageing begins near puberty and is a continuous process thereafter, without any discontinuity which might provide a rational basis for separating a particular group of adults as the elderly.

There are several theories of ageing and for those who want more scientific detail, Dr Grimley Evans' article quoted above is a valuable source. Briefly, theories centre round the loss of irreplaceable cells and the limitation of the capacity of division of existing body cells in later life. Some believe that errors in cell division produce unsound cells, other that we produce increasingly antibodies to our own tissues. This auto immune phenomenon is also thought to be responsible for the increase in some infections and cancers in old age. Further possibilities are alterations in cell supporting tissues or the accumulation of waste produce within cells themselves.

Though physiological theories of ageing seem bewildering, they are at least easier to pursue than those underlying its psychological concomitants. Among the deterrents to researchers in this field are the need to mount very large population studies and the effect of the very varied life experience of different cohorts of old people living through a century of dramatic changes.

[6] John Grimley-Evans in *Recent Advances in Medicine,* eds. Dawson, Compson, Besser, Churchill, Livingstone.

It is held that the old are less adaptable and slower to accept changes, that they 'disengage' from society and have more difficulty in carrying out complex mental activities. In the area of memory it is the common experience that as we age we develop difficulties in remembering names and faces, but the concept of 'Benign Senescent Forgetfulness' postulated by Kral has been repudiated by some psychologists comparing performances of old people and young students. It was found that in similar circumstances both groups performed equally in memory based tasks. There seems little proof of differences in intellectual functions in healthy old age other than those which are explained by inherent variation in ability, education and experience.

Illnesses in Old Age

Drs. Coni, Davidson and Webster in their lucid and enjoyable book *Lecture Notes on Geriatrics* describe illness as 'more and more something that happens to you when you grow old'.[7] Curiously, those who complain bitterly that present day hospital beds are full of 'geriatrics', seldom pause to give thanks that these same beds are no longer occupied by rows of young adults suffering the effect of rheumatic disease, tuberculosis or incurable infection. Nowadays, apart from what may be termed self induced illness, including self poisoning, addictions or accidents on the road and sports field, threats to health in young and early middle age have receded.

The elderly on the other hand are particularly vulnerable to environmental insults which could be shrugged off earlier in life. The very old do not easily withstand dehydration or alterations in temperature and have difficulty in metabolizing and eliminating drugs required to treat their illness.

As well as those illnesses common throughout life, the elderly are particularly afflicted by bone and joint disease, Parkinson's Disease and diseases of the heart and blood vessels. Such illnesses represent not only a threat to physical health, but often to a precariously maintained independence.

[7] Coni and Davidson, *Lecture Notes on Geriatrics* (Blackwell)

Care of the Physically Ill

The speciality of geriatrics which has grown rapidly over the second half of this century aims to provide medical care for older patients, more especially the very old. The goal of doctors working in this field is the prevention of chronic disability by early effective treatment and active rehabilitation. When restoration of function proves impossible, geriatricians hope to provide long term care and the optimum quality of life for those requiring such care. That performance lags behind desire in the field is to a great extent due to the failure of society as a whole to earmark sufficient funds from already scarce resources for the care of the elderly.

Doctors are being urged today to look at 'the whole person' and geriatricians are among the prime practioners of this art. They need to decide which of a number of simultaneously present illnesses to treat and which to leave alone. They may have to acknowledge that in some cases the cure may be, if not worse than the disease, at least as bad. Above all they have to consider not only the patients but their home and family circumstances and resources available to them in their neighbourhood.

This is why geriatricians must include in their teams, experienced nurses, social workers and occupational and physio-therapists. There is little point in curing the patient's illness and sending him back to the unheated house and poor nutrition which caused it.

Mental Illness

Until the 1950s, it was assumed that the old did not experience mental illness. They either 'went senile' or survived as the grown-old schizophrenics in long stay mental hospitals. During the 1950s and 60s, a research team working in Newcastle and studying hospital population and those living at home, showed that as many as 25% of the elderly suffered from mental ill health. One in every ten people over 65, and one in every five aged over 80, suffers from one of the dementing illnesses which lead eventually to total dependence. For every one of these in hospital care, there will be six to seven living at home.[8]

[8] Elaine Murphy 'Depression in the Elderly' (*Medicine in Practice* [1983]), 755ff.

The surprising finding of the Newcastle and subsequent studies is that depression is the commonest mental illness in old age. Average findings are that 30 – 15% of the population suffer from depression severe enough to warrant medical attention, and 2.5% will experience those forms of the illness which need hospital treatment. An interesting finding is that these rates for older women are comparable with those of other age groups but that in men, rates of depression and suicide rates rise with age. So called neurotic illness is common in the elderly, most of it related to depression or anxiety.

As with physical illness, so with the psychiatric problems of old age, special medical services have come into being to meet needs. In the early 1970s, there were no more than a dozen psychiatrists specializing in this area. A recent survey concluded that there are now at least 120 psychogeriatricians practising in the UK.[9] It is now NHS policy to appoint such a specialist in each health district. Most work with teams of expert helpers similar to those described for geriatric services. Most also depend heavily on home assessment and on keeping patients in their own familiar surroundings where possible.

In addition to assessing the demented and to treating the depressed, psychiatrists must work closely with geriatric physicians in dealing with the many cases of apparent mental illness resulting from physical causes. The old, like the young, are vulnerable to delirium and often the old person who suddenly 'goes mad' is suffering from pneumonia, heart failure or something from the adverse effects of medication. Such attacks can be extremely frightening to families and neighbours and have resulted in inappropriate admissions to mental hospitals.

Primary Care Services

For the majority of people whatever their age, the first recourse in illness is to the general practioner, often nowadays the leader of a primary care team of practice nursing staff and social workers. Community or more familiarly District Nurses, carry a heave caseload of frail elderly and may prove the best source of information about their needs.

Health visitors and Social Service Departments have a

[9] Wattis and Arie, 'Psychogeriatrics: A National Survey' (*British Medical Journal,* Vol. 282, 1529-1534).

tradition of care for families and young children. Both have been slow to adjust to the needs of the old, but fortunately an increasing number of social workers are turning towards this speciality and away from the 'generic pattern' proposed by the Seebohm Committee.

Long Term Care

The twin pillars of home care are the Home Help and Meals on Wheels services. Most workers would like to see an expansion of these with the addition of night and day 'granny sitting'.

Residential Care

Those who can no longer manage at home but do not need nursing care may be referred for residential care in local authority or private homes. Places in what is known as Part III accommodation have always lagged disastrously behind even the meagre norms proposed by the DHSS. Today these places originally meant to provide hostel type accommodation are increasingly filled with the moderately demented and are inadequately staffed to deal with their need for greater supervision. Private homes, in which central government is now subsidising the elderly, provide a 'let out' but may later pose problems because of difficulties in monitoring their standards.

A constant proportion of the dependent elderly will need long term care in settings where professional nursing is available. There may be patients who have problems of behaviour which are not tolerable at home. There may be those who cannot perform the simplest functions of self care, or they may have outlived their relatives or antagonized those who cared for them by lifelong quirks of personality. For these, the only resource available at present is the long stay psychiatric or geriatric ward. Much has been done to upgrade these settings but much remains to be done.

When all is said and done however, the bulk of the care of the old is in the hands of 'the community'. In plain English, this may mean an ageing spouse, a middle aged or elderly son or daughter, sometimes even a devoted neighbour. At the turn of the century, there were ten middle aged active people available for every one over 65. Now the number is more like three to one. An increasing burden devolves on a smaller army of supporters.

Nor is it true that people want to 'put away' their grandparents. In many cases, devoted care is given until the supporter dies, moves away or crumbles through sheer exhaustion.

Implication for Pastoral Carers

I have devoted the major part of this chapter to 'setting the scene'. This is because I believe that the first duty of those advising on help to the elderly is the provision of a body of knowledge and the dispelling of myths.

It is hard to give general advice to Pastors who will be working in conditions as diverse as those found in inner city tower blocks and south coast 'retirement ghettos'.

First it should be stressed that the needs of the majority of the elderly differ in no way from those of the rest of the community. They require food, warmth, shelter, affection from close friends and relatives and from the rest of us, respect for their rights as human beings. Meeting those needs may well depend as much on the economic circumstances of the country as a whole, and on fiscal politics of government, as on charity, however that word be interpreted.

It is said that old people who are rich, revered or lovable will find that their needs are met. Unfortunately there are those who are poor in beneficial personality traits as well as in money. Some are rendered unlovable through the effects of illness. For these people, the statutory services are more likely to bear the responsibility.

Special Problems

There are special problems of old age which need our attention:

(1) *Bereavement*. There is extensive literature on this subject. Two points need to be made – one is that in general the old may be better adjusted to deal with loss than are the young and middle aged. Humility is therefore an essential ingredient of bereavement counselling.

The second is that resentment and apparent ingratitude may be natural features of mourning. Those who wish to help the bereaved must realize that their maximum effort will not bring back the dead and that they may have to act as willing scapegoats for the resentment of the bereft.

(2) *Loneliness*. Being alone is an almost inevitable experience for those who live long. Some tolerate and even welcome solitude. Some studies have shown that those who complain most bitterly of their isolation are people living in the midst of a family circle. In short, loneliness can be the result of personality factors. There is a difference between isolation and desolation.

The best that community helpers can do is to make sure that no one is deprived of opportunities for social contacts. It is worth remembering that for many old people, moving to a new area is the norm. It is also as well to consider that the recently retired may welcome requests for help as much as offers of aid. 'Uselessness' is a common complaint of the aged.

Carers

It must follow from what has gone before that the people most in need of pastoral care are those who themselves care for a frail elderly relation.

I would see as the most urgent task of any parish, the setting up of a panel of volunteer visitors, and night and day sitters, people who will allow families time off to shop or to go to family gatherings or places of entertainment. The organization of voluntary day centres can be a boon.

Above all, voluntary carers should be armed with information about local provisions. It would be valuable to ask local medical, nursing and Social Service workers in this field to talk to parish groups about their work. The ounce of practical advice about how to obtain a walking aid or apply for the Constant Attendance Allowance may well be worth the proverbial ton of sympathy.

I am naturally diffident about proffering advice on spiritual and psychological counselling to such a readership and will simply conclude by reminding you that with today's improved life expectancy rates, old age will be the common lot. There is no 'them' and 'us'. Enlightened self interest at least should make our approach to the old one of 'Do as you would be done by'.

Simone De Beauvior:

'It is the meaning that men attribute to their life, it is the entire system of values that define the meaning and the value of old age. The reverse applies; by the way in which a society behaves towards its old people it uncovers the naked and often carefully hidden truth about its real principles and aims'.

Further Reading

Colin Murray Parkes, *Bereavement Studies of Grief in Adult Life* (Penguin Books [1975]).

Alison Norman, *Mental Illness in Old Age*, Centre for Policy on Ageing, Nuffield Lodge, Regents Park, London

The Rising Tide (Published by Health Advisory Service).

D.B. Bromley, *The Psychology of Human Ageing.*

Ronald Blythe, *The View in Winter* (Allen Lane)

Balzac, *Pere Goriot.*

Saul Bellow, *Mr. Sammler's Planet.*

12. Suicide

By Barbara Swinyard,
Ex Director, Samaritans, Beckenham

First aid is emergency help. Suicide, be it an attempt, a threat, or a seemingly vague wish, calls for emergency treatment, emergency caring, immediate help. Suicide is crisis.

Suicide care involves anticipating the act and recognizing a tendency, it is care after an attempt, and it is also caring for the bereaved after a successful attempt. It cannot be stressed enough that the more we know ourselves the more effective will be our care of others. This self-knowledge, this awareness of our own attitudes and feelings is essential to suicide care.

For centuries suicide was seen in Europe as an abominable sin. England was one of the last countries to change the law which made it a crime, and that not until 1961. In a successful suicide the corpse was refused a Christian burial and more often than not desecrated. The unsuccessful, would-be suicide was severely punished. Is it surprising, therefore, that we can still view it with a primitive horror?

Unless we can recognize and accept these deep feelings in ourselves, how can we accept fully the suicidal person? And acceptance is what he most needs as he struggles with his own feelings of guilt, unworthiness and rejection. A study of this complex subject can go a long way to changing our attitudes and helping us to accept, if not fully understand, our feelings so that we can begin to share the state of mind of a suicidal person. Study of the subject will also enable us to recognize the factors likely to lead to suicide so that it can be anticipated and, we hope, prevented.

Why does one person learn to live with a great personal tragedy whilst another cannot face what appears to be a comparatively minor problem and chooses death as a way out? To answer this question it is necessary to look at the various underlying factors common to many suicides. Among these are feelings of isolation and rejection, of shame or inadequacy, guilt and anxiety, loss of faith, a lack of a philosophy of life. The apparent 'minor cause' is usually not the whole story but merely the precipitant, the last straw. Even when the immediate problem itself is devastating, there are usually underlying factors that will make the distressed person decide to end his or her life. Awareness of this fact will help the carer to concentrate as much on the feelings as the problem.

For example, the loss of a job and continued unemployment can produce feelings of shame, inadequacy, loss of confidence and hope. Hardship, lack of money and boredom will not be the sole cause. The suicide rate amongst the poor and under-privileged is found to be no higher than in other groups. According to research published in 1984 more than half of all men who attempt suicide are unemployed.

The shame induced by a sexual problem, be it deviation, fear ·of homosexuality or sexual inadequacy, makes it difficult to share the problem and increases the feeling of isolation, so often a factor in suicide.

Severe relationship problems of long standing produce feelings of rejection, loss of confidence and loneliness. Many people accused of shoplifting have chosen death rather than live with the shame, unable to face friends and neighbours. That the suicide rate amongst divorced women is high is not surprising if the feelings of loneliness, rejection, loss of status and guilt are considered. For many of the same reasons the bereaved person is liable to feel suicidal. The over fifties are particularly vulnerable, feeling useless and frightened of a future without the support to which they have been accustomed. In each of these examples it is the deeper feelings which determine the reaction to the problem. Suicide is usually a method of opting out, of running away from what seems a situation impossible to live with.

In a different category are those who wish for death because a medical condition makes the thought of the future unbearable or because they wish to spare the distress of those caring for them. Chronic pain, insomnia, progressive disease, and terminal illness can understandably provoke these feelings. It is important in these circumstances for a counsellor to examine his own reactions. Feelings on this subject are so complex and profound, involving disturbing ethical issues, that it can be difficult to remember that it is the person's feelings that matter. The carer may believe that suffering is an essential part of life and may have difficulty establishing a good relationship if the person is made to feel guilty for being unable to cope or for not agreeing with the carer's point of view. It cannot be said too often that establishing a trusting relationship is essential and can only be achieved if acceptance is complete whatever the person's feelings.

An essential part of suicide care is an ability to recognize the intent. To disregard the verbal clues is to deny the person's need to express those feelings and to suggest that the listener has a desire, conscious or unconscious, to reject the subject. 'They'd be better off without me', 'I don't feel I can go on', 'I feel I've nothing to live for'. In this context these are obvious clues, but slipped into a tale of woe their significance can be overlooked and yet are vital in recognizing a potential suicide, the clues that when followed up can allow the person to share fully these feelings and intentions.

The need to get a suicidal person to talk of feelings and plans, if any, cannot be overstated. It is commonly believed that if you bring up the subject of suicide you will 'put the idea into their head'. This is not the case. The very thought that the idea of suicide would be taken up from someone else's suggestion indicates a lack of awareness of the depth of feelings that provoke suicide. Experience has shown that when a question about the possibility of suicide is put to a person who has no intention of taking that way out the response is immediate and unmistakable, 'Oh no, I wouldn't do that', 'Oh no, what about the children'.

Perhaps a carer's reluctance to ask lies with his or her own feelings and fears. The question does not have to be posed directly. A gentle progression can be made. 'You sound very low, as though you don't feel you can go on', 'How do you feel about the future?', 'Have you ever felt like ending it all?' Sometimes you will sense that a direct question is in order. 'You sound desperate, do you feel you want to finish it all?' Anyone who has seen and heard the overwhelming relief that this question can elicit will recognize the same taboos, the same fears in the suicidal person that can inhibit the carer. Fears that had made it seem impossible that the feelings could be shared, that the idea could be accepted without horror, without ridicule but with understanding.

There can be no more lonely feeling than that of a would-be suicide. To quote A. Alvarez in *The Savage God*, 'that total loneliness which is the precondition of suicidal depression'. If a bond can be established to enable the threatened person to talk there will be a chance of reducing the stress under which they are making life and death decisions. Once having established this bond it should be sustained at all costs. Sometimes the helper, alarmed by the enormity of having someone's 'life in his or her hands' feels like giving up, handing over. This would be yet another rejection. A supervisor or support group is particularly valuable to the carer in these circumstances not only for support and encouragement but also to help assess the threatened person's risk.

The responsibility of assessing a person's suicide risk weighs less heavily if there are guidelines which will help to differentiate between those who are in immediate danger and those who are long term suicide risks. A valuable tool which is used by the Samaritans for training is the Lethality Scoring Table. This was originally an American idea and it is invaluable for impressing on the mind the suicide danger signals. The table is deliberately simple to enable it to be retained in the mind easily. It also suggests lines of enquiry for assessing risk. In no way is it suggested that the carer sits before the person with the scoring table marking up the points.

LETHALITY SCORING TABLE

Start by scoring the Suicide plan (chief indicator of immediate risk) then add points for anything relevant under Other Factors (mostly long term factors)

SUICIDE PLAN**

Imminent sudden death	8
Imminent slow method suicide	7
Planning sudden death	6

Planning slow method suicide	5
Planning a suicide gamble	4
Planning a suicide gesture	3
Definite suicidal thoughts, no plan	2
Toying vaguely with idea of suicide	1
No suicidal thoughts	0

OTHER FACTORS

Previous suicidal acts	4
No hope; loss of faith	3*
Recent broken relationship	3
Isolation; rejection	3*
Possession of means of suicide	2
Putting affairs in order	2
Depressive illness (endogenous)	2
Dependence on alcohol or drugs	2
Over 60; male; ill; chronic pain	1*

**Choose one figure only   *Score everything that applies

ASK ABOUT SUICIDE RISK IN EVERY CASE AND AT EVERY CONTACT!

Other factors could be added since this list was made. Loss of job, in view of the statistics mentioned, must rate highly. A previous suicide in the person's family should rate at least one. It is suggested that scores over 12 mean serious risk and call for someone to stay with that person until the risk is lessened. If the score is above 5 contact should be maintained. It is important to assess each time as the risk will not remain static.

It is important to be aware that an apparant rise in spirits in the suicidal person must not lead to a relaxing of attention. It can be a danger signal. People experiencing the very depth of depression cannot even summon up the energy to kill themselves. As they begin to surface a little they can find that energy and there must be extra care and observation at this time.

We are warned of what might be a serious defect of the lethality table. A false sense of security can be reached if we fix too low a figure on a suicidal person. It is difficult to find a way to avoid this danger except by over-estimating rather than under, by careful enquiry and, as always, careful listening.

It is as well to be aware of certain fallacies which have developed in relation to suicide in case they influence attitudes. The most common one is, 'people who say they will kill themselves never do'. The reverse is true. A large number of successful suicides have been found to have talked to someone about their feelings and intention. 'People who have made one attempt will not make another'. Quite false. It is easy to be misled by an apparently cheerful person. Many deeply depressed people cultivate a jolly manner to hid their real feelings. Look for the brittleness, the false ring. There is an idea that a person is more likely to feel suicidal in the winter or dismal weather. The highest suicide rate is in Spring or June. Christmas is also a bad time, when isolation, rejection and loneliness are felt more strongly in contrast to the general air of jollity, family reunions, and so on.

When assessing suicidal risk it is good to be aware that certain groups are more susceptible than others. There is a marked increase in successful suicides as people grow older, the peak period being 55-65. At the other end of the age range suicide is the second highest cause of death in young people, university students being patricularly vulnerable. Doctors and psychiatrists have a high rate of successful suicides, successful, perhaps, because they have access to and knowledge of the best methods to achieve their aim.

It is worth mentioning, and perhaps appears surprising, that the rate is low in N. Ireland. The reason is that national tragedy is shared tragedy and this fact underlines once more that a feeling of isolation is one of the main factors in suicide. Similarly, there was a low suicide rate in concentration camps where horror and tragedy were shared.

Suicidal thoughts and intentions in the elderly pose particular problems. We tend to think of old people in terms of their physical welfare, the conditions in which they are living – or just existing. How often are we truly concerned with their state of mind? Old people usually cope with their problems stoically or just grumble about what appear to be minor problems. Seldom do they have a chance to open up on their innermost feelings. Their fears, their frustrations at not being able to function as in the past, the indignities that old age can bring, the effort required to perform quite simple tasks, humiliation over their mistakes and above all their knowledge that nothing will ever improve but only deteriorate. Finally their fear of dying, even when they would welcome death which they can see as a sleep, a relief from the burden that life has become. First aid here means someone giving time to develop a relationship of trust so that these fears and frustrations can be brought to the surface and acknowledged.

The taboos surrounding suicide, especially for the Christian, leave many old people lingering on, unhappy, lonely and often in pain until they are allowed to die. This is no place to discuss the moral issues surrounding euthanasia, aiding the suicidal, and many other related questions, but these add to the big responsibility placed on the clergy and others when caring for the elderly suicidal person. Is suicide always to be deplored?

Suicide is the second highest cause of death in young people and the numbers have grown steadily in the last decade. Maybe the threat of nuclear war or worsening economic conditions give them a feeling of hopelessness, but whatever the cause they need to share their despair and often find it difficult to do so. Little will be achieved unless you can command their absolute trust, trust that you will treat their confidences with such confidentiality that they feel that you will make no move without consulting or informing them. Confronted by a young person deeply troubled or in danger it is difficult to control and hide our anxiety and to drop the parental or authoritarian role. They need a calm accepting listener to whom they can reveal their feelings in absolute confidence as to an equal.

It is not surprising that some young people who have led sheltered lives at home find life overwhelmingly difficult when they go to University. There will be natural homesickness, pressures to achieve and satisfy parental expectations if not their own, a feeling of inadequacy if they are not joining in the social life, and money problems they have not encountered before. Fear of letting their parents down prevents them looking for support where it has been natural to seek it in the past. The friendship of people who can be more concerned with how they are in themselves than how they are getting on can be a valuable antidote to these fears and anxieties.

Bereavement is responsible for many suicides but it appears that widowers are particularly vulnerable. I believe the reason for lower incidence of suicide for widows lies in their ability to talk of their grief and share their pain. A man will more often feel he must 'be brave' and not grieve, keep his feelings to himself, and certainly not seek out someone to talk to. If this is the case, then a pastoral carer ought to keep an especially watchful eye on men with such a tendency. The great need is to encourage talk about the person who has died, and to explore feelings of guilt and recrimination. Perhaps, also, to accept that some people will wish to 'die' to be with their relative and find no incentive for life. The discovery of areas of life where they could be valued and their skills appreciated can be of great help if offered genuinely and at the right time.

When counselling a suicidal person an attempt should be made to try to assess how serious the attempt was, whether they really meant to die. If the client jumped from a height, under a bus, or used another violent method, we can be pretty certain there was a genuine intention to die. One indication would be whether with gassing, drowning and even hanging, the client knew someone would be likely to discover the attempt in time to prevent death. Most difficult to assess is overdosing in view of a possible ignorance of dosage. In trying to assess by examining the causes it can help to have the Lethality Scoring Table in mind. Most of us can cope with adversity in small doses, but problems arriving one after another can precipitate a breaking point, particularly if it is all kept within and not shared.

Common sense steps to follow when the risk is judged to be high will be:

i. moving (with the person's agreement) any obvious means.
ii. Tell the person what you plan to do to help, avoiding panic and rash promises.
iii. Seek permission to tell the relatives.
iv. Where such permission is not given it may nevertheless be considered necessary to tell the family – just tell the threatened person you are going to do this.
v. If the individual is under the care of a professional then it is our responsibility to tell them.
vi. Don't claim to take care of everything – you can't, and you need them to have something to look after to avoid relaxing all their inner controls –leave them with some responsibility.
vii. Reinforce strengths in the person.
viii. Encourage positive emotions – explore those things which have

made life important and good for them.

ix.   Have a good knowledge of mental health facilities – Samaritans,
       and so on – so that you can move toward referral as quickly as
       possible.

People under treatment can use this 'suicide' appeal in an
attempt to manipulate their own treatment situation. If you are
told you are the only one who has really understood 'and of
course you won't tell the psychiatrist will you' then avoid the
trap of pseudo-confidentiality and say clearly you will inform
the primary helper. Our best response to everyone concerned
is to inform the others involved and make them part of our
response.

Parasuicides, i.e., attempts at suicide which are not meant to
be successful, are frequently referred to as 'cries for help' –a
violent attempt to get a message across when communication
seems impossible in any other way. In many, many cases they
have achieved their aim. Friends, parents, spouses have been
rudely jolted into really listening, really seeing the distress for
the first time. Such listening may be very painful when the
'suicide' is an act of anger against the relative and is aimed at
'punishing' and producing guilt. Relatives can need strong support, not simply from the shock of the suicide itself, but also
from the confrontation by which the suicidal person may be
saying, 'you did this; it's your fault'.

Having said that, however, it must be recognized that there
are people who continually threaten and appear to attempt
suicide to get their own way or to get attention, or to get the
mothering they need. Dealing with this kind of manipulation
requires skill and courage, skill in distinguishing between the
'cry for help' and the manipulations, and courage to refuse to
respond to the latter and to help them to stand on their own
feet. It requires courage because it can be a daunting
experience waiting to see if you have made the right decision.
To play into the hands of the manipulator is to reinforce the
behaviour pattern.

'Can you give me one reason why I should go on living?'
This question has been asked by the suicidal and is often the
unspoken question. How does a Christian carer respond? Does

he try to talk about his own faith which he believes would sustain him in similar circumstances? The desire to share the great motivating power that works for him must be overwhelming. For the person who has lost faith and has no hope, any attempt to do so could be an indication that the carer was not able to listen and to understand. The result could be further alienation, greater isolation, and a loss of hope of ever achieving a real answer. It is not possible to transfer one's own faith or philosophy to someone else.

Should a caring situation be used to impose one's own belief on a person? All carers and counsellors have their 'beliefs'. The advantage for the pastoral carer is that he is a symbol not only of healing, as a doctor should be, but also of God, that is of love and acceptance, justice and mercy. That message is there of itself. Too hasty an offering of the resources of grace may break the last straw rather than provide it. When a person's own faith has failed the sense of 'I am a failure' can easily find renforcement. Perhaps he has or has had a different faith. What of the atheist or agnostic? To assume that your faith is the answer to the other's problems is to show a lack of respect for him at a time when he lacks all respect for himself and to alienate him when he needs acceptance above all else. For the minister the question of faith in caring for people in suicide situations poses particular problems. It is not safe to assume that because the distressed person has chosen to come for help to a known believer that he is asking for spiritual help or help with the resoration of his faith. It may be that the expectation of compassion and understanding from this source has prompted the choice. Only listening and gentle questioning will reveal his real needs.

Another problem arises from the fact that for centuries suicide has been seen as a sin, that it is impious to take one's own life, that it is for God to decide and wrong to anticipate his actions. This might lead the client to expect condemnation from a representative of the church. It would not, therefore, be surprising if a person tried to hide his suicidal intentions and feelings from a minister, making it much more difficult to recognize the suicidal pointers. Thus extra sensitivity and knowledge of danger signals will be required. Only by

maintaining trust and convincing the person of his uncon-
ditional acceptance will he be helped to reveal his suicidal
intentions and to talk about his inner feelings. As to the question of faith, only by allowing your own faith and love to be
evident in this total acceptance will the client have a chance to
regain a lost faith in a religious belief or in mankind from
whom he feels so isolated.

And to the original question 'Can you give me one reason
why I should go on living?' The caring situation is no place for
evangelizing. It is important to stress here that it is often the
expectations of life that are felt to rest on the person that lead to
hopelessness or despair. The person himself must be allowed to
choose a spiritual solution to his dilemma if he so wishes. It is
appropriate, however, to say to the client in response to that
difficult question that perhaps by talking with you he will move
towards finding his own answer, which of course is the only
answer that will mean anything to him.

On the other hand it may be that the client asks for spiritual
help or that the minister senses correctly that this is what is
needed. Chosen with care the moment may arise when the
minister may choose to say, 'As I see it, all life is a gift of God
and given to us in trust. You may feel that people have let you
down or even that God has let you down, but it is still open to
you to discover that you can trust yourself to take responsibility
to live your own life just as you wish to take responsibility to
end your life.' A minister may wish to go on to offer clients
some outward sign of God's forgiveness and acceptance such as
the laying on of hands or prayers with them. This may be the
first aid that some suicidal clients will respond to, but the counsellor must be sure it is the need of the client and not just his
own wish for the client that is being acted out here.

The laying on of hands needs to be prepared for carefully
and seen as an opening up and presentation of the whole of that
person's situation to God for their 'renewing' and that they may
come to a 'sober' estimate of themselves.

To be *understood* is paramountly healing. So it is that those
scriptures which shown understanding and acceptance of the
feelings of suicidal states can be of inestimable value: The depression of Elijah (1 Kgs 19^4) the anger and despair of Jonah

(Jonah 4); the evocative passages of the Psalms that speak of feeling like 'a bottle in the smoke' (Ps 119[83]) or 'a sparrow alone on the house top (Ps 102[7]). Psalm 42 with its dialogue between despair and trust may provide a useful tool, picking up the dialogue of the temptations in the wilderness and Gethsemane.

Such parables as the lost sheep, which speak of a seeking, valuing, returning may be appropriate. Greatest of all points of meaning for the potential suicide who is in any way open to the resources of grace must be the presence of Christ on the Cross, since here is One who experiences rejection, darkness, scorn, thirst, failure, despair, shame, who empathizes in his way with our alienation and distress and so can be with us in our darkness. Don't preach, be prepared to share your faith and the resources of grace if these are really asked for. What must be avoided are philosophical arguments about the faith or the person's situation since these will only serve to mobilize argumentative strengths rather than the positive emotions we need to seek to reinforce.

Ministers and others with faith will have their own ways of giving spiritual support, but the strongest evidence and expression of prayer in this situation will be in the attitude of respect and care for the person before them more than any words.

In any caring situation it is extremely important to be aware when referral is needed – when a client is so seriously disturbed that help more expert than yours must be called for, a doctor or a psychiatrist. In the case of a suicidal person it is literally a case of life and death. If the person is psychotic the carer may not be sufficiently trained to deal with this. Similarly, if the person is so withdrawn that no verbal communication is possible medical aid should be called. If in immediate danger on no account should the person be left alone. If the person agrees, mobilize the family or contact friends if you are unable to stay yourself. Remember that the Samaritans are trained to help in this situation but will not cooperate unless the person is willing to receive them.

The need for caring does not stop when a person succeeds in committing suicide. Shock, guilt, regret and anger are part of all grieving, but for the family and friends of a suicide these feelings are intense. Shock for obvious reasons, guilt over some action or words which might have caused the distress which led to the death, regret over what might have been done to prevent it, anger that they could do this to you, and often utter bewilderment over the unanswered 'why?' Add to this distress the involvement with police and an inquest and it will be realized that bereavement caring of great sensitivity is required.

Recommended reading:
Alvarez, A., *The Savage God: a study of suicide* (Penguin)
Stengel, Erwin, *Suicide and Attempted Suicide* (Penguin)

13. Death and Dying

By the Reverend John Perryman,
Chaplain, Withington Hospital, Manchester

I. *How do we care?*

What do you say when somebody asks, 'Am I ever going to get better?'? What do you say to a parent whose child has just died? Should people be told they are dying? Questions like these arouse a sense of inadequacy, panic and helplessness in most of us. Even if we have been through a bereavement ourselves, that remains our experience; it may not be somebody else's. Even if we have read books on death, that knowledge remains theory; it may not fit the particular circumstances of .the next dying or bereaved person we meet. Even if we pride ourselves on being good listeners, that may not be enough; there may be a need for more than just listening. Pastoral care of any kind is a hazardous enough task, arising so often in the middle of something else (a discussion group, a telephone conversation, a quiet drink) and lacking formal structure. Pastoral care of people before and after death demands in addition the willingness to expose oneself to a variety of feelings and to stay with them. Too often we prefer to avoid the hostility, guilt, perplexity or depression of the dying and bereaved. The fear is that we too might be overwhelmed.

Traditionally, the church has entrusted the care of the dying and bereaved to its ordained ministers, who have assumed without question the role of 'shepherds of the flock'. Even where shared ministry has developed, ministry to the dying and bereaved has been confined to the ordained person and a small circle of selected carers. The result has been twofold. First, the practice of ordinary care by ordinary people has been denigrated, a point well argued by John Elford: 'The shepherd is one who can always cope with any eventuality and the sheep are never capable of doing so for themselves.'[1] People do not

[1] 'The care of All for the souls of all' (*ET* 92 [19809-81], 333-336).

believe they can be effective in this area, whereas in reality they can and frequently are. One task for every ordained pastor is to recognize his or her own need to be omnipotent, to let go of that need, and to let other people care. With occasional supervision, most carers manage very well.

A second consequence of the church's pastoral tradition is that the role of the official pastor and his authorized assistants is idealized. They see themselves and are seen as all-coping, all-knowledgeable (especially about scripture), and always available. In reality of course they are not. Nor does the purveying of scripture meet every need. Like the sacraments of holy communion and holy unction, scripture is precious primarily to believers. Pastors, though, deal with increasing numbers of people who are at the fringe of the church and beyond it. It is not enough any longer simply to say prayers and use scripture, even at funerals. The pastoral carer needs to go beyond the received traditions and to enter into relationships with the dying and bereaved, costly though they might be.

In fact, much good pastoral care of the bereaved goes on unnoticed; people write letters, talk, listen, make tea, pray, etc., etc. There is less chance for ordinary care of the dying, though ministers and priests are called for in hospital or at home by many families. But all of us, professional or ordinary carers, need to be aware of what we do, and of what the dying and bereaved do. The better we understand ourselves and those we try to help, the more effective our pastoral care will be.

What we do with the dying and bereaved

	Causes	*Effects*
Avoid	Reluctance to intrude	*Isolation* They [hospital staff] didn't realise
	Fear of causing distress	how their silence increased my distress'
	Fear of becoming involved	(social worker after stillbirth)
		Frustration This [need to speak about dying]
	Fear of being overwhelmed by feelings (own or theirs)	may by frustrated by your aversion or unwillingness to face such a situation yourself.[2]
	Sense of helplessness 'What can I do or say?')	*Inhibited communication*

[2] Alex Comfort, *A Good Age*, (Mitchell Beazley [1977])

Generalize (happens to everyone)	Need to reassure Urge to demonstrate knowledge Need to escape from immediate distress	*Sometimes reassuring* e.g. newly bereaved person seeing the dead person about the house – 'Is it a ghost? Am I going mad?' *Sometimes devalues/dismisses the person* –takes the focus away from their immediate concern, e.g, 'One writes that "other friends remain", That 'loss is common to the race' – And common is the commonplace And vacant chaff well meant for grain'[3]
Personalize ('The same happened to me')	Need to show solidarity credentials Need to talk about ourselves	They – can't hear because preoccupied with themselves – hear but quickly return to self – feel ignored
Theologize	Need to bring hope Need to show and encourage faith Need to defend God Need to appeal to external objective reality	They may – tolerate but not internalize it, – reject it outright (cf. Job's reaction to the comforters) – find comfort – come back to it later (timing is important) – feel that the present reality is all that matters – imitate and theologize from their own experience.

II. Reactions to death and dying
Denial and disbelief

When faced with a life-threatening illness or a bereavement, most people begin by saying 'No, not me.' Few people are able to take in such news immediately without some resistance. 'I don't believe it; there must be some mistake – it can't be true.' Such denial sometimes persists in the dying even when some degree of acceptance has been reached and some people resolutely continue to act and live as though they were going to live for ever, which most of us do most of the time anyway! For example, a Christian woman who knew she did not have long to live and who had even prepared her funeral service with the vicar, spent a weekend shortly before her death selecting her paintings and drawings for an exhibition six months ahead and talking about being there. Denial like this regularly serves a useful purpose. It enables people to control the pace at which they come to terms with such devastating knowledge, in a situation where control seems to have passed to the medical profession or to the illness.

[3] Robert Lowell *After the Funeral*

Denial does not necessarily have to be challenged in the dying, but if it persists in the bereaved after the first few days of shock and disbelief the pastoral carer needs to start confronting the person gently with reality. The process of 'realizing' i.e., coming to terms with the reality of the death of someone close can take several months. Mr B. was on a business trip with his wife in Japan when he died suddenly in late May. In late February the following year Mrs B. said, 'It was a few months ago that it hit me. Until then, after the shock, it felt as if he was just away on one of his world trips – he often went on them. But in December I realized he wasn't.'

Anger

Another response to the prospect of death or the fact of death is anger, often enshrined in the question, 'Why me?' This anger gets directed at doctors, at family, at pastors, at anyone in the firing line. This is the point at which some pastoral care falls down. We all know how to give comfort but anger does not demand comfort. It demands acceptance and expression. Lindemann wrote about the bereaved: 'The fear of insanity, the fear of accepting the surprising changes in his feelings, especially the overflow of hostility, have to be worked through.'[4] Pastoral carers tend to feel that the anger is personally directed at them instead of being free enough of their own need to please, and tough enough to withstand the angry feelings and work with them.

One terminally ill woman in a corner bed of a hospital ward was consistently argumentative, cantankerous and hostile towards all the staff, and regularly lay facing the wall, presenting a defiant backside to the world. Frequently close relatives of a dying person will express anger as if on their behalf – with a G.P. for not doing more, with specialist nurses for not controlling pain better. Similar anger occurs after a bereavement. 'My sister called God all the names under the sun when she heard Mum had died', said a woman to her minister, carefully distancing herself from her own angry feelings. Less obvious but equally an indication of anger is the common reaction against the 'modernization of death' in crematorium chapels. A

[4] American Journal of Psychiatry [1944]

clergyman who felt stirred enough to write in the national press complaining about 'silly purple pamphlets', 'black entertainment' and 'Bachzak' might profitably have reflected on why he felt such righteous indignation about this funeral. He seemed to be mirroring powerful feelings of anger which were around in the family but could not be expressed.

Anger is the response to dying and bereavement which pastoral carers most frequently ignore, perhaps because they ignore it in themselves. In care of the bereaved this may hinder the griefwork. Very often the hardest feeling to get at is the anger with the dead person for leaving, for doing this (and perhaps other things in the past) without consultation and on their own. In the early stages of grief, such anger is unthinkable, the unconscious fantasy being that we may destroy further the one who has been destroyed. This leads to idealization of the dead person and repression of strong feelings. The more someone remembers their lost loved one and remembers them with love, the more it becomes possible to discover and express their anger with them. The astute pastoral carer will have opportunities to pick up and acknowledge that anger. The professional pastor needs to be particularly aware of any hints of such anger, since people may be reluctant to reveal these feelings to God's representative, the fantasy being that faith has no place for anger, or at least that it is unacceptable to God.

Depression/sadness

When the awful reality of the situation is acknowledged, whether temporarily or for good, whether before death or after, people become sad. Sadness can usually be worked through (though if it persists and there is long term depression, medical help may be needed). Pastoral carers who are not afraid of the sadness within themselves which may be activated by other people's tears, are usually very good at allowing people to cry. Some carers however feel duty bound to cheer people up. This is usually response to a need within the carer to avoid pain and rarely relates to the needs of the other, as in the case of someone who said in January to a mother whose sixteen-year-old daughter had been ill for a year and died in December, 'Do try to have a better year this year'.

Because most of us are good at comforting sad people, we need to be aware of the danger inherent in this sort of care. It is widely assumed that expression of sadness is the proper grief-work. 'The traditional burial (enables) genuine grief and mourning', wrote a clergyman, presumably meaning tears. Carers doggedly pursue the goal of tears and catharsis while failing to pick up the other equally important signs of grief in process. This stems from their need to be in control of others and to see themselves as strong for the weak, helper to the help-less, etc. Learning how to minister to people in their strength needs to be a priority for pastoral carers.

Acceptance

People vary greatly in the degree to which they accept a life-threatening situation or a bereavement, and in the speed with which they learn to accept. Some never do. Acceptance can feel like weakness and capitulation. It can also be felt as strength and a free choice. Christians are thought to be able to accept death more easily than those with no faith, but it is not always so. C. S. Lewis charted his feelings and reactions after his wife died and found the precepts of the resurrection faith as offered by kind friends ('she is with God', 'do not mourn like those who have no hope', 'she is in God's hands', etc) of no help or comfort to begin with. A recent study of the elderly bereaved[5] concluded that people with commitment to Christian faith did not differ significantly in their ability to face death from those with no faith. Everyone goes at their own speed, and the carer has the difficult task of assessing that speed and taking cues from people indicating how far they have moved towards acceptance. Kubler-Ross regarded acceptance as a final phase in coping with dying, but dying is rarely as neat and tidy as we like to think. A Christian woman shortly before her death told her minister one day that her favourite psalm was 139 with its assurance of the omnipresence of God. Two days later she said her favourite was Psalm 22, particularly the verse, 'My God, my God, why has thou forsaken me?' The relatives of dying people too may swing from denial to acceptance and then to

[5] Life after a death, Bowling and Cartwright (Tavistock [1982]).

angry questioning or they may be so different from each other in their ways of coping that several different responses are present in a family at one time. This underlines the need for careful timing in pastoral care, especially in the offering of scripture. It may take people a long time to adjust their understanding of God in the light of their loss.

III. *Special needs of the dying*

'Bargaining' is the title of a very short chapter in Kubler-Ross, but it describes a common way of coping used by the dying. It is half way between denial and acceptance, a conditional acknowledgement of reality. There is normally a condition ('If I am spared . . .') attached to a promise ('I will go to church more often/become a hospital volunteer/give money to cancer research'). Frequently the negotiation is with God (cf. Gen 18[20-33].

A second type of bargaining occurs when the family of a dying person begin to acknowledge the seriousness of the situation and then throw themselves into looking for other ways of dealing with the illness, e.g, seeking a second opinion medically, going to America, bringing in faith-healers, etc. This is usually a way of coping with helplessness and the feeling of not being in control by over-activity designed to help and regain control. While it is reasonable to say that bargaining is usually 'not very helpful'[6] we should beware of dismissing such a powerful coping mechanism. In facing this behaviour more than any other the pastoral carer needs to remember Erich Fromm's words about respect in love: 'I want [the loved person] to grow and unfold as they are, and not for the purpose of serving me'.[7] The danger here again for the carer is over-control. Bargaining may be necessary.

There is a third type of bargaining. Sometimes dying people will set themselves a target, in defiance of the difficult circumstances (and of death). This target may be a date or a family event (e.g., the birth of a grandchild, a wedding, an anniversary, etc.) or a task (one cancer sufferer set out to raise £1m to pay for scanning equipment to achieve earlier diagnosis of

[6] *Letting Go*, 23.
[7] *The Art of Loving* (Unwin Books [1962]).

conditions like his own; he had raised about £600,000 when he died). This too is bound up with the wish to be in control. A critically ill widow set herself two major tasks: first, to prepare for confirmation (she was confirmed in hospital a month or two before she died). Secondly, she was determined to live to keep an appointment with her solicitor, at which she gave detailed instructions about how her house was to be sold and her daughter provided for. She died less than 24 hours after keeping it.

This way of coping is similar to that recognized in concentration camps, where goal-setting enabled some prisoners to master the uncertainty of camp life and survive. Viktor Frankl wrote: 'Any attempt at fighting the camp's . . . influence on the prisoner . . . had to aim at giving him inner strength by pointing out to him a future goal to which he could look forward . . . The prisoner who had lost faith in the future – his future – was doomed . . . he let himself decline and became subject to mental and physical decay.'[8]

The pastoral carer needs to recognize the significance of goal-setting in a family struggling with accepting limits to their time together. Rational argument can rarely be heard when bargaining is in process. Sometimes, though, the process of letting go of the chance of alternative treatment, miracle cures, etc., serves as a rehearsal for letting go of the loved person and the loving relationship later, and families of dying people frequently go through anticipatory grief on different occasions before the death occurs. It is as if they 'try on for size' the prospect of life without the loved one.

The use of allusion

In a recent study of the elderly bereaved, 85 per cent of the widowed said that neither they nor anyone else had talked with their spouse about the impending death. This may indicate a high degree of denial, or it may point to a phenomenon that sensitive pastoral carers discover, namely that although no explicit reference is made by the dying to their own death, there may be much implicit meaning in the words used. A minister had been visiting a retired railway signalman ill in bed

[8] *Man's Search for Meaning*. (Hodder and Stoughton [1963]).

at home. One evening he said hardly anything, but as the minister was about to leave he looked at the clock and said, 'Well, it's about time for the last train to come through'. He died that night. A woman with a terminal illness told the pastoral visitor from church about a pot plant which had almost died during the winter but had been 'brought in just in time' and had survived to burst into bloom though the flowers were now starting to droop and fall. The timing corresponded with the progress of her illness in a vivid way and she was clearly identifying herself with this plant. When the visitor pointed that out she refused to acknowledge it and continued to talk in detail about the plant: but as the visitor got up to leave she said, 'Thank you for listening, and I know what you mean'. The link may have been an unconscious and unacknowledged one, but the important thing was hearing the actual words she used, albeit about the plant and not herself.

Such allusive statements need not be interpreted openly or picked to pieces. In this instance the visitor did not gain much by trying to be explicit, though it is always worth indicating that you have heard two levels of meaning when people use allusion and oblique language. The valuable thing is to be able to enter someone else's world of meaning and spend time there. That is felt to be tremendously supportive.

'Hit or miss' care

Care of the dying can be a very 'hit or miss' affair. We learn what each individual requires only by being with them. Some will want to relive sad memories (e.g. wanting children but not having them, slipping into bad habits of smoking, drinking, self-neglect, etc., wartime experiences). Others will not be able to speak much and we will find ourselves regretting the lost opportunities as well. More often than not we will be unaware of whether our care has been useful. Some of us may find out afterwards, and be surprised. One dying man summoned the strength to say just one sentence to his minister during a visit; 'We never really *know*, father, do we?' 'No, we don't Peter', replied the minister – and he went home feeling awful, inadequate, that he'd let the man down. Two days later the man died and the minister felt worse. Afterwards the family revealed that in those last two days he had found the inner peace which had eluded him for months before, and had spoken of his deep gratitude for all the minister had said that day!

This uncertainty about the effectiveness of pastoral care, this not knowing immediately, is paralleled in the resurrection-appearance stories, where the presence of the risen Christ is a very hit-or-miss affair. Twice the disciples fail to recognize him, the road to Emmaus, (Lk 24^{16}) and the sea of Tiberias (Jn 21^4), and once Mary mistakes him for the gardener (Jn 20^{14}). On each occasion recognition comes through a symbolic gesture – the breaking of bread, a miraculous catch of fish, and the speaking of a name. There was a need to look beyond the physical encounter to meanings. But even when the meanings were clear, there was no guarantee that the risen Christ would stay, and no control over his appearance or disappearance. He could not be localized or monopolized in the stories any more than the Holy Spirit can be. Pastoral carers need to be humble enough to abandon notions of 'bringing Christ' to the dying and bereaved, and open enough to discover him within pastoral encounters (Lk 24^{31,32,45}).

'To tell or not to tell?'

Alex Comfort in *A Good Age* short-circuits this debate in an admirable and convincing way. He writes: 'Nobody "needs to be told" that he or she is dying, but (people) may be looking for an opportunity to tell you'. It is most important for the pastoral carer to be open to what the dying person is trying to communicate, whether with words or without.

IV. *Special needs of the bereaved Yearning/searching*

While this is restricted to literal searching for the lost one's face in a crowd we can accept it. But sometimes the search extends to consulting a spiritualist to make contact with the dead one. At this point the pastoral carer's hackles rise! We invoke O.T. prohibitions and suddenly become authoritarian without trying to explore the underlying need, which is the need to hold on to the loved one and not let go. For those whose belief in life after death is tenuous, or operates on a model of literal survival and revivification, a 'message' from the 'other side' may be not only comforting but also a means of strengthening faith. After all, Thomas was not denied the opportunity to see and touch the risen Lord. Usually, a single visit to a spiritualist or a spiritualist church is enough. The danger of course lies in the possibility that the bereaved will continue to need such reassurance, will get stuck with the compulsion to search for more evidence of survival, and will not negotiate the tricky business of letting go. The need to hold on is part of human loving. The risen Christ has to tell Mary in the garden, 'Stop clinging to me.' Pastoral carers need to recognize the complexity of the task of letting go and to avoid hasty judgments.

Guilt

Pastoral carers often cope with guilt in the bereaved by invoking the mercy and forgiveness of God irrespective of the nature or the circumstances of the guilt. If it turns out that guilt ran through the whole relationship with the dead person and predated the death by a long time there may be a need to offer all available resources – sacramental confession and absolution, pastoral counselling over a length of time, perhaps even psychiatric help. But much guilt in the bereaved is temporary guilt stemming from one of two sources:

(1) the time immediately before the death and the death itself ('I should have done more/noticed the illness earlier/stayed with them all the time until they died');

(2) idealization of the dead person. This regularly begins straight after death ('he was such a good man/he never hurt anyone'), lasts while the survivor is working through the memories, and brings with it the corollary of self-denigration in the bereaved. Both these types of guilt will wane as the survivor reviews the relationship with the deceased and formulates a way of resuming life.

Internalizing

One way of understanding the task bereaved people face is to describe it as 'Establishing in your internal world the externally lost person'. Even temporary parting requires us to do that, and we use photographs, letters, memories, personal effects, to help us build a picture inside us. When the parting is final, a strange paradox occurs. The only way of starting to internalize the lost person is by letting them go externally. Holding on holds up the progress. That is why little progress can be made until after the funeral. Within the funeral service though there is provision for a ritualized letting go, in the commendation and committal. After that, people vary in the time they take to dispose of clothes and other belongings. Some do it straight away; others preserve things as in a shrine. Some bereaved people begin to adopt the traits and characteristics of the dead person, identifying strongly with them in an attempt to perpetuate their existence. The whole process of internalizing and letting go takes a long time, and the widow who said, 'A marvellous thing has happened; today I didn't think about him once', was celebrating a milestone on the way.

Theologically, we see this process at work in the post-resurrection events. The resurrection appearances cease, Jesus is lost physically at the ascension, and the Holy Spirit comes to dwell within. Luke describes these as a series of events following naturally from each other, but John goes further and sees the loss of Jesus as a necessary prerequisite for the sending of the indwelling spirit: 'If I do not go away, the Comforter will not come'.

V. *Models of pastoral care*

There are two widely used models which need questioning.

The forerunner

Here the carer, like John the Baptist, sees the task as preparing people to meet Jesus. The primary aim of the pastoral encounter is to point people beyond oneself and make oneself redundant. Though this may be an admirable approach to spreading the gospel, it is no satisfactory in care of the dying and bereaved. First it devalues the pastoral encounter by seeing it as a means to an end. Secondly, it does not come to grips with the real pain and depth of feeling that may be present. Thirdly it denigrates the carer by suggesting that only God can help.

The evangelist

Here the carer encourages the dying or bereaved person to empty themselves in order that God might fill their life. This is a false emptiness because in reality the person may be full of powerful feelings which are crying out to be heard and accepted before any progress can be made.

A far more effective model of care for the dying and bereaved is that of

The fellow-traveller

The risen Christ on the road to Emmaus is the archetypal fellow-traveller. There are four elements to the story:
(1) He came near.

Eugene Kennedy writes about the need in the counsellor to cultivate 'the sense of what it means to be in relationship to someone else'. The same is true for pastoral care. The focus is the other person; they are in the centre. Instead of emptying them, the effective carer starts by emptying himself or herself, real 'kenosis' in which we leave our own preoccupations aside and concentrate only on the other and the relationship.
(2) He listened.

The words people use are not just accidental. Nor are the unspoken communications. Both need careful attention. The person who says, 'I feel cut in half', is talking about a different experience from one who says, 'Something inside me had died', though both may be describing the death of a spouse. A third focus is the feeling or the meaning behind the words. 'Seeing with the heart' is one writer's phrase for it.[9]
(3) He made connexions

By 'opening' and interpreting scripture, Jesus made links between the present calamity and the word of God. People make their own connexions much of the time. 'It's a punishment,' 'I can't think of anything I've done to deserve this.' A young woman said when her mother died, 'I'm 32. I'm married, have children, yet I still haven't grown up. But now I'll have to.' The pastoral carer needs to spot links and join the struggle to make sense of things.

[9] Saint Exupery, *The Little Prince*: On ne voit bien qu'avec le coeur, l'essential est invisible pour les yeux'

(4) He went away.

Pastoral care often happens 'on the run'. The reality is that we will not be able to stay for ever with people. Every time we leave people we model something about letting go. Short regular visits to a dying person and their family are better than long intermittent ones. Each goodbye can be a rehearsal for the final one.

Conclusion

Paul writes that Jesus 'emptied himself, not grasping at equality with God'. Pastoral care of the dying and bereaved needs to follow that self-emptying. Sometimes that may mean enduring silence. Often when we rush to fill silences with words, texts, prayers, anything to bring comfort, we comfort ourselves only. Paradoxically, by concentrating on the other person and resisting the temptation to rush in with words, we model the love of God. The word becomes enfleshed.[10] The very action of coming near someone, sharing their journey, listening and making links, and going away again, instils hope. A new system has been established, 'You-with-me', which mirrors the incarnation truth 'God-with-us'. Of course we will never refuse to speak of God; we will simply be more aware of when we are using God-language to protect us from real encounter with the other. The risks are enormous. But the truth in the resurrection is that the way of the cross can turn out to be none other than the way of life and peace.

Further Reading

The three basic textbooks are: *On Death and Dying* by E. Kubler Ross (Tavistock [1970]), *Bereavement* by C. Murray Parkes (Pelican [1975]), and *Letting Go* by I. Ainsworth-Smith & P. Speck (SPCK [1982]). But there is no substitute for listening to dying and bereaved people!

14. The Skills of Pastoral Care

By Leslie Virgo

'In order to enter a personal relationship with the absolute, it is necessary to be a person again, to rescue one's real personal self from the fiery jaws of collectivism which devours all selfhood.'[1]

When I was asked to help in the revision of a prayer card for people in psychiatric hospitals[2] I took to the patients the card in use which was a 6 x 8 folded card with a picture of Salisbury Cathedral, several Collects and a reading. Their comment: 'It is too large and asks us to think too much – couldn't we have something smaller and that says something for us?'

Torn in half the card made a neat 6 x 4 book. This became the basic shape whilst the contents aimed at taking the situation in which people were living and letting that form the prayer.

The mid-day prayer:

The day goes on...
    has it been all rush and confusion?
        Be still and know that I am God.
And there are people around-
    the crowds pressed on Jesus -
        then let me bring to God these persons,
            this place,
                this person next to me,
                    the disturbed,
                        the desperate,
                            the orderlies,
                              the nurses, the doctors,
                                  those passing by; those I
                                      wish were here with me now.
Father, into your hands, into your love,
    into your generous peace,
      we bring ourselves.

[1] Martin Buber, *Between Man and Man* (Fontana [1968]).
[2] Copies may be obtained from CIO Publishing, Church House, London, SW1P 3NZ.

Come unto me, all ye that suffer and
    are heavy laden, and I will give you rest.

For the night prayer:

It is dark, Lord.
I am afraid
        lonely,
            anxious,
                restless, in pain, lost.
I said to my soul
        'be still,
            and let the dark come upon you,
                which shall be the darkness of God'.

The people who were to use the card became completely involved in its creation. In the end they felt it cared for them. More importantly it helped them to be pastorally caring as they brought the needs of others into their thoughts and prayers. Many thousands now use the card.

The card was successful because it developed through the application of some of the basic principles of pastoral care, particularly because it started where people were, not where they were assumed to be, it spoke to how people felt, and helped them care for others.

Feelings are not things we are very much at home with in the church. Our emphasis tends to be rational. As anyone who has cared for the aged, the dying, the handicapped and the severely ill will know, you don't have to be rational to be relational. We best relate to someone by really attempting to know how they feel in themselves. Pastoral care is to do with good relating and the language of such relating must include the language of feeling. Everyone engaged in pastoral care has an instrument to use, the instrument of himself. I don't have to know how to deal with people's problems to 'care'. I don't even have to have had similar experience, although it is a help if I can really share with them how they feel. The one language we can share with everyone is the language of feeling.

The study of the skills of pastoral care is based on the belief that 'relating' is at the heart of the gospel; that pastoral care is the action of the gospel in relating person to person and persons to God. Such care will be concerned not simply with what people say but with the feeling behind the words, the hidden and the inner world of the person.

Two weeks after her husband had died Mrs Hurst was in church. After the service someone asked how she was. 'Oh, I'm feeling fine', she replied. The words were positive – the way they were said, the feeling behind them was bleak. In fact Mrs Hurst had been thinking of taking an overdose to escape. The first step in her first aid for her was for someone to hear where she was, not just in her words, but in herself. Fortunately the questioner listened and help was given.

The skills needed for good pastoral care are no different from those we use to live an effective social and emotional life. Our aim is to develop these skills, and to recognise that pastoral care can be for good or ill, depending on how we use our informed common sense.

It is possible to be as destructive in caring for others as an un-skilled driver might be on the road. A young curate once des-cribed with satisfaction and some pride the way in which he had responded to a pastoral call one evening and had spent the night holding the hand of the young lady in distress. A month later he was pleading to be rescued. We can say we know better than to be drawn in like that, but do we? People involved in pastoral care have to struggle with the expectation which is felt to be implicit in the role, that we shall be available to all people at all times, and that such availability will not count the cost of time. Both attitudes can be devastatingly harmful.

It is well for pastoral carers to think of themselves as a homing signal for inadequate persons and people who are afraid to be unnoticed and alone. Attempts to meet the demands of these people on an 'all things to all men' basis can lead to a 'clinging vine' or to the increasing demands for care and attention which eventually are refused with an ensuing fury from the one rejected.

The Background to Pastoral Skills

For me Dietrich Bonhoeffer in his *Creation and Fall* provides the basic question of pastoral care and counselling and therapy in general, in fact the question that faces us all day in daily life.

Commenting on Gen3$^{8-13}$ he says

> 'Adam, where are you?' With this word the Creator calls Adam forth out
> of his conscience. Adam must stand before his Creator. . . 'Come out of
> your hiding place, from your self reproach, your covering, your secrecy,
> your self torment, from your vain remorse. Confess to yourself, do not
> lose yourself in religious depair, be yourself, Adam. . . where are you?
> Stand before your Creator.'

Whenever one person comes to another for care they are
answering *this* question. To speak of yourself to another openly
means coming out from behind the defences, from the screens
and barriers we put up to avoid looking at ourselves or letting
others see us as we really are. Before good caring can take place
it is essential that the carer answer this call 'Where are you?' for
himself, standing as openly before his Creator as self-
knowledge can allow.

In a look back at a man's beginning we recognize that people
have always 'cared' for one another, so why write about it now?
Gerard Egan writes:

> 'Pastoral Care is not a neutral process: it is for better or for worse. If the
> distressed person finds a skilled helper he is likely to improve, that is, to
> begin to live more effectively...However, if he is invloved with a ' low-
> level' helper it is quite likely that he will get worse.'[3]

For this reason the researches of C. B. Truax and R. R.
Carkhuff in 1967 were generally welcomed in the counselling
world. In their *Toward Effective Counselling and Psychotherapy
Training and Practice* (Chicago, Aldine [1967]) they maintain
that effective care or counselling does not depend on technique
but on the presence of elements or skills, and three in particular: empathy: genuineness: non-possessive love. They
maintain that when these are present growth and healing can
take place. The importance of this for pastoral care is that it is
not only in one-to-one relationships that these skills can be
exercised but across the whole range of ministry.

Seward Hiltner in his *Preface to Pastoral Theology* (Abingdon
Press [1958]), points out that Zwingli's book *The Shepherd* used
'pastoral' as a funcional extension of the noun 'pastor':

[3] Gerard Egan, *The Skilled Helper* (Brooks/Cole [1975])

'Whatever the pastor or shepherd did was pastoral or shepherding. Functions followed from title. By implication everything done by one called 'pastor' was shepherding.'

This invites us to recognize our pastoral care as an attitude of shepherding: of respect, concern and care for the people we are involved with, whether in a pulpit or committee, by a bedside or at a civic reception.

In this way the 'pastoral' element of care may be likened to prevenient grace: the grace of God present at all times and in all places; 'care' then corresponds to actual grace: those occasions when a response is made to that general presence in a particular relationship.

As well as empathy, genuineness and non-possessive love Truax and Carkuff detail four other 'skills' needed for good counselling or care: respect; concreteness; immediacy; confrontation. In 1975 Gerard Egan in *The Skilled Helper* produced a mode for systemactic helping and interpersonal relating based on Truax and Carkhuff's work. These two sources provide the background for this consideration.

The Nature of Care

Pastoral care tends to be nebulous, bitty and uncalculated, unlike counselling which usually involves an agreement to work together at specific times, in a certain place, and with mutually recognised goals. The need to respond in care may spring out like the proverbial bear that is waiting for the unwary who step on the lines of the pavement. So it is that the pastoral carer needs an attitude of care, and some clear ideas of how to respond.

Most people will give *listening* as the most important part of care. Certainly unless we are ready to listen we cannot care at all.

In the 6th Century BC Seneca wrote of the need for someone to listen:

'For who listens to us all in the world whether he be friend, or teacher, brother or father or mother, sister or neighbour, son or ruler or servant. Does he listen, our advocate, or our husbands or wives, those who are dearest to us? Do the stars listen, when we turn despairingly away from man, or the great seas, or winds of the mountains? To whom can any man say - Here I am! Behold me in my nakedness, my wounds, my secret grief, my despair, my betrayal, my pain, my tongue which cannot express my sorrow, my terror, my abandonment. Listen to me for a day - an hour - a moment. Lest I expire in my terrible wilderness, my lonely silence. Oh! - God, is there no one to listen?'

What is the listening for? A doctor will listen and probe with his questions to hear the symptoms, make his diagnosis and offer his prescription. The classical or clerical model of counselling follows this medical model with fatal results:

'Can I help you, Mrs S.?
'Well, Vicar, I am so tired with all the work to do.'

may be followed by a series of questions on the nature of the work, the availability of others to help, and so on, followed by some suggestions as to cure: 'Get the children to help.'I'll get someone from the parish to come in.'Even,'I'll come and help you myself' - a last desperate fling since all the other suggestions have been met with a 'Yes - but . . .', leaving our vicar feeling frustrated and useless and Mrs S. frustrated and not understood. This is 'computer' listening. The person punches in the program and the vicar displays the solution.

Listening can be a polite silence while you rehearse what you are going to say when you get the floor. Listening can mean waiting alertly for the flaw in the other fellow's argument so that you can mow him down. Or listening can be empathetic. It is in empathetic listening that both care and counselling find their core - which needs full fleshing to be a finished fruit.

All relationships established with empathy can be the basis for growth and change when linked to understanding and action.

Carl Rogers, The first to fully underline the importance of empathy, says, concerning the counselling process:

'It is a relationship in which at least one of the parties is intent on promoting the development, maturity, improved functioning, improved coping with life, of the other.'[4]

[4] Carl Rogers, *Empathy* [1958].

Empathy need not in any way be confined to the practising of skilled therapy but can be seen as an essential healing agent in all relationships. It is, therefore, a basic element or skill which can and should be practiced and learnt by all who are involved in any way in the care of persons.

It is possible to discover examples of empathy in many fields not least in the arts, in such books as *The Inheritors* by William Golding and in this empathetic response by G. K. Chesterton on behalf of the woman who was seen by Frances Crofts Cornford only as a pitiful object walking through the field in gloves

'Why do you rush through the field in trains,
Guessing so much and so much?
Why do you flash through the flowery meads,
Fat-headed poet that nobody reads?
And why do you know such a frightful lot
About people in gloves as such?
And how the devil can you be sure,
Guessing so much and so much?
How do you know but what someone who loves
Always to see me in nice white gloves
At the end of the field you are rushing by,
Is waiting for his Old Dutch?'[5]

Empathy is an extention of listening but empathy takes listening one stage further in that this is the means by which the listener enables the one who is talking not only to know that he has been understood without judgement, but also that the person listening has been able to enter into his world and knows what it feels like to be him. An essential prerequisite for effective empathetic response is the ability of the listener to be in touch with his own feelings. If he cannot allow himself to be aware of feelings of loss, or anxiety or anger, for example, it will be difficult for him to accept or understand them in the other, since they will be threatening to him, and the more he is aware of himself the more he can be aware of the other and share this awareness in an empathetic manner. In her *A Handbook of Counselling* (Paternoster Press [1980]) Evelyn Peterson mistakenly suggests that it is easier to enter into the

[5] *The Collected Poems of G. K. Chesterton*, 39

experience if one has had a similar expereince. It is not the experience that needs experiencing, however, but that we have the ability to enter the feelings inherent in the experience.

Practice will not make perfect in our development of these skills – there will always be room for improvement. Useful exercises in empathy are to take portmanteau words and unpack them, asking 'How do I feel when I feel depressed?' ranging from sad to suicidal, and flat to completely squashed. A long list of feeling words can help us to be aware of the different states wrapped up in the one word. This is also because we have, at some time, used a word to describe our own state – like 'depressed', or 'bereaved' – we can too easily assume the person sharing with us is in the same place that we were.

The value of the empathetic response can be experienced by unpacking the word 'accepted'. Write down a list of all that you feel and experience when you experience being accepted.

The goal of all our aid must have within it the aim of helping others to be more authentic in themselves and in their faith and so we need to practise authenticity, *genuineness*, ourselves. How easy it is to hide behind the role, fitting in with the old pop song 'Here comes the vicar walking down the aisle, putting on the agony, putting on the style'!

If we are to help others to be more real we must endeavour to be 'real' ourselves, and not cloak our own ignorance or aggression under platitudes of avoidance.

> 'We must not deceive ourselves by believing that the disease can be cured by formulae which assert that nothing is really as the sick person imagines. It is an idle undertaking to call out to a mankind that has grown blind to eternity: "Look at the eternal values!"'[6]

'I know I am going to die and that I shouldn't be afraid, but I am still frightened – do you get frightened Vicar?' may be met with: 'Just rest on the promise of eternal life', or 'Yes, I find the thought of dying fearful – but not death itself somehow!'

A genuine response will do far more to be with and acknowledge where the questioner is in their own fears and uncertainties. Pastoral care is reassuring by not fearing to be genuine. Most often reassurance raises anxiety as it seeks to play down

[6] Martin Buber, *Between Man and Man*.

fears and can suggest they *are* too fearful to be faced openly.

One test of genuineness for ourselves is to ask how much do I benefit from the help I give to others? After some years working with disturbed people I realized I should not ask, 'What can I do for them?' but 'What can they do for me!' I then discovered that people I help:

> Give me an additional sense of value
> Make me feel powerful
> Satisfy my need to be wanted
> Give me a sense of 'service' and so of spiritual well being.

Recognizing that makes me a little more humble, and opens the way to that most gratifying of all pastoral experiences which I can only liken to the Burning Bush. Moses, seeing the fire which burnt without consuming, takes off his shoes, and approaches delicately, carefully, awefully (Ex 3²⁻⁶). Entering into dialogue he makes two great discoveries: the name of God, and something more of his own name. So it can be with us as we approach all who come to us in care with our due care.

Let us return to our young curate and the danger of *possession*. Letting ourselves be possessed by the person in need, or possessing them, can lead to endless complication, recrimination, resignation, despair, thoughts of murder, and sometimes actual suicide as the only way out.

Faced with an overly possessive person, the carer does well to read the signs early. Such signs are a tendency to create crisis, demand attention, flatter the carer as 'the only one who has ever understood me', make increasing demands for attention and time, involve many others in support roles, constantly bringing helpers to screaming pitch and the desire to reject, but making them feel that the consequences would be fateful. Such a person has been described as an archipelago ego – so split up in themselves that they require as much attention as they can get as often as possible from as many different sources in order to maintain a sense of self.

The first aid response to this need is clear but by no means easy. The need is to exercise strict control, to provide a boundary of care within which the person can know themselves to be related to, but also know that they will not be allowed to spill over. Such control is not easy, particulary for those of us who are raised in an ambience of Christian love where availability would seem the keynote. However, it is this exercise of acceptance with clear control which alone can help such a person gradually lose the fear of losing control themselves and begin to trust.

It is salutary to ask ourselves whether we fit into this pattern, the work that we do gives us ample opportunity to feed from others, and so possess those we care for, always remaining in control ourselves, perhaps hiding a fearfulness of genuine relationship under our caring responses.

The model for non-possessive love is the love that God has for us, the emphasis in the Lord as Shepherd (Jn 10$^{1-17}$) is a responsiveness of known and knowing in an interdependence. It is as well to remember that progress to maturity, both developmental and spiritually, is one from dependence, through independence to interdependence. 'I call you not servants but friends' (Jn 15^{15}). Christ 'respects' his disciples and ourselves in these words.

Such an attitude to others assumes and requires *respect*. Respect is another of the recognized 'skills' of Care. It may seem so obvious as to be beyond mentioning until we let ourselves become aware of the ways in which our own prejudices and bias undermine our respect for others. The desire to make people conform to our way of thinking under the sincerely held belief that this is the 'only' good for a person has led from the failures of Job's comforters through the enormities of the Inquisition to the present problems in fundamentalism.

Respect observes boundaries. The ease with which we use Christian names, the modern trend of exchanging the Peace, are two ways in which we may be assuming too close a relationship too soon. A volunteer in a hospice used 'love', 'dear one', 'precious' as her approach to every person she tended on her first approach. She came to recognize that this was a sort of 'cheap grace' and that the approach of respect would move more gradually from Mr Smith, to 'Jim', to 'love'. In another hospital situation a new member of staff was appalled at the sight of people sitting around on commodes or being carried dripping naked through the ward on a geriatric hoist, and met the scorn of the other staff when she tried to make a stand for the dignity of the person by providing screens in the one case and a blanket in the other.

Respect acknowledges defences and does not try to push people too far too quickly. A bereaved person may quite quickly pass through the initial defence of 'numbness' following the shock, but seem to go on and on repeating the happenings surrounding the moment of dying. Remaining ready for the next movement in bereavement, the carer will respect the need for this defence.

Defences are our natural way of avoiding a flooding of feeling and awareness before we are ready. Respect recognizes that there are psychological 'distances': we can get too close to someone and embarrass them. 'I know just how you feel and understand completely' are overstatements that get too close. We can remain too cool and dismissive and depersonalize others: 'Don't worry about it, it happens to us all'. Respect acknowledges a person's right to be themselves and to take responsibility for their own life. Respect acknowledges that others may have different views of faith or morals to ourselves and will respect those differences.

Martin Buber shows the dynamic nature of respect as he says:

> 'If I face a human being as my *Thou*, and say the primary word *I-Thou* to him, he is not a thing among things, and does not consist of things. . . Just as the melody is not made up of notes nor the verse of words nor the statue of lines, but they must be tugged and dragged till their unity has been scattered into these many pieces, so with the man to whom I say *Thou*. I can take out from him the colour of his hair, or of his speech, or of his goodness. I must continually do this. But each time I do it he cease, to be *Thou*.'[7]

Christians are directed to 'love themselves'. a proposition which seems to be at odds with the injuctions to deny ourselves. The apparent contradiction is resolved when it is realized that we cannot deny what we do not know. It is a human characteristic to hide from ourselves and, even more, to hide

[7] Martin Buber, *I and Thou* (T. & T. Clark [1958]).

ourselves from others. Self rejection and lack of self valuing is a frequent cause of distress for people. To know and accept is not to condone behaviour, it is rather to lead towards that 'sober estimate' talked of by St Paul which, as he says, comes from a continual offering of the mind to God for its renewing. Such self acceptance helps us to avoid repressing aspects of ourselves which we find difficult or unpleasant and which we often put into other people or groups and condemn in them: 'I really find these "high"/"low" church people so insufferably intolerant'.

A failure to know the self leads us to set up defences to prevent ourselves and others looking too closely. It also means that we lack *'immediacy'*.

In the context of 'skills' immediacy is understood as that ability to be aware of and to acknowledge how one feels in this moment. To have the ability to acknowledge, 'I feel angry – furstrated – sexually excited', means that we can own the feeling; we don't have to act it, or repress it, but can acknowldge that we feel like this, and, if it is appropriate, we may even say that that makes me feel angry (or hurt or . . .).

Repressed feelings become active volcanoes building up to explosion, swamping and destructive. The Green Shield Stamp days provide a good illustration: in those days it was possible to collect books of stamps and then hand them in for a gift. When we fail to acknowledge our feelings immediately to ourselves if not to others we tend to 'collect stamps'. An apparent or actual slight will start a good day's collection of resentments which will, perhaps, find fulfillment at an awkward PCC, and a wife who says innocently and sympathetically 'You're late tonight' – now is the time to cash 'stamps' in for the 'present'. Now the explosion building up all day seems justified, frustrated rage can erupt. Pity the bemused wife, child or other victim. Helping people to be immediate is to help them avoid the ills attendant on repression; and depression is not the least of these. It is to enable someone to say, 'Here and now this is how I feel'. In groups with the relatives of alcoholic professional people I often need to underline this need for the spouse to own their feelings. The feelings are exposed not to change the other person's behaviour but to show how that behaviour affects the spouse.

Immediacy and genuineness go hand in hand with the communication which is essential to good relationship which depends on the proposition, 'How can you know who I am unless I tell you?'

Feelings are a universal language; though often feared, they are ignored to our peril. Provided we keep our feelings well attuned, the strings of the instrument neither too slack nor too shrill, we can get some sense of where the other person is in themselves.

When we are 'caring' for another we need to be aware of our immediate feelings about them. How does this person make me feel, what is he doing to me, am I feeling parental, judgmental, depressed, impotent, strong and protective, bored and confused. Our feelings will usually give us a clear sense of what the other person is feeling, and what feelings they are putting on to us.

In our meeting with others we need to avoid woolly emotionalism or vague expression. *Concreteness* as a basic skill aims at directness. 'I shouldn't really have come, I know you're busy', could be pulled to earth with 'If you take responsibility for your time, then I will for mine. Settle down and share what's on your mind'.

Concreteness is needed when expressions like 'I've had a bad day', or 'I feel terrible' are used. What is 'a bad day?' - a day full of disaster, or simply one in which feelings have been low. 'I feel terrible' can range from indigestion to impending death.

Finally, *confrontation*. Placed last because needing greatest care in its use. Confrontation can be an accurate instrument of care or a steam roller squashing a nut. Confrontation can only be effective when there is a good relationship between two persons. Just to tell someone they're wrong is a blunt instrument, to help someone face up to reality they're pointedly avoiding can lead to release.

The woman of Samaria, is a classic example of accurate confrontation once a relationship had been established (Jn 4). In his confrontation of David, Nathan made a most delicate approach (2 Sam 12).

The Model of Care

Care is most effective when it can move through the three phases of relating, pattern making and acting. Put the person in the centre and with accurate empathetic responses build a relationship of trust. As the feelings are expressed and the situation unfolds help the person see the pattern in themselves and their actions. As they can see themselves more clearly lead onto action, helping them to see how they can act more constructively in their attitude to themselves, their problems and others.

The aim of care will be so to accept another that they will be free to explore themselves, to understand themselves better, and to decide their own course of action.

First aid may include intervention as an appropriate response, since crises may well require a practical action to ease the situation. It is vital that such intervention should be first aid and that the persons helped should be encouraged to use their own muscle and take responsibility for their own lives as soon as possible.

Finally those who are engaged in pastoral care must be ready to refer: The Samaritan didn't go on collecting needy people on his donkey, he passed the traveller on for someone better fitted than himself to continue the care (Lk 10[29-37]). Referral requires a good knowledge of resources and a careful use of skills so that the person we refer may not feel rejected. A good referral will prepare the ground both in the person in need, and with the recourse referred to, so that the transition may be smooth and positive.

Always we can remember that first aid is God's - He has already made a referral to us; we are privileged to be part of his movement of healing and growth with others and so within ourselves.

15. Breakdown and Referral

By Professor James P. Watson,
Guy's Hospital, London

I. *Introduction*

According to my dictionary, 'breakdown' means 'collapse' or 'stoppage'. As this book is about pastoral care, we are concerned here with breakdowns in the functioning of people, not cars, fuel supplies, or other inanimate systems whose integrity is important to us. Up to a point, however, breakdowns in people resemble those of cars, which frequently stop through failure of a part of some complex mechanism or because components cease working harmoniously with each other. One kind of human breakdown occurs when parts of the individual's bodily and psychological structures fail to function. We shall call these 'individual system disorders'. They have various forms depending on which parts are affected. It is helpful for the pastoral carer to be able to tell when one of these disorders may be present.

Human breakdowns, or the appearance of breakdown, are also of two other kinds, to which the 'car breakdown' analogy does not really apply, and which I call 'coping difficulties' and 'relationship disorders'. Both these types of breakdown acknowledge that people are more than collections of bodily parts, but are social beings situated in worlds or relationship with others in families and groups forming networks of infinite potential. 'Coping difficulties' appear as breakdowns when the social network fails to sustain the individual trying to deal with life's demands. 'Relationship problems' become breakdown when the marital, family, or other multi-person system malfunctions; the system itself may ask for help, or one individual may be symptomatic of the wider problem. It is helpful for a pastoral carer to be able to distinguish between the three classes of breakdown, even though the distinction may be by no means easy to make. An understanding of processes whereby people seek help for personal problems is useful, and this is discussed next.

II. *Help Seeking*

The starting point is the individual experiencing something; often a sense of unease, uncomfortable bodily sensations, or disagreeable feelings, which indicates a problem. ('Problem' in this context means 'something requiring attention and possibly action'.) The person first identifies the experience as *signifying a problem*, and there follows a process of *appraisal* which provides a provisional explanation and a judgment of what, if anything, needs to be done.

Consider an example. I wake in the morning experiencing disagreeable sensations. I note headache, nausea, dizziness, and unsteadiness on walking. My appraisal is 'hangover', with relief expected in four to six hours. Now suppose in similar circumstances I say, 'hangover', but then realise there was no drinking to cause it. I would need a new explanation. I might say, 'I must be ill', and retire to bed expecting 'influenza' to take a familiar course. Alternatively I might be unable to think of a satisfactory explanation and want to ask someone. If I can ask my wife and obtain a satisfactory formulation from her, then again some coping action may suggest itself. If I have no wife or other confidant to ask, or if my wife's formulation is unconvincing, I may decide to seek outside advice. This could be from doctor, pastoral carer, grandmother, friend – or indeed from anyone I regard as capable of giving good advice. (I might have different expectations of professional and 'lay' advisers and choose between different helpers for different sorts of problems.) The conversation with a helper would allow a reformulation of the problem with an opportunity to consider new possible actions.

Cycles of reappraisal and reformulation may recur until an explanation leading to useful action is arrived at. At some stage in the process referral to an agency may be proposed.

Consider another example. I have an argument with my wife one evening and have a headache next morning. The atmosphere at home is tense and I feel unable to confide in my wife that I feel unwell. As the day goes on my headache feels worse and the thought occurs to me that I may be developing severe blood pressure or a brain tumour. I therefore consult my doctor and tell this story to him. Inevitably he selects from what I say choosing items partly in accord with his own predilictions. So, as might many doctors, he may examine my nervous system, take my blood pressure, and then either tell me my anxiety was unfounded or refer me to a specialist neurologist for investigation. (The latter course would almost certainly strengthen my fears that I have a serious brain disease.)

Alternatively the doctor might focus upon possible connections between events and symptoms, making suggestions such as, 'Is it possible that these bodily feelings are consequences of the argument the previous night?' This would suggest something quite different from referral for neurological advice.

These examples are intended to indicate that statements of personal problems emerge from process of formulation and appraisal; and that these processes may involve several converstions with people who select from their own repertoires of ideas about people when they offer explanations of the problems they hear about. The examples also remind us that helpers apply to what help-seekers tell them a mixture of any professional ideas they may have with what I call their 'generally personal' sets of ideas about people. What this means is this. In ordinary life people learn from an early age to talk about people's behaviour and problems in ways which they find meaningful. Many of these ways of talking have moral connotations, or refer to supposed personal characteristics: 'He lacks willpower to do this'; 'It's all right, you can rely on such a conscientious person'; 'He's a pleasant man', etc. It seems to me that people bring to professional training 'ordinary language' approaches evolved from past experience and regarded as personally meaningful, and that any professional frames of reference are added to these but do not supersede them. These frames of reference will include some medical ones in doctors, some theological ones in ministers, and ideas selected from a wide range of psychological systems among psychotherapists. But the first task of the helper is to establish a mutually intelligible language with 'ordinary life' concepts. The addition of 'professional' concepts may or may not add to what can be done on an ordinary language basis.

This approach implies that anyone with a 'generally human' capacity to establish mutual understanding with another person can help people to the extent that they can be helped without professional expertise. A basic rule of caring is to acknowledge when the problem is beyond one's personal competence. This is one fundamental reason for referral.

To summarize so far. Help-seeking occurs when a person has identified themself as (1) having a problem which (2) cannot be dealt with personally or (3) within the immediate social network. Help giving begins with a conversation to establish a mutually intelligible language about the problem to provide a reformulation which will either (a) suggest action or (b) inform referral for relevant expertise.

We can now try and apply this view to the three classes of breakdown labelled earlier.

III. Coping Difficulties

'Breakdown' implies an idea of urgency, of crisis, and coping difficulties usually present this acutely. Typically, an event pushes the support system beyond capacity. Sometimes the stressful event introduces crisis into a previously stable system: unexpected bereavement, for instance, a sudden illness, an accident, burglary, or house fire might precipitate urgent breakdown. Whether or not it does depends on several factors, as well as the number of supportive people surrounding the stressed person, as already noted. People are not equally capable of withstanding all stresses; what is especially threatening for one may mean less to another; and events may mean different things at different time. Also, events have individual features which may influence responses to them.

The example of bereavement may clarify some of these points. The effects of loss of a loved one often depend, among other things, upon the age of the deceased – death of a mother is usually more traumatic for a person of 15 than for one of 50, and when the mother is 40 than 80; and death of a child, especially when young, is for many people more grief-provoking than of the spouse, parent, or any other person. Effects of bereavement will also depend on the unexpectedness of the loss, the closeness of the relationship and its characteristics, and the immediate circumstances of the death. One basic principle of caring in 'coping breakdowns' is for the helper to encourage sharing in conversation of the details of the distressed person's experience. This requires time and the capacity to listen and tolerate being in the presence of another's intense painful feeling. In this group of breakdowns there is a natural tendency for the intensity of distress to subside with time in the presence of an attentive other person.

A second principle is to explore possible constructive actions with the help seeker when the acute distress has subsided. The actions would aim to provide support whose lack had contributed to the breakdown – temporary residence with a friend, or refuge elsewhere, or someone to join the sufferer at home, for instance.

It is sometimes difficult for even the experienced care-giver to distinguish a coping breakdown from 'individual system' or 'relationship' ones. The intensity of distress, and the way it is expressed may suggest to the helper that the person is 'ill' (has an individual system disorder), whether 'mad' or ill in some way. Sometimes of course people with coping difficulties attempt to solve their problems with the help of alcohol or drugs; these activities can add an element of 'illness' to a breakdown which began as a coping problem. For many, coping distress is extremely intense and can suggest the possibility of a psychiatric illness, such as depression out of proportion to the provoking event. However, the utmost caution is advised in ascribing distress to illness. It is very difficult for the helper to be sure the distress being presented is outside the normal range. This is a particular problem with people whose cultural background differs markedly from the care-giver's. For instance, people's responses to an event such as bereavement are partly determined by the norms and customs of the person's cultural group, and a middle class Londoner, for instance, might find it very difficult to understand the behaviour of a Lancashire man, Jew, or Jamaican after bereavement.

IV. *Individual System Disorders*

Thus far I have emphasized close relationships between

events and the feelings and behavioural responses which they evoke, and between these responses and the available social supporting network, in determining how people cope and whether or not breakdown occurs. It is also possible, for people have mechanical aspects as well as social realities, for breakdown to reflect failure in a process within the individual. These are the psychiatric illnesses. They form three main groups of disorders, which in medical terminology can be termed psychoses (varieties of madness), neuroses (varieties of nervousness) and 'organic' mental illnesses (where mental problems reflect disturbed brain function).

For the pastoral carer, it is not necessary to worry about the niceties of psychiatric classification or to be afraid of being overwhelmed by psychiatric illness. Three guidelines are helpful.

(i) If as a layperson the impression is gained that the help seeker may be 'mad', consider the possibility of a psychiatric opinion about the case.

(ii) If the help seeker's level or kind of distress appears – as an informed 'lay' judgment – to be out of proportion to the provoking situation, to be more intense or more prolonged than would be expected in the circumstances, or to be of an unexpected quality, then a variety of nervous illness (neurosis) may be present and a medical opinion sought.

(iii) If the person appears ill, or confused, or both, in an informed 'lay' sense, then there is a possibility of some brain problems warranting medical opinion.

Of course, non-medical carers become increasingly expert at recognizing individual disorders, and, with experience, distinguish them from other sorts of breakdown, so the threshold for referral – the frequency of doubt – may change for the individual.

It is advisable to be cautious about ascribing distress or problems to illness, even when an illness is present. It may take much knowledge of the individual and of their situation before connections between illness, relationships, and events can be discerned with confidence. On other occasions, these matters are easy to understand.

V. *Relationships*

People with 'individual' breakdowns may also have 'coping difficulty'-type breakdowns. They may also experience relationship problems and acute presentations for help may reflect relationship crises. Thus a person with a depressive illness may experience marital problems as a consequence of this and a crisis might be precipitated by a husband separating from a depressed wife. (It may be difficult to distinguish this set of events from marital difficulty leading to depression which once evoked might make the marital problems worse.)

A useful guideline is this. If the help-seeker refers to a problem of intimate relationships, or if they don't and the carer is at a loss to understand the problem, the possibility of a relationship problem should be investigated. This grandiloquent phrase really means, if in doubt see the couple together, or the whole family together. An initial meeting in the service of increased understanding, where the helper's prime role is a listening one, requires the native 'human being' qualities of the carer and additional professional therapeutic training is not necessary. To aim at marital or family change through therapy, however, does require training. The same applies to specific treatments applicable to individuals, but pastoral carers may be particularly well placed to become (through training) therapists who can deal specifically with marital and family issues. One reason for this is that the pastoral carer may have easier access to the whole family system than a carer based at a treatment centre such as a hospital.

VI *Referral*

Referral, then, follows identification of a problem beyond the coping competence of those involved. Once the need for it has been identified, the principle is to try and select the agent most appropirate to the individual's problem as presently understood.

As indicated in the foregoing paragraphs, there are circumstances in which a medical referral may clarify the nature of a breakdown. This may be general medical, at family doctor level, or a hospital specialist such as a psychiatrist. A vital principle here is for the individual carer to know their local talent.

Regretfully it must be acknowledged that some psychiatrists are not good at helping certain sorts of patients who should be kept away from them; and some physicians are given to inappropriate sequences of physical investigation in preference to even the simplest psychosocial assessment. The availability of help varies enormously in quantity and quality from place to place. The carer should be aware of the resources available within social services, counselling centres, and self help facilities among non-medical facilities within the locality.

Further Reading

Stafford-Clark, D. and Smith, A.C., *Psychiatry for Students* (Allen & Unwin, 7th edition [1983]). (A readable outline of psychiatry suitable for 'lay carers'.)

Skynner, A.C.R. and Cleese, J., *Families and how to survive them* (Methuen [1984]). (An unusual, serious, charming and at times amusing exploration of families and problems which may arise in them.)

16. Ethical Dilemmas

BY THE REVEREND BERNARD MOBBS, SYDENHAM, LONDON

IT is now many years since Dietrich Bonhoeffer suggested that an apparent lack of interest in ethical systems arose, not from moral indifference, but because his period was oppressed by a superabundance of ethical problems. This is even more true of our time. An increasingly complex society forces upon us ever more baffling ethical dilemmas. What is more, the old moral authorities are either questioned or considered irrelevent to situations which are unprecedented. The religious and ethical pluralism of Western society also presents us with a bewildering array of view points from which to choose. The result of all this for the individual who faces a concrete ethical dilemma ranges from severe loss of confidence to near moral paralysis.

A whole range of ethical dilemmas has to do with sex, reproduction and marriage, and many of them are linked with improved techniques of contraception and increased control over reproduction. Sexual relationships outside marriage,the nature of the homosexual relationship, abortion, artificial insemination by donor (AID), the medical response to the severely damaged or deformed baby, are but a few of the issues in this area.

At the other end of our human existance there are problems relating to the responsibilty for elderly or senile parents and relatives. These problems, made more acute by inadequate housing and cuts in the social services, seem bound to increase. Who can doubt also that the question of euthanasia and suicide will become more urgent?

A further range of problems arises because the sensitive conscience can never be restricted to questions of personal morality. To protest about such iniquities as the arms race, or unfair discrimination, can cost a person his or her job.

There is in the Christian church a centuries long traditon of spiritual direction and guidance. The modern pastoral care movement has roots in that tradition as well as in more recent developments in psychology and other human sciences. The

giving of moral advice and direction was, of course, an important part of the director's task. It was often given in a
straightforward and authoritative way. The director was well
versed in moral theology, the discipline of Christian ethics was
relatively stable, the authority of the director was unquestioned. The penitent declared the moral question which
troubled him and the director, drawing upon both his
understanding of the penitant as well as his knowledge of the
teaching of the church, declared an answer. But both the director and the penitent lived in a world of fixed moral landmarks
which few inhabit today. In any case, we stand on the other side
of important developments in the understanding of human
nature. We now realize how important it is for human growth
and maturity that a person should be enabled to make his own
moral decisions. We recognise how stultifying it is for a person
to act upon the moral convictions of someone else, convictions
he has not assimilated and made his own. We are more aware of
moral ambiguity and uncertainty than were some of our
predecessors.

The Christian exercising a pastoral ministry will sometimes
be called upon to care for those perplexed by ethical dilemmas.
In view of the kind of world we live in these situations seem
likely to increase rather than diminish. How shall we make the
most adequate response possible? This is the question this chapter seeks to address.

First of all, something must be said about our terminology. It
is unforunate that no word has been found to describe the
recipient of pastoral care. That person may well be a
parishioner or church member. He or she may be receiving
regular counselling, in which case the label used might be client
or counselee. None of these words is totally satisfactory
because they are all limiting. The word client will sometims be
used in this chapter when a counselling situation, formal or
informal is envisaged.

What is more important than the label used, however, is that
we do not regard the recipient of pastoral care as being
inevitably *the other person*. At certain times we ourselves will be
the recipient of pastoral care. We will be the clients in a counselling situation. We will be facing a critical moral dilemma

and needing help to understand it and come to a decision. Pastoral care is distorted when it is seen as the strong helping the weak, those with resources helping those who have only questions. Pastoral care is about a relationship in which we will be involved ourselves at different times in different roles. This is good because quality in caring springs partly from knowing well the experience of being cared for with compassion and expertise.

Ministry to those perplexed by moral dilemmas will require both some ethical knowledge and counselling skills. The one without the other will hardly make for an adequate response.

The examination paper in Christian Ethics set for ordinands in the Church of England used to have one question called 'The Moral Case'. In about 400 words a situation involving a difficult moral decision was described. The person sitting the examination was expected to make a proper analysis of the situation from the point of view of ethical principles and to describe what response should be made. This type of examination question had advantages in stimulating ethical reflection and revealing what resources of ethical knowledge the examinee has at his dispoal.

Yet the difference between 'the moral case' situation as described in an examination paper and a real life ethical dilemma which might confront us in pastoral care is enormous. Many factors which would be absent from the examination question are the very ones that a pastor or counsellor would attend to closely: emotions, motivation, degree of emotional maturity, capacity for action, social support. Yet the realities the examination question was designed to focus upon also demand proper attention: ethical principles, the difference between right and wrong, the proper recognition of the whole ethical dimension which is important to a full humanity.

Consider how ethical issues, personality factors and social environment are all interwined in the following examples. Both counselling skills and ethical understanding would be engaged in each situation.

A young, unmarried woman is pregnant and her parents want her to have an abortion. Her doctor agrees with her parents. She herself has considerable misgivings about this prospect but is uncertain to what extent these misgivings are ethical scruples, or simply desire to have her baby, or both. She is worried at the thought that if she does have her baby it will often be her parents who will have to assist her to care for it. Has she the right to expect them to sacrifice for her moral principles? And is it really moral principle that motivates her resistance to the proposed abortion?

A woman with teenage children has a mother who is no longer able to live on her own because of increasing infirmity and confusion. Her husband expresses concern at what it will mean in the family if his mother-in-law is brought to live with them but says it must be his wife's decision. They cannot afford to pay for nursing home accommodation, and the council home into which the mother would be sent fills her with alarm.

A young man with a family works for a firm which produces and installs fire alarms. He is an electrical engineer, His contentment with his job he is shattered when he is asked to do some work at a missile base. He has been active in the peace movement and has a passionate commitment to disarmamemt. When he refuses to do the work on conscientious grounds he is immediately suspended. He loses a day's pay and is asked to resign. He refuses. He is told that if he ever declines to do work again his employment will be terminated. He asks himself whether he is concerned most about the principles invloved, or is he driven by a need to suffer for the cause to which he is committed?

A man who has been unhappily married for many years begins a relationship with a woman whose husband recently died. The man is a Roman Catholic and has always regarded divorce and remarriage as wrong. Suddenly the possibilities of happiness seems to be offered and there is a part of him which suggests it would be wrong to forego the fulfilment offered. Moral principles, a definitive code of Christian ethics in the form of the teaching of the Roman Catholic Church, personal happiness, fear and hope all seem to be at odds and to produce total confusion.

It is the fact that concrete issues of right and wrong cannot, in real life, be isolated from other human realities such as emotion, motivation, psychological maturity and social support, which requires that patoral care in such situations is ethically informed and psychologically sensitive.

Let us consider what should be some of the goals we set before us when counselling someone facing a moral dilemma.

First, we will try to help the client to explore the dilemma as they see it, with all its ramifications. This will include their feelings as well as their thoughts about the various options before them. It would not serve the purpose of mature decision-making to allow the exchange to become only a discussion about ethical principles and their application. It is the whole person who will decide and that means emotions as well as rationality.

It might help at this stage, not only to facilitate the expression of feelings, but to clarify the ethical principles the client is consciously or unconsciously using. We might make such comments as 'Perhaps you believe that to try to do the loving thing is the only thing that matters, even if that goes against what has usually been thought right': It seems to me that you are saying God has made his will known on this issue and there can be no exceptions under any circumstances'; 'Maybe you feel that this principle is so important that everything else must be sacrificed for it'; 'It seems you are working on the principle that doing the lovable thing is what is right but that in this situation some people are going to feel very unloved'.

Many of our ethical responses are made without a great deal of reflection. A kind of ethical 'style' develops over many years and in a moral dilemma we may need help to recogise the kind of ethical tools we usually employ and to know that there maybe other tools we should at least consider. So as well as trying to clarify the way the client at present views the dilemma, we will try to offer alternative perspectives. We might say, 'Of course, there are some Christians who would view this kind of dilemma quite differently'; 'Let's think for a few minutes about some alternative ways in which Christians approach this particular issue'. It is important that people know that there is a variety of ethical theories, even within the Christian church. This may, of course, initially add to their sense of confusion and the consellor will have to be prepared to stay alongside them in that confusion. But the final decision is much more likely to carry a sense of being the result of work well and truly done.

Another factor which needs making explicit is the degree to which we will be drawing upon our childhood associations with regard to right and wrong, and particularly the degree of rightness and wrongness attached to certain acts or omissions. Many adults witness that they have irrational feelings of unease over actions which their parents regarded with horror but which they have ceased to regard as wrong. A truly moral decision can be taken only when there is some degree of freedom from such constraints, and it is the work of counselling to help us to become more conscious of these powerful influences from the past.

Possibly one of the factors which will need to be faced is the fact that relatively few decisions of this kind can be made with an absolute certainty of being right. Alternatives may be considered at some depth, our feeling about the various options properly weighed, the dilemma analysed with the aid of different ethical theories, but the result will not have the inevitability and finality of a mathematical problem duly worked through.

Of course, some people cannot bear this degree of uncertainty, and they will be most at ease with an ethical stance based upon an uncritical acceptance of the Bible or the teaching of the church if these authorities have addressed the particular problem they face.

The person who is offering pastoral care to someone who is facing a moral dilemma will hopefully try to keep the exchange within the wider dimension of God's grace and forgiveness. A desire to make the right decision, and an awareness of the high importance of the ethical dimension in the life of man, can accompany an assumption that salvation is by works. No matter how seriously the Christian takes the ethical requirements of his faith he must also set those demands in the context of the loving compassion and forgiveness of God. Perhaps the gospel of God's grace will be made explicit in the counselling itself, but it should also be powerfully implicit in the relationship between the pastor and the person receiving care.

It sometimes happens that a person faced with an ethical dilemma finds himself quite unable to come to a decision. This may well be because of the complexity of the dilemma but it may also be a psychological difficulty about making any important decisions. The client may need to be brought to see his or her difficulty in this instance as part of a more wide-spread problem of commitment. Helping and supporting a person towards making a difficult ethical choice will be effective if all the goals we have considered are kept in mind. Empathy, as well as knowledge, is required. The person needs to feel that the pastor is truly with them feeling the weight of uncertainity and the conflict between opposing courses of action. Doubt about the right thing to do can be shared and its power to paralyse action will then diminish. A great deal of living has to be done without the benefit of certainty. What we can be sure of in these situations is that we have honestly tried to face all the alternatives, to weigh the ethical principles involved, to search our motives and consider the consequences. When the right action seems to be clear, or as clear as it will ever be, a person will need support in making a decision. However, if the counselling has been thorough the support will already be there. It probably cannot be added on as something additional to the counselling itself.

Of course support may also need to be given after action has been taken. The instance of the unmarried pregnant girl mentioned above is an excellent example as are all occasions of possible abortion. An abortion decision is also irreversible as also, beyond a certain point, is the decision not to have an abortion. Most women will have some doubts about their decision if they felt it to be a real moral dilemma. They need to know that doubt is not guilt though the two emotions can easily become confused. Most momentous decisions have an element of uncertainity and we need to be able to accept this and live with this.

Sometimes a person may become convinced that a wrong decision was made and may feel guilty. Even then it is important to help them see that we can never know the extent of our guilt. A certain agnosticism about our guilt is theologically right and pastorally sound. 'We never know where in the world we . . . should be forgiven; we can never say with an absolute judgement: there is sin, it happened right there' (Karl Rahner). Of course, whatever the degree of guilt the true answer for the

Christian lies in an experience of God's pardon and forgiveness. Pastoral care will aim to make that experience real
through the relationship itself and in any other way that
seems appropriate.

In giving Pastoral care to someone facing a moral dilemma
we must, as with all counselling, attempt to monitor our own
attitudes and feelings. Although we may have resources like
alternative ethical tools to offer, and although good listening
will certainly assist anyone who is confused and uncertain, the
dilemma is still not our dilemma. It is not we who must decide.
No matter how keenly we feel the dilemma, and recognize that
equally agonizing decisions come our way, this remains
true.

In this area of moral uncertainty and dilemma we might
especially be tempted to feel powerful as the one who is looked
to for advice, for an answer. But if we take on the role of the
guru, rather than one who stands alongside the person with the
problem, we will have to pay a high price. Both the responsibility that the right decision be made, and the responsibility
for the consequences of that decision, will seem to be ours.

In counselling or pastoral care which involves moral issues
the word conscience is likely to enter the discussion. Probably
it is best not to take it for granted that both partners in the
dialogue mean the same thing by conscience, or indeed that any
of us mean the same thing all the time.

When we use the word conscience are we thinking of a
seperate faculty within us, a kind of moral compass? Or do we
imbue conscience with even weighter authority and, with
Milton, regard it as the voice of God within? Are we more
analytical in our reflection about conscience and, with Nowell-
Smith, make a distinction between the office of a judge and the
office of an advocate? Grant to conscience the office of judge
and it must inevitably be obeyed, what ever the consequences.
See conscience as an advocate whose case must be carefully
listened to but not always acted upon and the results may be
very different. Do we think of conscience as simply the whole
man in the act of making a moral decision? Or do we confuse
conscience with the Freudian super-ego and regard it with suspicion as the potential enemy of psychological well-being?

It is this last confusion which might militate against good counselling when we are faced with moral questions.

In his book *Ethics and Belief* Peter Baelz says, 'The psycho-analytic and the philosophical concepts of conscience must not be confused. They are obviously different from each other. We need always to be clear in our minds, when we are talking about the conscience, which concept we are using.' He points out, for example, that Bishop Butler's concept of conscience is clearly closer to Freud's ego than to his super-ego ' since it is the attempt of reason to order the basic inclinations and desires according to the realities of man and the world'.

What so often complicates a moral issue is the question of motive. Just when some clarity seems to have been achieved concerning the principles involved, a person facing an ethical dilemma may be plunged into further uncertainty by a suspicion that the 'right' course is also the one that will yield more personal satisfaction, or bring most inconvience, even pain, to others. Has ethical reflection, then, been merely a rationalization of self interests? Can an authentic moral choice be made when the motivation has become suspect? Of course, this complication is most acute in introspective people with a tendency to judge themselves harshly. They may even quote the well known lines of T. S. Eliot:

This is the last and greatest treason
To do the right deed for the wrong reason.

(Murder in the Cathedral)

Good counselling can hopefully help to disentangle these issues of inner motive and outward action. Normally right should be done and evil avoided irrespective of which course of action appears most attractive. Yet knowing what we really want, understanding our deepest motives, is very important indeed and may make a difference to which course of action is seen to be right. We also need to recognize that any action which runs totally counter to our own desires requires us seriously to face the question, 'What resources do I have to sustain me in such costly action?

Issues of right and wrong are rarely absent for long from

counselling. Man has been called 'the ethical animal' and it is part of his greatness that he can find himself poised between different courses of action, and concerned to assess those courses in moral terms. To be with someone facing a real moral dilemma is an awesome privilege. It is a situation of great potential either for growth or diminishment. It calls for all the skills we may possess, but especially for the qualities of sensitivity and humility.

17. The Charismatic Movement

By the Reverend Dr John Ponter,
Chelmsford

THERE is, on the face of it, something very odd in writing under the title 'First Aid in Pastoral Care – The Charismatic movement'. All Christians believe that the Holy Spirit of God himself has been promised to us in Jesus Christ. As the church began its life, it experienced a new, direct and enabling relationship with the Father which turned a message of mere words into a living witness to the kingdom of God.

In our generation the charismatic movement has called us to a renewed faith in and experience of this primal truth about the church. It has said that whatever else we do about rethinking our doctrines, restructuring our institutions, revamping our liturgy, it must be the quality of our relationship with God through the Holy Spirit which alone offers true hope of being the church called to such a vital role in the purposes of God.

And so, at a time when society feels so unsure, and so confused about where hope lies, the renewal movement has been heard to promise power, certainty, healing and joy. Something in each of us responds to that message as it touches a deep need.

And so it might seem very odd to include 'The Charismatic Movement' as occasioning a problem in pastoral care. That seems to imply that the movement is harmful rather than a source of new life and hope. In fact it has the potential to be both. The stance adopted here is that the basic message of the charismatic movement about a renewed relationship with God through the Holy Spirit is vital and timely, but the way the movement has developed has meant that the actual experience of it has been a source of deception and harm to many.

If people who have been so misled and hurt are to be

helped, it is necessary to understand what it is about the charismatic movement which can produce such casualties. So I shall outline some of the persistent characteristics of the movement on the basis of personal experience. Readers must judge how much this rings true for them. Some understanding of this can then indicate how people who have been perplexed or disturbed by their experience can be strengthened, and led into a fuller understanding of the Holy Spirit. Finally I will suggest some ways in which the charismatic movement speaks to us of what God is calling us to in our generation.

The Nature of the Charismatic Movement

At the heart of the movement is a deeply felt need for growth and renewal. Many have found it, and their own lives and that of the world around them have been greatly blessed. At one level, it is natural that others should have been hurt and damaged. The same thing happens, after all, in secular 'growth' movements. Something of great power is being handled by those who are not always mature and experienced enough to understand what they have unleashed. The weak and desperate become attracted to such movements and discover their terrible vulnerability.

But there are *particular* characteristics of the movement which give cause for disquiet. These emerge both from the pressure which comes from those within or others, and also in the nature of the problems and difficulties experienced by people who come into contact with it. These characteristics are fairly well defined and widespread.

(1) Narrow interpretation of 'experience of the Holy Spirit'

This has most frequently been characterized as an experience of 'baptism in the Spirit', understood within the context of the movement, after prayer and perhaps laying on of hands. It is a particular experience, unique somehow in character. It is associated also with the experience of 'gifts' which have a powerful experiential character, like speaking in tongues, prophecy and healing. Even where such exclusive narrowness has been played down, it still tends to be identified with experiences which can acquire the label 'religious' and take place in the context of believers' fellowship.

It is easy to see how such a narrow understanding of the Holy Spirit fosters a sense of 'special blessing' to those who are part of it. If one has a persistent problem in affirming the presence of God and the experience of the Holy Spirit promised to us in our baptism, then it is an enormous help to focus on a deep and repeatable emotional experience. But such a justification arises out of spiritual weakness, not strength.

This narrowness has been the basis for others feeling threatened, because it implies a denial of different experience. A Christian who has valued his spiritual life and not questioned very deeply its limits and assumptions can be put on the defensive or seduced into believing that what he has believed and experienced is invalid. These attitudes are not necessarily consciously held by those involved in the charismatic movement, but they are the basic assumptions which they convey to others.

(2) *Authoritarian Outlook*

It seems a contradiction that a movement which spoke of freedom, openness and exploration should become particularly associated with literal fundamentalism. This characteristic of the pentecostal renewal is not just in the attitude to the scriptures but in the way fellowships are structured and in a prevailing ethic about family life. Hierarchical regimes are experienced as the way that the authority of God is transmitted. The validity of an individual's experience and his or her standing in the fellowship of the redeemed are often judged by external authority. Once again, those who feel insecure and unsure can find in this great strength. It can equally be experienced as very threatening, or at least excluding.

Such authoritarianism frequently cannot enter into fruitful and enlightening dialogue either with the world, or with Christian brethren. Its assumptive world includes unquestioning acceptance of external authority. It is extremely difficult to help someone who feels 'caught' by this authority but at the same time is distressed by it. It is often tempting to be authoritarian oneself as a protective counter-balance. We always have to remember when someone is seriously a casualty as part of any powerful movement that it was something about *themselves* that made them get into that position. They have to question the authority themselves. They need to find their own authority within themselves.

(3) *The Search for Personal Identity*

The last remark leads on to something which is at the crux of the problems which people experience in relation to charismatic experience. The movement uses the language of mature spiritual development and the deepest, most mystical relationship with God. It talks of 'letting go' and allowing the power of God, Creator and Redeemer, to bring life and growth. It aspires to transcend rational thought and human plans with the wisdom and purposes of God. 'Tongues' are defended as important, since they signify the relationship with God in the Holy Spirit within which these things can take place.

In order to reach this level of maturity, you have to have a very clear appreciation of your own identity. You must value yourself, as well as experiencing a deep trust in God. You must know who you are and what you are without too many illusions.

It is by no means uncommon for people to seek and to gain some kind of powerful experience in the charismatic movement precisely because they are *not* sure of themselves. A number of evil and ugly things can follow. These can be the spiritual pride of counting these experiences as marks of favour and superiority. So we have the corruption of Pharisaism again. Much more seriously, the person concerned might be covering up a deep sense of guilt, or an almost total loss of any sense of identity. On the one hand they long for the blessing and power that is promised to them, but on the other hand they are deeply pessimistic about themselves. The talk of 'letting go' and allowing the Spirit of Christ to take over is a kind of spiritual act of suicide. When it all goes wrong they become desperate.

One of the ways in which this playing down of personal identity operates is in the emphasis on corporateness. People who are unused to charismatic worship are sometimes frightened by it because it seems to threaten to overwhelm them and take them over. Those taking part are longing to get caught up in something which is bigger and greater than themselves. The fellowship can become the most important group they belong to, more important than the family. It is in this culture that the authoritarianism flourishes. It is as if the individual will is being overridden by the will of the group, identified as the will of the Spirit. Differences of opinion, even of personal style, cannot be tolerated. When it becomes like that, there is a culture into which people have come out of weakness and within which they are very vulnerable. It is very far indeed from the maturity of the NT language about the Spirit. Many times, in dealing with people who become casualties from such a culture, I find them discovering that while they were promised power, gifts and victory, they did not experience love. Above all, they need to be stayed with, accepted, listened to with serious attention and loved for what they are.

(4) *Splitting*

There is one more characteristic that is worth isolating. This is expressed theologically as a black and white definiteness about good and evil. Personally it is experienced as failing to hold together different aspects of ourselves and our experience, which is something called 'splitting'.

It can almost become a basic principle in drawing one's map of reality. Thus God is seen as at work in the Christian and in particular kinds of experiences and events, but 'the world' might be felt as an essentially godless sphere in which God might from time to time 'intervene'. Personally this is experienced as a feeling that unless God shows his intervention in your life there is no reason to suppose that you 'have' his Spirit. If you are very unsure of yourself, the feeling that you personally are, or might be, part of the godless world, the domain ruled by the Devil, is very threatening indeed. Not infrequently individuals in a fellowship feel pressure to get caught up in expressions of joy, peace and love which suppress any feeling of pain, despair or anger. This is another aspect of 'splitting' which is both spiritually and psychologically harmful. Mature spirituality cannot come through lack of honesty.

It would be difficult to deny that the characteristics described are features commonly met in charismatic groups, both within established churches and also in pentecostal sects and house-churches. Many who believe in the movement would argue that these are examples of its going astray. They might also suggest that those who are put off seeking charismatic experience by these factors are being defensive and conservative. That could be true. It is a faith we share that there is a Holy Spirit of God whose power and potential for growth we perceive only dimly, and that our ordered rational ways can be barriers to exploring the riches of being a person created and redeemed by God. There are those who have entered deeply into a renewed relationship with God in the charismatic movement.

Nevertheless, I would argue that what has been described, and the fuller experience that underlies it, are grounds to look very carefully on the charismatic movement as a popular religious movement of the present time.

The main reason for this is that the individual causes for disquiet build up into a picture. They can be seen as symptoms of something which underlies them all. All of them speak of the experience of the dependent infant. They reflect on the utter weakness and vulnerability of those who are attracted to it. They exhibit loss of personal authority and loss of a sense of boundary between yourself and others. Power and potency come from outside, either graciously given or terribly withheld. This is the background to the cry for 'healing'.

One striking illustration of how these aspects affect ways of thinking and feeling is in the talk of devils and demons. Such a way of understanding both personal problems and psychological disturbance is encouraged by scriptural fundamentalism. If the world of our experience is somehow godless, it is a domain for the devil, 'the prince of this world'. This sense of the pressure of the Devil and devils is then used in 'splitting' to see oneself as some sort of battle ground of the Spirit against the Devil. One's own sense of identity and personal responsibility is diminished, perhaps to the point of extinction.

Such a way of describing what happens is simplistic and crude. But it serves to point out how the talk about devils is part of the pattern of characteristics. The standard way of dealing with devils amongst charismatics is, once again, by external authority, deliverance or exorcism. One way in which pastoral help might be sought is because of a desperate need to find someone who can do this effectively. Perhaps *this* person might have the 'magic'. To respond by attempting deliverance or exorcism on demand would be a disaster, since it is the whole pattern of thinking and reacting which needs to be re-examined. There might be times when an authoritative word from a representative ministry speaks with power. But the last place for it is in a situation where a person has become so vulnerably dependent on external authority.

The overall picture which emerges is of a deep underlying sense of helplessness and vulnerability which is either picked up from those around you, or else is very particularly your own experience.

How can pastoral aid be given?

Some time has been taken on describing charismatic experiences because it indicates the manner and level of an appropriate pastoral response to someone seeking help. This might be someone who desperately needs help as a result of experience within a charismatic group. It may be a congregation member scandalized or attracted by what such a group within their church is doing. Yet again, someone might be experiencing pressure from a group in relation to some aspect of their lives. Although these are all very different, they share certain things in common:

(a) It is about the persons themselves. They are troubled or curious because of something in their own consciousness. Above all, that has to be understood. Why does this trouble you? Why do you feel attracted or repelled?

(b) This encounter with them sets up certain things in ourselves, to whom the person has come. The forces at work here are very powerful indeed. It can take all our reserves of faith, maturity and sanity to cope. It will not be helpful to become defensive or partisan.

(c) The issues have to be dealt with in the end at the level of personal search for spiritual growth. It is no use pretending that it is really about what sort of hymns we should sing in church, or what a 'correct' theology of pentecostal experience might be, or whether *my* experience is better than *yours*, or whether spontaneous gestures, words and unintelligible sounds are appropriate and helpful in worship! We believe we are made to have union with God, and that Christ through his Spirit invites us to grow into that. The road is personal, and often perplexing and strewn with mines. What others gain from us as ministers is much more about what they sense as the reality of what we are, than our knowledge and abilities. There are no sides to take in this. The seduction to make it a matter of being in or out of a group or a set of beliefs has to be resisted. 'The time approaches, indeed it is already here, when those who are real worshippers will worship the Father in spirit and in truth.'

It might be helpful to earth some of these comments in examples of pastoral support. I shall mention two very different ones.

(A) A young man, Richard, was a member of a house-church. He was highly intelligent and articulate, and he was very committed to a 'charismatic' Christianity. He had never belonged to a different tradition. I was a personal friend and chaplain to the place where he worked. He had a doctrinal disagreement with the elders of his house-church which concerned the way those elders had treated a teenage couple. As a result of this, Richard and his wife were put 'out of fellowship' with the house-church. This meant that they could not worship there, and that their entire circle of friends were forbidden to speak to them. It was crushing cruelty.

Richard and his wife turned to me for support. I would like to have persuaded them that what had happened said something about the whole basic outlook of the tradition in which they had immersed themselves so completely. But they could not see it that way. It seemed to me that if they and myself became polarized over a theological debate, then I could not easily help them pastorally in this situation. They would have to respect the reality of my faith and spirituality and I theirs. We could 'agree to differ' over other things for the moment. The anguish I could feel for their present predicament was a point of sharing. Somehow I could represent the possibility that God himself understood and shared that anguish. Behind all this was an issue about how God exercises his authority. Richard could not accept fundamentalism, just as he could not accept the external authority of the elders as moral judges. Together, he and I could affirm to each other that the presence of God's Spirit in a person was the hearing of an authentic voice which had to be wrestled with.

(B) Joan had been a member of a church where I was vicar. She had become a close family friend. She was about ten years older than my wife and I. She later became intensely involved in an Anglican church with a charismatic vicar. After an initial period of great joy, purpose and hope, things began to go wrong. She had feelings of depression and guilt. The house-group where she tried to work these problems out did not seem to accept her 'negative' feelings. They pressed her to hang on to the fruits of the Spirit, and tell the Devil to go away. They acted this out in prayer and laying on of hands. As her condition grew worse they began to say that she was not prepared to deny the Devil and that they could not help her unless she did.

This outline is, of course, ridiculously oversimplified, but it gives a rough idea of how what developed was understood within the charismatic church.

Joan had been precipitated into a spiritual crisis of life and death proportions. Her own bad feeling about herself became so magnified that her sense of identity, personal worth and authority had been effectively crushed. She attempted suicide. She had entered the world of thought and feeling of the charis-matics. The external authority of the group, backed by a way of using scripture, was the only reference point of reality she could have. The message which eventually came – that a devil was dominating her, which *she* had to deny before the church could help – left her without reserve or recourse to avoid final annihilation. She came through only by a spell in a mental hos-pital and transferring to another 'fringe' church which was somewhat more sane.

How could I help? She tried both to convert me, and to appeal to myself and my wife for help at those points where there was no one else. We spent many hours listening, unable to say very much. One thing we had which seemed to help.

Joan believed that we really loved her, which was true. However much she felt that *truth* came from the house group, she did not feel that they loved *her*. It was not she herself as a person that ultimately mattered to them.

She was victim of something very evil at work in the heart of our church. There are many more like her.

The message of this experience

There is finally a much deeper question to be raised by all this: What is the meaning and significance of the rise of the charismatic movement? In terms of pastoral situations it is those who are vulnerable at various levels that we have been thinking of. But the charismatic groups do not consist just of such people. Many of the most gifted and potential in the church today claim themselves to be part of the movement. They are not especially vulnerable and they are not cranks. Many of them bear witness to growth in the Spirit which they have experienced themselves and observed in others. All this is positive and in line with the opening paragraph. Nevertheless, the characteristics of renewal groups described here, and the kind of casualties they produce, are widespread enough to suspect that there is something at work in the movement as it has actually developed which required deeper insight. It could be that even the best intentioned leaders can sometimes be subject to pressures in them and upon them which are not properly understood.

So we need to know why the movement has arisen and has become the hope and despair of the church. If we can at least begin to answer that, then we have a context into which we can put our assessment of its value, and the feelings about our own spiritual pilgrimage which are affected by it. In proposing my own answer, I am outlining a possibility to be considered. This is not the place to describe it fully or to argue it out, I am personally satisfied that the evidence for it is substantial and that it is on the right lines.

The clue lies, I believe, in the basic experience of helplessness and threatened chaos which so often underlies the charismatic experience. The kind of characteristics and experiences that have been described here imply that it is the power and the fear which dominate, not faith in God. When this happens, colossal expectations are put upon the leaders of the movement and upon God himeslf. These expectations of God are called 'having faith' in him, but they are in fact fantasies about an all supplying Giver, who can bear little resemblance to the God of Job and the Father of Christ crucified.

The source of these underlying feelings is our whole experience as a society today. We experience a deep longing to be able to return to the certainties and securities that we imagine existed in the past. The experience of war and massive social and cultural changes have left a climate of confusion and moral decay. In such a setting of loss and helplessness, the church experiences almost irresistible pressure to be strong, powerful and certain. It has declined in influence, size, power and self-confidence, but it counteracts this actual experience by a felt desire, amounting to desperate need, to exhibit numerical growth, visible signs of power and influence. This is a pressure recieved from the community of which we are a part.

The nuclear bomb has perhaps become a symbol for our age because it expresses the apparently irresolvable contradiction of our present experience. On the other hand, it speaks of incredible capacity to produce and utilize great power which has required revolutions in exploratory science and in technology. On the other hand, it speaks of our ultimate helplessness before destructive forces that we cannot control.

The truth is that we cannot unmake the nuclear bomb, or unask the disturbing sceptical questions of our age any more than we can uneat the fruit which brought knowledge of good and evil.

If we react unreflectively and at an unconscious level to the pressure to pretend that things are different, we are inevitably caught up in deceit, escapism and immature dependence. God seems to require two basic responses from the church in a situation like ours:

(1) to experience fully the dilemmas, the impossible decisions and the irresolvable contradictions of our times without posing anachronistic or facile solutions;

(2) to acknowledge and proclaim the truth of man's ultimate helplessness, while holding trust in God the Creator as we see

him in Jesus Christ. It is a paradox at the heart of our faith that to accept powerlessness is the road to real strength. 'When I am weak, then I am strong.'

It is necessary to ask this basic question, 'Why the Charismatic Movement?', because the answer to it enables us to evaluate what it is doing and not ourselves be conned by talk of new power and effectiveness. We do need to understand more fully the potential of God's promise of his Holy Spirit without responding uncritically to slick and popular answers under pressures of which we are barely aware. It also follows that we can be more aware of the nature of these pressures when we can see how they operate on ourselves. The subtle pressures to be 'successful', popular, strong and relevant that the churches experience can all be seen as related. They lead to a competitiveness between churches which endangers all the ecumenical advance of a few years ago. We all find it hard to relate to that inner feeling of disorientation and powerlessness which is at the heart of our present experience as a community. The spiritual leaders of a true renewal in the Holy Spirit will be those who can both relate to it, and respond with faith.

For further reading:

[1] There are many books written out of charismatic experience. It is worth reading some critically to ask what basic unexamined assumptions are being made which might confirm or deny the view you have. A useful one is *Greater Things Than These* by John Gunstone (Faith Press), but there are many others.

[2] There have been several outstanding books on the Holy Spirit in recent years based on a mature spirituality. Nothing could be of greater help. For example: *The Go Between God* by John V. Taylor (SCM Press), *Smouldering Fire* by Martin Israel (Hodder & Stoughton). The strength of each of these is that the discernment of the nature and activity of the Holy Spirit is wide and deep.

[3] The history and nature of Pentecostalism as a modern movement is fully documented and commented on in *The Pentecostals* by Walter J. Hollenweger (SCM Press).

[4] The outlining of a sensitive and intelligent experiencing of the culture of our age from whithin Christian faith can be found in *The Forgotten Dream* by Peter Baelz (Mowbrays).

18. Psychic Disturbances

By THE VENERABLE MICHAEL PERRY,
ARCHDEACON OF DURHAM

WHAT should a clergyman or minister do when faced with a person seeking help over a problem which seems to have a psychic element? This whole area stirs up deep emotions in many counsellors (we shall use the terms 'counsellor' and 'client' in this chapter; those who prefer some other words can substitute their own choice as they read on). Some may feel distaste, or even fright, when encountering such cases. Others immediately sense the presence of evil which they want to counter with a greater power of good. Some feel pastorally out of their depth and want either to terminate the interview as soon as they can, or to pass the client on to someone who has a greater experience of Christian ministry in this field. Some are equally certain that the whole business is nonsense and should be immediately dismissed as such.

None of these attitudes is pastorally helpful. In most cases, it has taken a great deal of courage for the client to 'open up' at all. He half expects to be greeted by ridicule, or – if the counsellor is a Christian minister – condemnation. If he is met by the attitude he fears, he will clam up altogether and any hope of resolving the pastoral situation will be gone. In any case, counsellors with much experience in this area know that the psychic element is often no more than the 'presenting symptom' and that what is really needed is a searching probe into what might be called the interpersonal psychodynamics of the situation, in which the counsellor will find that he can minister to a troubled soul by the tried and tested methods of spiritual guidance. If he stays with his client and listens to the story as it unfolds, his very attitude of non-judgmental openness may be the most pastorally healing thing about the whole encounter

If a client is immediately shipped off from his chosen counsellor to a supposed 'expert' in the psychic field, it could

encourage the belief that he is in the grip of something excep-
tional, or even that he is in trouble with evil spirits who need
the kind of treatment that the 'ordinary' Christian (even the
'ordinary' Christian minister) is not capable of giving him. He
may think that he is being sent to someone who is a wizard
more powerful than the forces that have him in thrall, and that
he is to be invited to play 'piggy-in-the-middle' in a scene
redolent of the contests between Moses and the Egyptian
sorcerers. That encourages a wholly sub-Christian (but pain-
fully common) view of the whole business. The counsellor may
at some stage have to admit that he has not come across anything like this case before, and ask for time in which to think
about it and discuss it with someone whose experience is wider
than his own. As a Christian, he will wish to emphasize that no
problem is beyond the power of Christ to deal with, and will
commend the situation to him in prayer. But first he will
encourage the client to tell his story in as full a way as possible,
and tell him the facts as they seem to him. The minister who has
done even a small amount of counselling of this sort will know
that what he is being told is far less unusual than the client
believes. The assurance that others have had similar experiences without ending up in a psychiatric ward can bring enormous
relief to a worried client.

What kind of situation is the counsellor liekly to be confronted with? Psychic disturbances come either sought or unsought.
Of the spontaneously-occuring kinds, the four common ones
are bereavement experiences, psychic sensitivity, personality
changes, and hauntings. Let us take them in that order.

1. The bereaved frequently have a sense of continuing presence of the departed partner. There is nothing unusual about
hearing one's partner's voice, or smelling his pipe, or even feeling him in bed, seeing him about a familiar task or sitting in a
familiar chair – sometimes in the early stages of bereavement,
sometimes even a long time afterwards. The experience is more
often a comforting one than a frightening or threatening one,
and is not usually presented to the counsellor as a
'problem'.

Whether these experiences are to be interpreted purely

psychologically (like the phenomenon of a 'phantom limb' felt by a person who has undergone an amputation), or whether this is to be interpreted as a genuine communication between two people who still love each other though they are separated by death, will depend on discussion between counsellor and client and upon their general beliefs as to whether this kind of communication is possible or not. It is best to accept that the phenomenon occurs, for the counsellor to be uncommitted as to its interpretation in any particular instance, and for the client to make of it what he will. It should not be taken as evidence for anything morbid or evil or as a sign of incipient mental illness unless it becomes so frequent and insistent that the client becomes unable to discern between this experience and normal conversation with those who are still alive in the present world. If that looks as if it is beginning to happen, the client should be urged to seek medical help.

There are useful guidelines as to what is normal and what pathological in Colin Murray Parkes *Bereavement* (Pelican Books) and Kathleen Smith *Help for the Bereaved* (Duckworth). The latter also tries to distinguish between experiences which are most likely psychological in origin and those which may have a psychic component – though, in this case, the boundaries depend much on the individual's own assessment of the *a priori* probabilities.

2. Some clients believe themselves to be psychically sensitive and may approach a Christian counsellor to know whether this ability of theirs is of God or not, and – even if it is – whether it is to be encouraged, repressed, or ignored. The phenomenon may amount to no more than the *rapport* experienced between some close siblings or married couples or especial friends, whereby each is occasionally aware of the other's thoughts or circumstances even when they are physically parted; or it may be that the client becomes aware of the thoughts of others in a group of which he or she is a member; or it may be that he or she is aware of future events in the life of others or in the more public domain.

Some counsellors believe such things to be possible, others do not. Those who do, may regard them as talents which are ethically neutral in themselves but which should be used, if at all, as Christians should use their other talents – only in such ways as conduce to God's glory and help others, and not so as to stimulate mere vulgar curiosity or as a parlour trick. Others see them as gifts so dangerous that their exercise should be discouraged. The counsellor faced with claims to such gifts should sort out his own beliefs and attitudes on these points before counselling others. He will be most use to his client if he first listens to the evidence with suspended judgment, is agnostic as to whether the phenomena happen at all, urges a critical stance in his client as to whether these experiments are the result of an accurate intuition or of genuinely paranormal powers, and then asks the normal questions of Christians ethics about the use of information one has acquired without the knowledge of those imparting it.

The counsellor will be particularly on the lookout for evidence of unbalance in claiming such gifts and of over-valuing them as practical guidance. Clients who claim to 'hear voices' may be recipients of paranormal information, or they may suffer from demonic infestation or psychiatric disturbance. Those who suffer from delusions can be very plausible in the way they build up a great superstructure of secondary delusions in order to prevent themselves from recognizing the true nature of their primary error. Counsellors who suspect their clients are losing their grip on reality should seek specialized help for them.

3. We have already strayed into the third area, that of changes in personality. It is here that some Christians most readily see evidence of demonic activity, whilst others see nothing that cannot be explained on psychological or psychiatric models. (Yet others – with more justification – do not see these two explanatory hypotheses as mutually exclusive.)

For instance, a mother came to me saying that her teenage daughter used to be (like herself) a keen Christian with few interests outside the church and its organizations, but that recently she had got into what the mother described as 'bad company'. She had become secretive, morose, and unwilling even to have a Bible in the same room as she was. Had she become possessed by an evil spirit? Or was she showing a strong adolescent reaction against overpowering parental norms? (Might there perhaps be a drug problem unrecognized by the mother?) The solution might lie less in the attempted exorcism of the child than in the healing of family attitudes which up till then had not allowed her the freedom to discover Christ for herself but had forced other people's way of life so strongly upon her that she felt suffocated by a Christianity with which she could no longer identify.

The Church of Scotland discourages any purported ceremony of exorcism. Its General Assembly on 21 May 1976 accepted advice to 'enjoin ministers to refrain from conducting a special ceremony of exorcism' on the grounds that all so-called 'demonic possession' was 'of a mental and psychological nature' and that 'a special ceremonial designed to expel evil spirits must tend to produce a misunderstanding of the role of the pastor which seems to give him magic powers . . . There is no place in the Reformed Scottish tradition for such a rite to be devised'.

Others, particularly those affected by the charismatic revival, take an exactly opposite view and attempt the exorcism of evil spirits as a routine activity if ever they are faced with a person whose spiritual state is not susceptible to reason. This seems to the present writer to err even more from the truth. He would urge that exorcism should always be kept open as a possibility, but one which would be appropriate only rarely. Before it is assayed, all other methods of cure should be tried – prayer, persuasion, preaching, psychiatric treatment –and there should be evidence of intended traffic with evil powers. If, as a last resort, exorcism is decided upon, the advice of Archbishop Coggan should be heeded. Speaking on behalf of the House of Bishops to a question asked in General Synod on 30 June 1975, he said:

> There are many men and women so within the grip of the power of evil that they need the help of the Christian Church in delivering them from it. When this ministry is carried out the following factors should be borne in mind:
> (1) It should be done in collaboration with the resources of medicine.

(2) It should be done in the context of prayer and sacrament.

(3) It should be done with a minimum of publicity.

(4) It should be done by experienced persons authorized by the diocesan bishop.

(5) It should be followed up by continuing pastoral care.

This acknowledges the sacramental approach which sees outward and visible signs as vehicles of inward and spiritual grace – what is of value purely psychologically to a disturbed person may also convey the healing power of Christ to him. The final point, about continuing pastoral care, is vital. The client may see exorcism as shifting the blame for his condition off himself and on to a demonic third party. No true healing can come about until the client learns many things about himself that he formerly found it unacceptable so to do, and until he learns the freedom to accept Christ for himself and, within that freedom, to accept responsibility for his own actions. That often needs 'collaboration with the resources of medicine'; it always needs 'continuing pastoral care'.

4. Hauntings are more common than is often realized, and the most common form to be reported is that of the poltergeist. A typical 'attack' begins with noises, raps, or footsteps heard in the house and often then proceeds either to physical phenomena such as the movement of objects or to visual effects like the sighting of vague grey figures in conditions of semi-darkness. The popular explanation is in terms of 'spirit' activity and the counsellor will usually be directly asked to exorcize the house. In the author's (probably limited) experience, this has never been necessary. Poltergeist phenomena seem to occur when there are inter-personal tensions within a household (marital difficulties, adolescent rebellion, or worries about work or the threat of unemployment). They may even be ruses invented by the client who wants a move to a more congenial council house, but that is another matter! The physical phenomena may be misreported, or they may be the result of those inter-personal forces being externalized. Visual phenomena are probably the result of the 'jittery' atmosphere within a family already under strain and further disturbed by the

unnerving poltergeistry. If this explanation is offered to the clients, and some work done on the reduction of the inter-personal tensions, the poltergeist will usually subside of its own accord. Only if they do not respond to this approach should poltergeist cases be treated as due to non-incarnate entities.

Sometimes there are reports of apparitions seen in a par-ticular house or locality – either once only, or repeatedly. They, too, may be caused psychologically as a 'cry for help' by the family concerned. Again, the counsellor listens carefully and tries to assess the psycho-dynamics of the situation. If he is open to interpretations beyond the psychological or psychiatric he may wish to consider the possibility that here is a 'memory trace' sticking to a particular site and showing no evidence of conscious activity; or that the apparition may be due to the activity of a deceased and earth-bound human spirit which needs to be prayed out of its obsession with its former abode and enabled to move on in its supra-mundane pilgrimage (possibly with the help of a Requiem Eucharist). Only in very rare cases are they likely to be non-human demonic entities deserving of exorcism – and then usually only because they have been actively invoked to that spot by ill-intentioned methods.

If the counsellor is unhappy with that particular range of explanations, let him deal with the phenomena in psychological rather than parapsychological terms. What matters is not the explanation, but the relief we can give to those who are bur-dened by happenings which they cannot explain and which can make a terror of their life. However we react, we must pro-claim the saving power of Jesus, who alone can release folk from bondage to whatever is not of God.

Psychic disturbances, we said, come either sought or unsought. So far we have concerned ourselves only with the spontaneous ones. What of those who actively encourage psy-chic phenomena, find themselves in trouble, and then come to a Christian minister for help?

A familiar object, especially amongst adolescents or the emotionally immature, is the ouija-board. Like planchette, or the upturned glass, or the table, it is an alleged way of obtaining messages from the 'the spirits' in answer to questions from a sitter or, more usually, a circle of sitters. It is often used in an attitude of daredevilry and a seeking after thrills in an atmosphere of undefined danger. Straight condemnation may be counter-productive, but it remains true that the whole procedure is inadvisable in the extreme. At the least, this is a method of allowing the control of the conscious mind to be bypassed so that material from the subconscious may come to the surface without the censorship normally exercised by the mechanism of repression. The material which comes out may thus be particularly disturbing to the practitioner, especially if he has yet unresolved emotional problems, and if this material presents itself to him as the utterance of an entity external to himself. Maybe, of course, more than this minimalist interpretation is true, in which case the person operating the board is allowing his mind to be open to stray influences of a telepathic nature which may be harmless but could just as well be malign; influences which may come from a human source or a sub-human and demonic one. It is for the same reasons that most Christians are wary of trance mediumship in which the medium claims to be 'controlled' by another entity. A Christian does not lightly hand over control of his personality to anything other than to Jesus or the Holy Spirit of God. The late Alun Virgin expressed the dangers pungently;

> Fumbling around with the unconscious mind has been happily compared with attempting to remove one's appendix with a can-opener. Doubtless it can be done but a considerable amount of skilled knowledge and judgment would be required – not to mention luck – and in any case there are better ways of doing it! . . . An ouija board is a very blunt psychic instrument indeed. Whatever our opinion concerning their ultimate origin, powerful destructive forces do operate within the human psyche. We risk releasing them in uncontrolled conditions at our peril.
>
> (*Common Ground* 4 [1982], 23)

Others may have come into contact with the psychic through organized Spiritualism. In this writer's opinion, this body of people is not so much wicked as limited in its apprehension of spiritual truth. Spiritualists ought not to have their previous experiences denied or denounced; rather, they need to be led to see how inadequate and partial a grasp of truth they have if they become fixated at the psychic level when they ought to progress to the spiritual. Psychic experience is real, but it cannot be the be-all and end-all of spiritual life. The Spiritualist is a little like Peter on the mount of the Transfiguration, tempted to cage the vision within tents which should make it permanent. The transfigured Christ is too alive to be kept in a tent. What we must do is to help people move on from their psychical experience, using it to help them to self-knowledge and the knowledge of God, which will involve a moral transformation and the acknowledgement of the seriousness of human sin and the need for an atoning Saviour (the sticking-point for most Spiritualists).

This chapter only mentions selected aspects of a vast field. Counsellors faced with problems beyond their experience or competence would do well to seek advice from others with a wider experience. Many of the English bishops have their advisers in this area. Most of them work with a very low profile, rightly believing that publicity is rarely helpful. Most believe that their business is not to take cases away from the parish clergy but to discuss them with them so as to enable the counsellor himself to tackle the client's problem at first hand.

Some bishops have teams of advisers, and I am fortunate to have been able to discuss this present chapter in draft with two other priests and a psychiatrist who form such a multi-disciplinary team and meet regularly to review their cases and discuss their approach to their clients.

There is also the (ecumenical) Churches' Fellowship for Psychical and Spiritual Studies, whose General Secretary, at St Mary Abchurch, London EC4N 7BA, may be able to put a counsellor on to someone locally who has experience of this kind of problem, and a sister body, the CFPSS (Scotland), which may be contacted at 27 Ramsay Gardens, Aberdeen AB1 7AE.

19. Prisoners and Delinquents

BY THE REVEREND ALLAN R. DRUCE, M.A.,
CHAPLAIN, H. M. PRISON, LINCOLN

JESUS related to prisoners. His betrayal and arrest, his public vilification and accusation, as well as the heartache of his family and the agony of his punishment – all combine to present a dramatic background which has inspired Christians to pursue pastoral opportunities among individuals on the wrong side of the law. Further motivation for this work is also provided by Jesus who showed a concern for all who were marginal to his society and who particularly commended those who visit prisoners (Mt25³ ⁶).

A paper about 'visiting' prisoners and delinquents should present the total scope within which this work could be considered and then indicate the particular sympathies which will be explored. Some who hold a wide view might argue that offenders are the result of unjust social structures and that their pastoral care can only be improved by a radical attack on the whole criminal justice system. Others will see this pastoral care on a narrow individual basis – equating it almost entirely with one to one pastoral counselling. There is a sense in which the processes of law and order lead to an isolationist approach in pastoral care; it is customary, for instance, to adjudicate each case 'on its merits' and then to handle every offender as an individual problem. This chapter broadly inclines to the latter interpretation in the belief that many Christians are in personal contact with the proliferating number of offenders in our society and that they need to articulate some of the delicate questions that arise for them when they offer support.

Within this narrower framework the general aim of pastoral care as presented in this chapter will be to help offenders find a more fulfilling life. In pursuing this objective, emphasis will be placed on ways of reordering the perception of an offender and on ways of resolving some of the strong moral opinions

expressed by courts, by newspapers and by the public conscience. This general aim will allow for different approach
roads across a field where individualism and accumulated
experience command respect. The sense of a general aim is
important for anyone who offers pastoral care, however
remotely, in the face of law enforcement, because it helps
define bounderies along side other professional workers and
gives guidelines within which exploitation might be avoided.
No mention will be made of the specific problems of ex-
offenders – but it is nevertheless obvious that many of their
pastoral care needs tie in with points covered in this chapter.

However, the wider context of pastoral care still has a
place alongside this general aim. The importance of developing
an understanding of pastoral contact with prisoners and with
delinquents is heightened by the global rise in criminal activity,
and by the compensating weight of repression from totalitarian
governments that see value in emphasizing the deterrent
aspects of legal sanctions. Biological and behavioural sciences
have provided negligible impetus for effecting redress in this
situation. It could well be that pastoral care – with its more
traditional community roots – can become an important coun-
terpoise to more alien tendencies that are so fashionable. Amid
the maelstrom of social and economic change, and increasing
geographical mobility, there has been a collapse of community
life in urban areas. It is in these areas that crime is
particularly rampant.

The etymological backgrounds to the words ' prisoner' and
'delinquent' pose questions about the nature of man. These
questions relate basic theological ideas to the ideas to the
general aim in this sphere of pastoral care. A prison, for
instance, is a place 'of prehension of seizure' and directly relates
to all the connotations of the word 'apprehension'. It can refer
to the human condition of 'doing prison' as much as to the
material structure. Delinquent not only means 'left down' – but
paricularly implies 'left down in dregs' and has the same connotations as 'deride' and detest'. Words such as these, infused
with both violent and judgemental sentiments invite theological interpretation. The importance of considering these questions is enhanced if one senses that the belief system of a person

who conducts pastoral care is communicated explicitly or implicitly to a recipient.

Tenets of the Christian faith are peculiarly relevent to those on the wrong side of the law. For instance, individual qualities are upheld amid a cosmic view of God's existance; this frame of reference militates against encapsulated small-mindedness so easily resorted to amid the pressures of prison. Again, the emphasis that man is in the image of God is a symbolic phrase, revealing the close contact between all human and divine life. Pastoral contacts in a prison can be made against a background belief that the prisoner is also my brother, a son of Adam, in the image of God; any thing in prison that tarnishes or destroys him and destroys me. God is also understood as trinitarian and is approached in relationship terms; therefore anything in a prison that perverts a man's opportunity for fellowship can become increasingly destructive of the whole body of society. The Christian understanding of sin helps a person involved in pastoral care among prisoners come to terms with the 'portrayal' of wickedness. The doctrines of sins confront the explicable tendency in the world to create wickedness, acknowledging that there are violent people who have to be coercively restrained yet allowing no one group to remain in a position of uncontrolable power. Paul's words can find an echo in hearts of all men, Christian and non-Christian. 'I can will what is right, but I cannot do it. For I do not do the good I want, but the evil I do not want is what I do' (Rom7[18-19]). The Old Testament portrays sin as in the structures of society. The prophets direct God's wrath at the way the poor and out cast are treated; this insight encourages all who have pastoral contact with prisoners to be aware of mankind's 'solidarity in sin'. Dean Inge once caustically ramarked that acquaintance with the prison world undermines 'the comfortable shudder with which the average congregation accepts the burden of sin'. Finally, the focus of Christian hope may not be this-worldly but it is used to express belief now in the measureless power and love of God. The challenge facing pastoral care in this field is to make theological insights realistically relevent to the situation of the offender.

Offenders have distinctive characteristics which affect the

pastoral care that can be offered. A common feature is the we/ they division in their view of life. They need sensitive handling because some might be immature, weak-willed, mercurial and violent, as well as unable to see issues in perspective. Anyone in conflict with legal authority can experience anxiety, self-pity, loneliness, and, particularly when in prison, a need to be pretentious. Prison is one of the extreme environments of life because of its physical characteristics, its sensory deprivation, its restriction on social and sexual intercourse, and its special psychological character as authoritarian, punitive and relentlessly regimented. The extremity of the situation can also be heightened by the inevitable 'hit and run' nature of much pastoral care. Inmates are not kept in one prison indefinitely and most sentences are served in several establishments. The dramatic extremity of a prison situation makes it a useful environment with which to compare aspects of pastoral care less evident elsewhere. The poet Richard Lovelace, for instance, wrote in 1642

> Stone walls do not a prison make
> Nor iron bars a cage

He wrote these words while in prison, using the environment of the Gatehouse at Westminster to mirror the experience of everyman

Some general attitudes on the part of the person who provides pastoral care in this sphere are important.

First, it is helpful if an offender can experience some feeling of dignity and worth. An arrest and reception into prison are dehumanizing. Those on the wrong side of the law can become stereotyped, classified, and viewed in terms of previous convictions. A Christian outlook should tend to focus on the present and the future rather than on the present and on the past. History taking may be imporant in a clinical approach – but it can be damaging in a context of pastoral care. The past may hardly be relevant because circumstances could have irrevocably changed, particularly as imprisonment for many is a clearing of the air. A reordering of the future can be more sensitively developed from where the person now is rather than where he represents that he has been. Work with those in conflict with the law stands or falls on what the pastoral carer emanates from his inner self. If he meets a person officiously, taking notes across a table, inferring that the papers are to be shown to others, the image he creates can vitiate the fragile opportunity in a penal environment for a mutually creative sharing of the Good News.

Secondly, the spontaneity and freedom of the person who offers pastoral care are significant. The church has a long history of independence of standing. Those who have traditionally offered pastoral care in its name have usually been in tune with a broad sympathy in society for decentralization. The impetus towards decentralization has been apparent in the United Kingdom since the 1870's when many government departments, including the Prison Commissioners, were brought under unified control. Those who offer pastoral care in prisons must have a sympathy with a 'muddling through' approach in which high value is placed on exchanging spontaneous individual opinions. The most effective pastoral care in a prison is offered in non-formalized situations which can appear slightly in conflict with institutional regimentation. The weakness of this position is that it may seem to be inefficient – but it gains strength from its freedom, its immediacy, and its flexibility. Pastoral care in this context can make use of irrational, intuitive and sometimes dream-like states of mind which affect men in a prison.

Thirdly, there is a need to balance a judgmental and an accepting attitude in the face of encounters that handle strong feelings of sin and guilt. Sometimes it is appropriate to take a firmer attitude, aiming to implant a framework within which an offender might find support. At other times an accepting attitude is more advantageous – using passivity to invite expression. This may accord with Paul's exhortation 'to accept one another as Christ accepted us' (Rom 15[7]). Yet judgmentalism, on the one hand, has tarnished the image of people associated with the church, and its association with a harsh theology has been described by Bishop Ian Ramsay as 'a polished system, which contains no water, no living water'. Acceptance, on the other hand, can appear as a weak attitude to men sequestered prison, shattered by a sense of loss, and it can register as a wish to minimize evil or not to become involved. Ultimately an accepting person is forced to choose between denunciation or toleration. In this delicate balance between being judgmental and accepting, the pastoral carer faces a risk which can often be appreciated by the person in need. It is advisable not to take a definitive stance too soon in any meeting so allowing for a development of opinion. Also in a prison context premature reassurance that guilt has been removed might be detrimental to the spiritual and mental health of an inmate. Whilst the converse can also apply – the invitable problem with releasing a prisoner from guilt is that it cannot be related to encouraging an increase in responsibility. One of the damaging features of imprisonment is the impossibility for an inmate to test out his responsibility in relation to the crucial reason why he is incarcerated – which is usually the reasons why he feels guilty. A judgmental attitude towards guilt and sin is helpful when made by the person who should receive it, and especially when it arises as a response to feelings revealed when an offender sets his behaviour in the context of an inspiring spiritual outlook. A moral judgment is worth nothing unless it mediates a moral ideal which freely inspires and wins over acceptance. Pastoral care must bring the offender to accept his situation and interpret it in such a way that he himself can pass judgment upon it, revealing in his new look a hope and possibility of redemption which together can induce a growth to maturity. Thus theological understanding can purvey a unifying vision helping the pastoral carer to balance judgmental and accepting attitudes.

Fourthly, offenders respond to a good listener. Listening is important in any counselling, but it has a special relevance to offenders because their situation evinces so much anger and anxiety. They are often in conflict with their environments or with facets of their own personalities. On a practical level, listening must be implemented with a knowledge of interviewing skills. Yet it also has an important dynamic level requiring concentration and a measure of responsiveness – so distinguishing pastoral care from treatment. Listening can make an important contribution to the atmosphere of a caring relationship in a prison where intense feelings might need to be dissipated. Listening also allows the person talking to present a wide background from which important themes can be extracted and might bring to light parts of a person's life of which they can be proud and on which future self-esteem can be built. Among prisoners, as elsewhere, a listener mirrors the whole of the Holy Spirit – the Counsellor, the Paraclete, titles which indicate in derivation, 'the one called to stand by'. Significantly Ezekiel described his ministry of pastoral care towards prisoners in Babylon in terms of listening and stand by: '...the hand of the LORD was strong upon me. I came to them of the captivity ... that dwell by the River Chebar, and I sat where they sat, and remained there astonished among them seven days' (3[14-15]).

Turning from the pastoral carer to the offender, there are inward and outward looking attitudes on the recipients' side that can play a part in helping him improve his well-being.

First, his attitude towards truth is crucial. In society there is a taboo on asking personal questions. Yet in a prison environment one can ask stark questions. Truthful answers are not always given; this is understandable if one is ministering among some people adept at evasion! Total denial or diversion in interpretation, especially in relation to a crime for which there has been a guilty conviction, can inhibit pastoral care. One can follow the line that God embodies truth (Jn 14[16]) and that he expects truthfulness in all relationships –Jesus himself not allowing the woman at the well the luxury of a half-truth (Jn 4[17]). Yet truth and freedom are connected. A mark of the image of God is that everyone has freedom of choice. In a pastoral care situation with an offender who appears to be seeking a more stable life the high ideal of truth may become stronger as a relationship progresses in security. In this context there can be a strong awareness that in the face of loss of truth the power of the spirit can be quenched (1Thes 5[19]) and grieved (Eph 4[30]).

Secondly, men in prison need help in coping with loss of self-respect. Regardless of the justification for the imprisonment it has many dehumanizing features, including physical conditions, enforced companionship and general regimentation – amid all of which psychological survival is the overwhelming consideration. In these circumstances the personal dimension of pastoral care has an intrinsic value in itself. Frequently it is in the presence of someone who treats a prisoner as human that the value of any help is primarily remembered. One can reflect on the verdict of the landlady of the Potwell Inn. When Mr Polly, the creation of H.G. Wells, admitted to having 'a bit of arson' before asking her for a job, she replied thoughtfully: 'Its all right if you haven't been to prison. It isn't what a man's happened to do that makes 'im bad. We all happen to do things at times. It's bringing it home to him and spoiling his self-respect does the mischief.'

Thirdly, group experiences can help pastoral care. Institutions like prisons do not easily accommodate group-work opportunties, partly because of the authoritarian structure and also because of the strong loyalties within an inmate sub-culture. However, when small groups have met voluntarily for a limited time, especially when there has been a unifying common problem among the men, worthwhile experiences can be achieved. A pastoral counsellor might help a group focus on themes and feelings relevant to imprisonment. These groups lead men to growth in trust, in risk-taking, in self-disclosure and sometimes in constructive conflict. A prison group of this sort demonstrates the double meaning of the word 'apartness'. These men are separate, lonely, apart from but also 'a part of'. One prisoner put it poignantly when he described himself as 'a lonely ship in the dark'. Although no physical mooring could be made it was nevertheless comforting for him, a segregated sex offender, 'to see the lights of other ships sailing in the same water'. Groups where remarks like this can be made can experience a close fellowship and struggle with deep existential questions.

Group-work with prisoners in a pastoral care context could include a reference to worship. The pastoral care in individual contact or in group-work is part of an overall ministry focused in liturgical worship and prayer groups, both of which can include preaching, teaching and fellowship. All these are part of a pastoral outreach that aims to enhance social and spiritual health. There are about 150 penal establishments in the United

Kingdom and all of them have at least one chapel which is at the centre in many of these buildings. Attendance is always on a voluntary basis and is proportionately very high in relation to general population's attendance. However one might rationalize this surprisingly high participation in religious worship, a challenging opportunity exists for implanting an interest in the gospel. All new prison chapels place an emphasis in their architecture on new life, inner light and a sense of resurrection. This contrasts with the more sombre penitential style in which the Victorians built prisons. Frequently individuals who have had a place in the prison during the week as pastoral counsellors working on a basis of individual contacts, have felt it is important to tie their wider ministering into a prison act of worship. The atmosphere within which individual care is offered to a man may help him follow it through on his release in a continuing association with a local church.

There are many practical situations of crisis and stress for offenders where pastoral care can be demonstrated. These situations are common to pastoral care in other sections of the community and cover death and serious illness, marital and relationship disharmony, anxiety about impending news or future life patterns. Some of these problems in a prison can be resolved through conventional welfare practices: other problems prove long-term and are not immediately amenable to resolution or relief. Pastoral care sometimes has to follow the example of Mary, who sat our Lord's feet 'and stayed there listening', rather than of Martha who 'busied herself' with what Emerson has called 'an unnecessary deal of doing'. Despite the large number of things 'done' for prisoners and delinquents it is surprising that it is largely their own maturity that prevents repetition of offences.

Those who offer pastoral care to people in trouble with the law need, in certain senses, to be cared for themselves.

First, there is a need for collective responsibility. In offering to share a vision of a better life the individual, through whom the care is implemented, is only an intermediary. He should be part of a bridge-building team based in one locality acting in communion with other Christians. When any individual is equipped with an opportunity to make contact with offenders this can lead to a degree of egocentricity. The person who offers 'pastoral care' alone increases his risk of feeling rejected. He may find any disappointment less acute if he is part of a body or team that will share this experience. The spirit and fellowship of a supportive group can not only help him resist the temptation to be cynical about revitalizing prospects for offenders but can be a beneficial forum for sharing the humor of many prison situations. The value of a collective mind is reflected in Paul's observation that 'the partial vanishes when wholeness comes'.

Secondly, continuous moral reflection can be useful for those who offer pastoral care within the orbit of any law enforcement agency. In this way the aims of pastoral care can be implemented creatively in accord with the goals of the institution. Those who have interpreted pastoral care in this field in the past may have done better to have resisted the idea of seeing this moral concern in an analogy with a prophet. Because of the autonomy which institutions like prisons have from the direct power of the church, the model of the ancient scribe or rabbi is more appropriate to the circumstances. The moral objectives of pastoral care in a prison could take the form of a 'midrash' (a search or inquiry) which can illicit the collaborative efforts of various professionals.

Thirdly, criminality and disruptiveness are, in varying degrees, part of everyone's inner life. Those who offer pastoral care in this field might reflect on these aspects in their own lives – especially if they are regularly presenting themselves as a 'still centre' in the presence of potentially dangerous people. Prospero's words are a useful reminder at this point – he refers to

> This thing of darkness I acknowledge mine.
>
> (The Tempest V, 1,275)

In a parallel way Freud has analysed the way society reacts to offenders and has explained punishment as a form of mass sexual gratification. In an exaggerated world like a prison those who sensitively offer pastoral care might at times find it hard to distinguish clearly between their own needs, society's needs and the needs of those they are trying to help.

Jesus the prisoner was also Jesus the victim. Consequently a consideration about pastoral care among offenders should aim to link their criminal activities with the suffering caused to their victims. Because the legal system in the West is overwhelmingly punitive towards the offender and largely excludes the victim, apart from a brief appearance in court, the impact of restitution (or, some might say, atonement) has been diminished. Although the ancient link between restitution and punishment has been severed, philosophers through the ages have tried to keep this interest alive. Sir Thomas More, for instance, in Utopia, suggested that restitution should be made by offenders to their victims and that offenders should be required to labour on public works to raise such money. Numerous facilities have recently been developed in the United States of America for victim offenders conciliation, and in the United Kingdom there have been substantial developments in the last decade in community service schemes. This seems to be an area of development for pastoral care practice, offering the offender purposeful activity to enhance his self-esteem, to relieve any sense of needy or victimized individuals. This restitutive approach reverts to ideas in pre-modern law systems where the criminal act is seen in terms that directly relate theological interpretation to the realities of estrangement between the offender and the community. Restitutive sanctions are designed neither to punish nor to treat but to provide an offender with an opportunity to recompense an injured party and to become more intergrated in the community.

As Jesus related to prisoners, churches today should continually consider how they might function in this sphere of pastoral care. Few who come within the jurisdiction of a court have had much contact with a religious organization; consequently the initiative lies with the church. Direct contact with offenders can result from personal introductions or from information culled from newspaper reports on court cases. Crime is usually a local affair and in the majority of criminal activites like burglary, which is the reason for the largest number of imprisonments in the United Kingdom, a considerable number of people in the vicinity of a church can be involved in dealing with matters affecting an offence, both before and after the actual incident. Local clergy can visit men in a police station or in a prison and can demand attention if they speak in court about their links with an offender. The majority of people who get into trouble are part of seemingly prolific local families, several members of which may have criminal records. Thus contact with one side leads to their associates! It can be profitable for churches to be acquainted with social work agencies supporting these families, because prisoners and delinquents are usually part of turbulent domestic scenes. In many areas there are meeting points with offenders at Day Centres and at activity groups organized by probation services as non-custodial sanctions. There is also a place for churches to relate to the wider context of pastoral care in this field by filling an educative role about offenders' problems within the society – possibly by receiving bulletins from political groups seeking progress for social groups that come into conflict with the law. Churches have an almost unique opportunity to bring together groups on both sides of the law that have the well-being of an offender in view. The possibilities within the grasp of a church to foster contacts across these barriers and to create understanding and harmony should never be underestimated.

20. The Needs of Those Giving Pastoral Care

By Irene Bloomfield Psychotherapist, B.A. Hon Psych, London

The idea that those who give pastoral care and counselling to others might at times be in need of support, care or counsel themselves was largely unacceptable to the majority of clergy and Religious before the 1960s. Although there has been a great change in the climate of opinion regarding help for the helpers, the old feeling still persists in some church circles. It is still not unusual to come across the view that ordination or life vows bestow a kind of immunity from the effects of stress, and that symptoms of anxiety or depression mean that something has gone wrong with the individual's relationship with God or their spiritual and prayer life, and if only they could pray harder or work more intensely on their spirituality, they would be alright.

The problem with this view is that severe anxiety or depression or other symptoms of emotional disturbance are often so all-absorbing that no other thoughts are possible, and the idea that people's symptoms are somehow their own fault, tends to increase the guilt and feelings of unworthiness which are generally an important ingredient of depression. The individual's self-hatred thus becomes worse, and the self-acceptance so necessary for love of neighbour becomes more and more impossible. Inability to give or receive love increases the depressed individual's guilt even more, and it becomes harder and harder to reverse the downward spiral.

In the days when this attitude towards emotional disturbance in the helper prevailed, it seemed that only complete mental or physical breakdown could bring any possibility of help.

Fortunately, these attitudes began to change in the early 1960s when Frank Lake brought the Clinical Theology movement into existence, the Richmond Fellowship offered training and counselling to clergy and Religious, and other pioneers like

Bill Kyle and Louis Marteau followed with their religious counselling centres. Since then, it has become much more widely accepted that clergy and Religious are just as likely to react to stress by becoming anxious or depressed or unable to cope as are other mortals. The stereotype of the 'invulnerable' priest or nun is gradually fading.

Needs of other 'helpers'

Clergy were not, of course, alone in their conviction that they had to be immune from emotional or psychological disturbance, and that it was unacceptable for them to be in need of care, counsel or support themselves. I recall with a measure of incredulity that it was totally unacceptable in my own department of psychological medicine of a teaching hospital for a member of staff to become depressed or to need psychological help for themselves. The climate of the 1950s and 60s did not allow for breakdown among staff. In the same way as the clergy, we too were expected to *give* help, not to receive it, and at that time there was an irreconcilable split between the 'helpers' and the helped. In theory, therapy for therapists was regarded as highly desirable. In practice, however, there were virtually no facilities for the therapist or psychiatrist who needed help for him or her self. When one of the junior psychiatrists in our department became depressed and committed suicide, it was impossible to talk about it. There was general feeling that it should not have happened, that he let the side down, and that it was best not to mention it.

All of this was deplorable, but it was very similar to the feelings which were expressed when a nun in a Community I knew killed herself in quite a violent manner. It was obviously a terrible shock to everybody in the Community, but here too there was an unspoken taboo on sharing and expressing the feelings which virtually paralysed the Community for a long time afterwards.

Changing climate in helping professions

Fortunately, there has been a very drastic change in the climate regarding emotional disturbance in society at large and the church and psychiatric services in particular. It is now generally acknowledged that those in the caring professions may need care for themselves at some point and should have easy access to help and support for themselves as a matter of course. I am not sure whether it is equally accepted that we can only care for others to the extent that we feel cared about ourselves and accept ourselves.

The idea of self-acceptance and self-love is one which is still viewed with a measure of distaste in many circles, including religious ones. Self-love smacks of narcissism, and although we talk very easily of loving our neighbour as ourselves, we ignore the fact that we can *only* love the neighbour *as much* as we love ourselves, not more. It is not possible to give love to others when we are filled with self-hatred or self-loathing.

Consequences of unrealistic expectations

I have met several clergy who have thought of themselves as servants of God who should ask nothing for themselves, have a permanently open door to all who express a need, should not expect to have days or hours off just for themselves or their families, and should never resent the continuous demands which such an attitude encourages. When such a man finally gets to breaking point and wants to throw it all in, run away or scream at the next person who demands his attention, he is seen as having failed, and himself feels that perhaps he is not up to the job, a disgrace to his calling, a poor priest. This is not a flight of fancy on my part. There are a number of clergy and priests who were in one group or another with me who expressed just those feelings.

Peter, who was a member of a diocesan support group for clergy, gave a picture of his life which did not allow for any privacy and left room for very little leisure. He had a strong belief that his life belonged to the church, his bishop, his parishioners. He was unmarried, and nothing therefore stood in the way of his total commitment to service. He enjoyed doing his work and many people came to see him with their troubles. It worked well enough, until one of his female parishioners discovered that the door was, metaphorically speaking, always open and decided she was in almost constant need of the vicar's care and attention, and that in fact she was going to marry him. After that Peter had no peace at all, and his ability to care for the rest of his parish became impaired. He was very angry with Margaret, the widow who had set her cap at him, but he did not believe in expressing anger to anyone, let alone one of his flock. Something had to give, and Peter became ill. After that he was more able to listen to the group and its encouragement to him to set limits to others and to himself as well.

Paul was another young vicar in the same group. He thought of himself very much as 'a suffering servant' who had to accept whatever was asked of him by the authorities, his parish workers or his parishioners. There was a perverse satisfaction for him in being the martyr who had to work fifteen hours a day until he collapsed in a state of total exhaustion.

Disappointment

There are those who try to find in the church or the Community the ideal family they did not have as children. They are generally disappointed and feel let down, because they can only give and experience love to the extent to which they received it at an earlier stage in their lives. During deeper exploration, it often becomes evident that they see God either as a harsh, punitive father or as one who can love others, but not them.

Others find that they constantly fall short of their own and other people's expectations of the sort of saintly person they 'ought' to be. This cuases them to be angry or depressed, religion for them just adds to their sense of worthlessness and failure.

Forgiving oneself and others

Another problem which arises frequently is that members of any of the Christian churches find it relatively easy to forgive others, but when it comes to forgiving themselves for real or imagined misdemeanours, small omissions or failure to be 'as perfect as Jesus was perfect,' they cannot do it. It is the inability to forgive themselves which creates so many of the problems which clergy and Religious bring to the counsellor or thereapist when they eventually have to seek help. Often there is not even really anything they have to forgive themselves for, except for not being what others wanted tham to be, i.e. a saint or a daddy or a prophet.

Psychotherapy, counselling, sensitivity or therapeutic groups generally start with the individual as he or she is, and accept him or her more or less without reservation, but in the expectation that he or she will struggle towards change, growth and development.

Religion generally starts with how we ought to be but cannot be. It therefore often leaves us with a great sense of failure. In therapy or counselling the individual may be helped to internalize a less demanding authority and thus become more accepting of him or her self and more able to love others.

Effect of delaying first aid

In the following pages I would like to give an example of someone who did not get the first aid which might have prevented the long and serious condition he suffered from for many years.

James was a curate who illustrated this very well. He came to see me as a last resort and very unwillingly. He saw counselling and therapy as an unacceptable self-indulgence and a weakness which only went to confirm the low opinion he had of himself in any case. He was very wary of all members of my profession, and I was only marginally more acceptable because a priest had recommended me. In talking about James, I would like to show what may happen if no help is available at the crucial time and describe how the process of counselling or therapy may work when it becomes necessary. I hope that this description will go some way towards showing that therapy is neither self-indulgence nor weakness, but that on the contrary it is generally painful, often frightening, and if it is to be successful it requires a lot of courage.

James had been hospitalized at an earlier stage of his life after making a suicide attempt, and just prior to seeing me, he had again become suicidal.

He was a very tortured person who felt that he was 'loathsome and should be crushed underfoot like an insect'. He seemed to go out of his way to make himself look as unattractive as possible. He dressed in a slovenly manner. His hair and beard were untidy and he gave a general impression of slovenliness. He felt dirty and scruffy but seemed unable to change his appearance. Feeling dirty went back to childhood when as a youngster he wet his bed and was made to carry the wet sheets through the house to the bathroom where he had to wash them himself. His brothers who had no such problems frequently jeered at him.

Feeling dirty had in later life become transferred to nasty, dirty thoughts and feelings. In adolescence he had had a few homosexual experiences. There had been no homosexual or heterosexual contacts since then, but he still felt attracted by young men, the kind of young man he would have liked to have been himself. He was very evnious of all the young men whom he met or just passed in the street who seemed to him clean and wholesome, athletic and good-looking, well off and self-confident.

Homosexual impulses and envy were to him sinful and added to his self-loathing, a term he used frequently about himself.

Seen objectively, James had in fact done extremely well. He came from a working class family in which he was the only one who passed the 11+ examination and went to a grammar school. His brothers were good athletes and mechanics and shared their father's enthusiasm for football, motor bikes and pubs in later life.

James disliked all these activities. He had never been any good at games, could never kick a ball straight and lacked the coordination to do anything with his hands. Poor eyesight and glasses did not help his image of masculinity. Father often grumbled, saying: 'This boy will never amount to anything. He always has his nose stuck in a book, instead of doing sensible things like playing football or mending a bike'.

James never did amount to much in father's or his brothers' eyes. They saw him as an 'odd ball', in spite or perhaps because of the fact that he had managed to get a good university degree and had been ordained as a minister in the Church of England. The family did not really approve of all this 'church business' either. The sad thing was that James could not really get any satisfaction from his very real achievements, because he shared the family's feelings about himself. He was bitterly resentful towards his father and very envious of his brothers, the envy which later became transferred onto all the good-looking, athletic young men he admired. He was also very wary and suspicious of women generally and did not feel he could trust a woman not to humiliate him in the way his mother had done when she made him carry his wet sheets through the house for all to see.

James did not have the first aid which could, I think, have prevented some of his distorted perceptions and the great unhappiness he felt for the ten years or so before he came into therapy. His resentment and bitterness found no outlet and could therefore only be directed against himself. He was being eaten up from within and felt violent and destructive. It was at the times when these destructive feelings were uppermost that he decided to end it all and to kill himself, but the attempt failed and he ended up in a psychiatric ward instead. He found this a totally humiliating and appalling experience which in his eyes put him beyond the pale.

James remained quite depressed for the next ten years. During the ten months in which he was in therapy we saw a very dramatic change take place. It was most noticeable in his appearance, in that he began to take more care of himself and to look much less scruffy. This coincided with feeling better about himself as he saw that he really had not done badly. He began to feel that he no longer had to live out the role of the 'no-good, denigrated self'. Feeling better about himself also meant that the signals he was sending out to others changed from 'Keep away, I am poison and will contaminate you', to signals which said 'Come closer, I would like to know you and to be approached', and to his amazement people did.

James was incredulous for quite a while and did not believe in the change. He was also frightened, because it meant giving up a familiar, if unwelcome, role and coping strategy. He had to find new ways of relating.

He went through a phase of hating me for putting him through such an ordeal. When he stopped seeing me, he looked very different from the scruffy character I had seen in the beginning. He held himself erect instead of slouching and dressed neatly. There was a new sense of pride in his achievements and at having overcome so many hurdles. He had more self-confidence and was no longer so envious of others, because he saw that he had things of his own.

I heard no more from him until I wrote to him five years later to ask whether he would object to my using his case as an illustration in a talk I was due to give. He gave his permission, and I quote from his letter. 'It was a most pleasant surprise to receive your letter two days ago. I apologize for not replying more speedily, but life in a monastery gives little time for such things as letters. My answer is, of course, in the affirmative. Although at the time my experiences of our sessions were extremely painful, I now view them as some of the most valuable time I have ever spent. I am not saying that they were 'magical', but I am not the same person you first met.

'For a start, I don't detest myself any more, nor do I constantly look at others and see myself in a negative light by comparison. I see that my parents for all their failings not only loved me but did their best for me. They were what they were and could be nothing else, and I on my part failed them often. It was I who was ashamed of them, not they of me. I can now see not only their defects but also their glories.

'I am not trying to say that the old problems do not emerge from time to time, but they are becoming increasingly rare. Life now has a quietness and gentleness and contentment which I would never have dreamt possible. Joining a religious community was the first action I have ever taken which did not have the unanimous approval of all those I depended upon for support. My entrance into religious life was in no way looking for a prop. I knew it would be difficult, and it was far more difficult than I could ever haved imagined.

'I am deeply grateful for all those sessions in which *you helped me to help myself*. From having a place of fear and as a 'pain bearer' in my thoughts, you now have a warm place in my thoughts and prayers as one who helped a frightened, hypersensitive and self-denigrating individual to being one who is at least approaching self-acceptance and self-love.

'I hope that your recounting of your experience with me may help others to cut through a veil of self-deceit which is so easy to build up, even on the part of those who apparently have many props, religious or otherwise.'

A year after writing this letter James came back to this country for a visit. He dropped in to see me, just to say how much peace of mind he had found in his life as a Religious. He looked well and serene, and this is a word I could never have imagined myself using about James when I first met him.

I have gone into James' case in such detail because it illustrates very well how relatively little help can have a very profound effect on clergy and Religious in order to reverse a downward spiral which can end in total breakdown or suicide. As I mentioned earlier, James had tried twice to end his life.

It may not be particularly helpful to speculate on the kind of first aid which might have prevented some of James' suffering, but I would nevertheless like to offer some suggestions, since they could perhaps be used preventively by others.

The thing which James might have benefitted from most would have been a relationship with someone, individual or group, who would not have been put off by his way of presenting himself, including his appearance, but who would have understood the message behind it, what it was saying. Such a person might have been able to stop him from translating his sense of worthlessness into sin, for this only aggravated the feeling of guilt and failure which he had carried with him since childhood.

There are, of course, many priests who can offer such a relationship and a number who are trained to see below the surface, but sometimes a priest may not be the best person to do this because of the individual's associations of him with 'punitive father figure, representative of God, upholder of the church's law'. A priest might have had greater difficulty in gaining James' confidence than did the more 'neutral' therapist, but more important than the role of the counsellor would have been his or her genuine interest, acceptance and wish to understand without judging.

Such understanding would have had to be based on some knowledge of the effect of family background on the individual's subsequent development, attitudes and behaviour patterns, including also his sexual development.

Understanding does not of course mean approval of attitudes and behaviour which are contrary to Christian mores, but understanding helps the individual to get things into perspective, to be less harsh with himself and to forgive himself for what may have been inevitable. This could have been the starting point for James' subsequent growth and development, as it is for many who have lived with similar burdens of distortion and misunderstanding.

Is there something special in counselling clergy?

It was the discovery that many of my clergy clients made very rapid and far reaching changes that aroused my interest in working with clergy and Religious, and although there are obviously some who are too badly damaged to benefit from short term work, there are many more who can use a relatively small amount of therapy, counselling or support to lift themselves up and go well beyond the point many other patients or clients do as a rule. I believe that this has something to do with motivation and with re-discovering or even discovering for the first time real meaning in their lives.

This may seem like a very strange statement about those for whom their faith might be expected to provide meaning. The trouble is that the 'oughts' of religion are not realized automatically because a person is ordained or enters religious life.

There is in the majority of religious people a strong wish to find meaning. This provides powerful motivation in therapy or counselling and may well be one of the factors which make the journey into their inner world more rapid. Moreover, being used to meditation may help to build a bridge between the outer and inner worlds which helps in the process of integration of different aspects of self.

Religious language may therefore have no real meaning until acceptance of self and others and pleasure in being him or her self enables the individual to find real meaning in the content as well as the language of religion.

21. Group Work As First Aid or Prevention

By Irene Bloomfield

In the previous chapter I talked of the first aid which may be very important for anyone involved in pastoral care, but the emphasis was on the individual, and on what consequences there might be if such first aid was not forthcoming.

In this chapter I would like to concentrate more on the different kinds of group which can be helpful, groups which exist already and groups which could be started in any parish, given that knowledge and experience of groups is present.

In some ways it should be the most natural thing in the world for us to function in a group setting. After all, we all started life in a group of a least two or three or many more. Most of our lives are spent in groups of one sort or another, in the nursery, at school, in Scouts or Guides, at university, at work in church or religious communities. Even Jesus had his group of twelve apostles.

It can be seen therefore that groups play an important part in all our lives, and that there is no way of getting away from them.

I would like to concentrate in this chapter on groups which can be used by pastoral carers for purposes of growth and development, support and affirmation and for pastoral care.

The variety and effectiveness of group work is immense, but it needs to be borne in mind that groups can also be extremely powerful instruments which need to be used with skill and sensitivity. Harm rather than good can come from working with groups if they are run by untrained or unskilled conductors. The term 'conductor' was coined by Michael Foulkes, the father of the group analysis in Britain. It is very apt and beautiful, because it conjures up the image of an orchestra which can function magnificently and harmoniously when conducted with skill and sensitivity or end up as a disaster of discord with an insensitive or unskilled conductor.

The term 'group' is used very loosely and may, therefore, be quite confusing. There is the primary family group and the wider family of grandparents, uncles, aunts and cousins and some of the others already mentioned; but the term can also have a more specific meaning, which is in use among the helpers in the community.

We talk of 'sensitivity' groups which generally consist of 8 – 12 members and which aim to increase people's self-awareness and understanding of their own and other people's feelings, needs, attitudes and behaviour. The result of this increased understanding is an improvement in sensitivity towards people generally. There are those who bring this kind of understanding and sensitivity to their encounters with others without having had any particular training. In some cases it is trained out of them, as in the cases of nurses, sometimes doctors and clergy as well. There are also those who will never have it, no matter how much training they get. They are often the very rigid, dogmatic, authoritarian or fanatical personalities, who are not able to change and do not wish to.

The majority of people, however can improve their understanding of self and others and increase the sensitivity which, hopefully, will lead to greater wholeness of the individual and the group in which he or she is a participant.

Supervision Seminars

There are supervision seminars which are designed to increase their members' counselling skills by getting them to bring problems from their parish situations. In other groups the emphasis will be more on looking at people's behaviour within the group. Some try to teach about group processes through the experience of being in a group, others emphasize the supportive quality for those who are under great stress and pressure. There are groups in which the stated aim is the growth and development of its members and others in which a particular task has to be achieved. The major difference is between those in which the largely problem-solving element predominates and others in which the growth and self-understanding aspects are more in the forefront.

In my experience, the most popular groups were those which started off as a forum to which people could bring problems arising in the parish but which gradually changed into groups in which self understanding became more important than the 'problem'.

I had experienced the problem-orientated seminar when I was an associate in a seminar run by Michael Balint, a well known psychiatrist/psychoanalyst who ran seminars for general practitioners. Doctors brought problem cases to the seminars and these were very thoroughly discussed. The doctors gradually also learned a great deal about their interactions and relationships with their patients. They learned to look for the message behind the symptom presented, and how their response to the patient's presentation could effect the outcome of the treatment. As a result, they felt that their skills as doctors were considerably improved. They also found their work much more interesting. They felt that the seminars helped them to become better doctors. It seemed to me that this model of working with doctors was equally suitable for working with clergy, and I ran a number of 'Balint groups' for clergy and Religious. Generally though, as members began to know each other better and to trust each other more, there was a tendency to become less interested in 'the problems' and more in the members' characteristic ways of handling problems and thus in understanding themselves. Not that these seminars turned into therapy groups, but the increase in self-awareness often led to theraputic by-products, in the sense that unhelpful attitudes and behaviour patterns could be identified and modified.

I would like to give an example from one of these groups. Dorothy was a deaconess who had considerable experience with church committees of various sorts. In one of our groups, she described an occasion in which she had been quite unable to get a hearing of her point of view. She was left feeling very hurt and angry, yet quite unable to say so. When she talked about it in the group, she became very distressed, and her anger seemed to be so great that it was quite out of proportion to the event. When this was pointed out to her, it brought back memories of many other occasions on which she had been unable to stand up for herself. Some of these went back to her childhood and to her position within her own family. Children could be seen, but not heard. The group did not attempt to explore Dorothy's childhood experiences in depth, but it helped Dorothy to recall her feelings then and to see how similar they were to the feelings she had experienced at the committee meeting. She could see that she was no longer the little girl who was helpless, but had other strengths and resources as an adult, and that the old pattern of behaviour of not talking when adults where around was no longer necessary or appropriate. Dorothy seemed to feel much relieved at having recognized these connections, and when she next reported to the group on the same committee and her behaviour in it, it was evident that there had been a marked change. She was heard and listened to. No one interrupted, and she was able to get her views across without difficulty. She had not been afraid to say things even if they might not be popular and had expressed herself forcefully and well. She expected to be taken seriously and therefore received different reactions from the other members of the committee. It was also important to recognize that the other members of the group felt more at ease with Dorothy and warmer towards her after she had shared her real feelings with them, even though they had been feelings of such intense anger.

Robert brought a problem which related to a curate who had been sent to him for training. Robert thought that it was quite wrong for a Christian to feel, let alone express, anger. He could not assert his authority with the curate who spent a lot of time on things which interested him but were not a great help in parish activities. Robert frequently preferred to do a job himself rather than tell the curate off for having neglected it. Cyril, the young curate, mistook Robert's unwillingness to remonstrate with him as weakness. He was a very self-confident and somewhat opinionated young man and was rather contemptuous of Robert's gentleness.

Matters came to a head, however, when Cyril turned up to a service dressed in T-shirt and jeans. Robert felt very angry then and was all set to ask for Cyril's removal. He felt guilty, useless and inadequate. When he brought this by-now inflammatory situation to the group, it tried to show him that it was appropriate, even for a good Christian, to experience and occasionally to express anger. Jesus himself had after all not been averse to doing so. When Robert finally managed to talk to Cyril and to tell him what annoyed and upset him, he was amazed to find that Cyril seemed quite pleased and relieved. He had been testing Robert and was glad to have some limits set to him.

I have had to condense interactions which sometimes stretched over several sessions to the point where it may appear simplistic or unlikely that one can simply say 'Be angry or be assertive or be genuine' and hey presto, all problems are solved. It was much more the experience of being accepted with all one's bad and one's good feelings in the groups which brought about change. It is what we *are* rather than what we *say* that makes the difference. That is why the work the helpers do on themselves is so important. It has a ripple effect.

Failures and difficulties in group work

The examples I have given so far were those in which group interventions were helpful. There are, of course, occasions when the group fails and people remove themselves. Not everyone can tolerate having a search light focused on them or sitting in the 'hot seat'. It can be uncomfortable, and not everyone is prepared for it or wants it. Most groups have their casualties, the people who fall by the way-side. In the groups I have been associated with, the group leader or leaders were always willing to offer time to anyone for whom the group was too difficult, too painful or not what they wanted, and I believe that such safeguards are necessary. The experience and skill of the group conductor as mentioned earlier is important and necessary, and he or she requires training and supervision. Moreover, ongoing situations have many advantages over the one-off weekend group, where it is generally much more difficult to enable people to deal with unfinished business or with feeling disturbed and upset as a result of an experience in the group.

Clergy Support Group

One type of group which has come into its own in recent years is the 'Clergy Support' or 'Pastoral Care Group', which has been set up in some of the Church of England dioceses.

Different dioceses have used slightly different models. Southwark Diocese's then Director of Pastoral Care and Counselling, Derek Blows, was the first to establish such a group and it attracted large numbers of clergy and lay workers. The London Diocese has had a scheme going for six years, but it took longer to get off the ground.

The word 'support' seemed to be unacceptable to some bishops and clergy who felt that they should not need support, especially if it came from such dubious outsiders as psychiatrists, psychotherapists, or even counsellors. In spite of the initial suspicion and wariness, a network of support groups for the training of group leaders has been set up in London Diocese, and those who participated whether as group leaders or as ordinary members have felt quite enthusiastic about it.

As I mentioned earlier, the idea that the need for support reflects weakness is quite fallacious. Attendance at a group which explores our characteristic but sometimes unhelpful patterns of behaviour and relationships with parishioners, friends, colleagues or clients requires far more courage and strength than does the denial of need. Those who expose weakness and acknowledge vulnerabilities are taking risks, risks which are not for their benefit alone, but also for all those who are in contact with them.

Other problems which may require prevention or first aid

The priest is frequently put on a pedestal and seen as saintly and perfect. He is expected to carry the goodness for all the parish. When he fails to come up to these unrealistic expectations, he gets knocked off and is perceived as a devil, even as devilish.

There is great satisfaction when his family presents an image of a 'holy family', united, loving, generous, devout – in short, perfect. There is great rejoicing if the vicar is honoured in some way. It is as if the whole parish shares in the reflected glory. But woe betide the vicar who is found to have feet of clay, who is discovered in some misdeneanour or whose marriage comes to grief. The feeling in the parish then is not just that he has let himself down, but that he had disgraced the parish and the whole church.

Where the priest starts with great good will, trying to be all the things people expect of him, he soon comes to feel that it is hopeless, that it is an impossible task, that he is a failure.

Because of the church's paternalistic structure, the minister will frequently project dreams of an all-giving, all-caring father onto the bishop, and of an all-nurturing ever-giving mother onto the church. He may become very disillusioned when he finds the bishop's diary is completely filled up for the next twelve months, and there is very little chance of getting the time, care and concern which he had hoped for. The bishop may then be experienced as a punitive, rejecting parent, very much as the vicar was when he could not meet all the parishioners' hopes and expectations.

A support group can be very helpful in showing its members that they are not alone in their unrealistic expectations of themselves as well as of their bishop. It is so much easier to see the mote in the other's eye, but once it has been seen, it can also be recognized in our own more readily.

A situation which can create great problems sometimes occurs when a parishioner becomes mentally disturbed. An acute and typical psychiatric condition is readily recognized by all concerned and can, on the whole, be dealt with by the appropriate authorities; but when the onset of the condition is insidious and gradual, it is much harder to recognize and to acknowledge, especially for the realtives.

Let me illustrate with an example. Thomas was the vicar of a large parish in the north of England. His vicarage was a huge Victorian mansion, designed for the married vicar of that period with a family of ten children. Thomas was single and found the house overwhelming. When one of his parishioners became temporarily homeless, he offered to let her have a room in the house until she could find new accommodation. The parishioner, a widow in her seventies, was very grateful to Thomas, and in order to express her appreciation she gave several large donations to the church.

Mrs M. had always found it difficult to make friends, and after her husband's death she became very isolated. Being mostly on her own made her wary and suspicious, and she began to misinterpret people's motives and behaviour. The vicar, who was one of the very few human contacts she had, became excessively important to her; but because it was quite unacceptable for her to acknowledge her own need and feelings for him, he being in his thirties and she in her late seventies, she projected these feelings onto him and suspected that he had designs on her. She felt that she was in great danger. The danger was, of course, from her own irrational impulses, but she experienced it as coming from him. She picked on odd words or phrases which he had used in sermons or talks with her and saw special significance in them, confirming her suspicions. Mrs M. was in fact becoming more and more paranoid, but as with so many people suffering from this mental condition, there was often a small grain of truth in what she said. Only the element of truth was so distorted that it was grossly misleading. She felt, for example, that she had in some way been compelled to give money to the church which she could not really afford, but that it was what Thomas was expecting her to do. There was no truth in that. He had accepted her donations in good faith and had not realized that she was depriving herself of necessities in order to do so. Mrs M. however, felt that he did know or should have known, and that he had some terrible hold on her, which she did not understand. All this would have been tolerable if she had not felt compelled to talk about it to people in the parish and others known to Thomas as well as to her. Most people probably discounted the sexual insinuations, but there were some who were concerned about the financial ones, thinking: 'Poor old thing, she should not have been asked to impoverish herself like this'.

The onset of Mrs M's paranoia was very gradual and therefore people took a long time to recognize it as such. Some never did. The gossip and insinuations were very unpleasant for Thomas, and he was very relieved to have his support group to relieve his great anxiety, for it all became thoroughly unpleasant. The group was able to help him get things into perspective and look at the worst that could happen and how he could protect himself without harming his unfortunate parishioner.

The situation Thomas got into was one that could happen to any minister, but it highlighted the importance of keeping some boundaries and the risks in becoming very involved with parishioners who may be in need of counselling in depth or of psychiatric help.

It may be very important and desirable for the minister to make friends with members of his parish, but because the parish situation evokes so many feelings which belong to our childhood experience within the family, it is very difficult to avoid feelings of envy, rivalry and competition for father's attention to be played out. The more awareness members of the clergy have of these processes, the more likely they are to deal with them sensitively and competently, but there are many situations in which a supportive network is invaluable and necessary; even the most highly trained counsellor or therapist needs others to help him see things clearly and get them into perspective.

To sum up

I have tried to show that clergy as well as other members of helping professions are often under the sort of pressure which makes it essential that they should have a forum where they can share difficulties and issues arising in their work, and get help and support without fear of criticism, ridicule, judgment or loss of face. It is now widely accepted that the more support, training or supervision the carers can get, the more it will benefit not only them – and that is important enough – but it will also help their families and all those who are in contact with them. Some of these supports may prevent a more serious breakdown of the individual or his marriage, and we are now only too aware of the strain that clergy marriages are under. It may also prevent the flight from the church altogether.

Sometimes support is not enough, and professional help has to be sought. This is often delayed for far too long, again out of a sense of pride and unwillingness to accept the vicar's human-ness and 'because it should not happen' to the good Christian person, let alone a clergyman. But does he not bleed as other mortals do when he is injured?

22. Worship and Pastoral Care

By Leslie Virgo

In the *Observer* of the 6th January, 1985, there appeared a moving account of Jimmie R., an alchoholic suffering from Korsakov's syndrome. Korsakov's syndrome is a disorder of learning and memory which comes about as the result of a long drinking history, usually to the exclusion of eating.[1]

Jimmie had served in the Navy during the war, but in 1945 his memory stopped functioning. Asked 'Do you feel alive?', he answered with sadness and resignation, 'Feel alive? . . . not really. I haven't felt alive for a very long time.'

Oliver Sacks, Jimmie's neurologist, once asked the Sisters in the nursing home who were looking after Jimmie, 'Do you think he has a soul?' They were outraged. 'Watch him in chapel', they said, 'and judge for yourself.' As he watched he saw a man totally held and absorbed.

'There was no forgetting, no Korsakov's, then . . . he was no longer at the mercy of a faulty and fallible mechanism – that of meaningless sequences and memory traces – but was altogether held in an act of his whole being.' Clearly Jim found himself, found continuity and reality, in the absoluteness of spiritual attention and act. He found his soul there. It then became clear that, for Jimmie, the same depth of absorption and attention was to be seen in relation to music and art: other realms where the soul is called on, and held and stilled, in attention and communion. Jim has the severest, most devasting Korsakov's; he cannot remember isolated items for more than a few seconds, and has a dense amnesia going back to 1945. But humanly, spiritually, he is at times a different man altogether – no longer fluttering, restless, bored and lost, but deeply attentive to the beauty and 'soul' of the world.

Sacks concludes: 'However great the organic damage and

[1] *'Encyclopedia Handbook of Alcoholism*. Pattison and Kauffman, p. 171 (Gardner Press, New York [1982]).

human dissolution, there remains the undiminished possibility of reintegration by art, by communion, by touching the human spirit'.[2]

I have a photograph in which Jimmie R. is multiplied by ten. It is a picture of a group of men in varying stages of senility in the ward of a psychiatric hospital. One man is in the act of receiving his communion. A spirit of relationship, given and received flows out of the picture. Again and again in these acts of communion in the wards people who were sunk in apathy came alive in a responsive meeting. People who usually remained enclosed in a silent world would join in the familiar prayers and give and receive communion. If, in this way we can see how worship can bring the solitary into families what is its place and value in pastoral care?

To discover the nature of worship we may look to both Biblical and psychological sources.

When Oliver Sacks says of Jimmie: 'He was altogether held in an act of his whole being', he is using the words chosen by Pedersen[3], in his study of Israel to describe the Israelites understanding of 'soul'. 'Soul', for the Jew, was 'man in his total essence'. 'Yahweh, as a potter, moulded man of clay or earth, and into the moulded image he breathed his breath, in which manner man became a living soul': a 'nephesh'. Man is not supplied with 'nephesh', he becomes a 'nephesh': a living soul. It is in the soul that holiness, or 'Kodesh', has its roots. For the Israelite all life needs the addition of strength gained through holiness.[4] It is a force which is felt in all spheres of life; it is, indeed, at the root of all other kinds of energy. 'Thus holiness becomes a regulating principle in life, because it constitutes the central points of life.' Holiness is necessary for the maintenance of life and the renewal and maintenance of blessing. Pedersen says of holiness in Israel: 'in the old days there was always the possibility of Holiness where there was soul life: in the life of the spring, the stone and the tree, in the life of

[2]The Observer Newspaper, 6th January, 1985.
[3]Pedersen, *Israel its life and culture*. Vols. I & II, p. 100. (Geo. Cumberledge, O.U.P., London)
[4] Op. cit. III & IV, p. 32.

animals and human beings. All forms of life drew their growth from Holiness, because their vital force emanated from it. The question was where it was especially to be found. It was important for man to realize this for it was the essential condition enabling him to get into the right relationship to it, to derive a blessing from it and not a curse . . . Holiness becomes a regulating principle in life because it constitutes the central points of life.[5]

In his book *I and Thou*, Martin Buber describes the experience of holiness as he looks at the relationship between ourselves and our world. People and things may be related to as successions of objects: as 'its', or as an 'I-Thou' meeting in relationship. 'When a man experiences the I-Thou meeting it is 'in-him' and not between him and the world that the experience arises. The realtion to the Thou is direct. No system of ideas, nor foreknowledge and no fancy intervene between I and Thou. The memory itself is transformed, as it plunges out of its isolation into the unity of the whole.'[6]

These descriptions of holiness in Pedersen and the 'I-Thou' meeting in Buber reflect the experience of Jimmie R. and the patients in the ward. Relationship does not depend on rationality.

Paul describes creation and people as 'groaning', (stenagmas), sighing deeply in a 'bound' state, and the spirit making intercession with 'groans that cannot be uttered' (Rom 8:18ff).

In the act of worship there is a release into the realms of the spirit and a remaking in the moment of concentration: caught up into unity in the act of worship. It is the experience T. S. Eliot describes as: 'The point of intersection of the timeless with time'.[7] To worship, pros-kuneo, is to prostate oneself before – in token of respect – to do obeisance to – to salute – deriving from 'pros', which is 'to move towards', and 'Kuneo' which is 'to kiss', 'to entreat', 'to beseech'.

Worship, then, is a movement of the soul, outward and into

[5] Ibid. p. 287.
[6] Martin Buber, *I and Thou*, 2nd Edn. p. 5 & 10, T. & T. Clark, Edinburgh, 1966
[7] T. S. Eliot, *The Four Quartets*.

all that is greater that itself. Worship is a movement inward, into the soul of all that is God, for not only does it describe our 'seeking' for God, but also that movement of life, of God, which draws us up and out of ourselves – the movement that seeks us as the Father seeks the worshippers: 'But the hour cometh, and now is when the true worshippers shall worship the Father in spirit and truth: for such doth the Father seek to be his worshippers' (Jn 4:23ff).

Experiences of birth, joining in marriage, and partings in death are times of crisis and change which touch the bed-rock of individual existence. At these times particularly, people are made aware of that which is greater than themselves. Suffering, fear of loss, fear of the unknown; moments of wonder, delight, moving out from the self into a sense of the greater than self. All are experiences of worship, experiences which are emotionally stirring. An act of worship, an outward ritual, takes up this sense of the 'greater than self' and objectifies the sense of value and meaning for the individual beyond the transitory moment. The act of worship also gives to the worshippers a greater sense of value in themselves.

Many of the people met with in pastoral care will have had the sense of their own value in themselves undermined in one way or another. Pastoral care is concerned with helping people to 'develop their own muscles', live more autonomously, take more responsibility for their own lives. Moses before the burning bush (Ex 3:1ff) and Isaiah 'In the year of King Uzziah's death' (Is 6:1ff) are Biblical types caught up in an act of worship at a time of crisis and desolation. Each shows both the individual moving out of himself into an experience of the holy, and the way in which the experience enlarges the individual's experience of the transcendent: of the Name of God. Both also gain a new sense of value in themselves: an enlargement of their own names, their personal value and ability (Ex 4:21; Is 6:7ff).

The fact that we discover something more of our own identity through an experience and act of worship is clear not only from the Bible but also from the perspective of human growth and development.

The experience of that which is greater than ourselves, of the transcendent, is an experience of going out from the self, of seeking that which is greater than the self – is an experience of worship, an experience of the Holy. The sociologist, Berger, describes the mother's acts towards her child as 'rumours of angels', as 'acts of transcendence'. Holding and comforting the crying infant the mother is saying 'all is well, and all will be well' in an ordering gesture which is either profoundly untrue, or yet more profoundly pointing to the transcendent – the sense of the 'everlasting arms'.[8]

Experiences of worship and of the holy link back to the experience of birth and an emerging sense of self-hood. At first infants are wrapped up and contained in an inner world of unselfconsciousness. Reaching out and seeking satisfaction for their most fundamental needs, infants are met by the 'mother' who 'seeks out' the child and brings something of the satisfaction it requires. For Winnicott, the 'paradox of infant-mother relationship' lay in that 'the environment (mother) makes the becoming self of the infant feasible'. He pointed out that a mother cherishes, enjoys and creates her baby.[9]

Mother brings to the infant the outside world, a separateness, and so the beginnings of selfconsciousness. A separation of I-myself-mother begins that growth of self-awareness, the process of individuation by which the personality is formed. From a self-absorbed inner world, an undifferentiated 'Garden of Eden', the infant becomes aware of objects 'outside'. Winnicott describes this early state as 'unintegration'.[10] He describes three processes: integration; personalization; and following these, the appreciation of time and space and other properties of reality – in short, realization. The child builds up a world of inner reality, which sufficiently corresponds to the outside world to make interpersonal life possible. Experiences of crisis for the child lead to times of regression. This regression is a moving back into an earlier sense of dependence on the

[8] Berger.
[9] D. W. Winnicott, *Through Paediatrics to Psycho-Analysis.*, Introduction xxxvii. Edited by M. Masud, R. Khan. The International Psycho-Analytical Library. (The Hogarth Press and Institute of Psycho-analysis [1978])
[10] Ibid, p., 149.

(M)other – the greater than the self – before moving forward again into a greater sense of self-awareness. These movements into dependence upon the other will, in later life, be properly described as experiences of worship and will lead towards the same increased sense of self-hood. We lose ourselves in mother and in God in order that we may find ourselves more fully. In order to love God it is essential that we know ourselves, yet to know the self I must also let myself go into that sense of the greater than self; in this experience I can find and love myself, my neighbour and my God. Worship is the royal road by which we may be lead into self-awareness, and so on to self-forgetfulness since what is expected is that I shall know and accept the self known and accepted by God. Now there is freedom to love the neighbour as the self is loved (Mk 12:33).

Until a person can accept him or her self there is no possibility of denying the self (Mk 8:34ff) since that which is not known cannot be given up. It is the unknown aspects of the self that are put onto those around us whether for envy or blame, since we tend to desire in others that which is potential but not yet realized in ourselves, and to condemn in others those aspects of the self which are perceived as negative or bad. These latter are seen as belonging to others and condemned in them. The need for the injunction 'judge not that you are not judged' (Mt 7:1) comes from this mechanism of projection which everyone uses. Worship should and can be a way to discover, know and own the self in a way that helps relationships with others to be unselfconscious and responsible.

For the child, the mother's dependable presence is a necessity for good growth. The development of meaning requires consistently repeated experiences so that the outer world happening can make sense in the inner world experience. General concepts are formed through the repetition of particular experience.[11]

The need for continuity, by which we establish meaning, underlines the need for continuity of worship in which we can see ourselves reaching out and seeking and being met by God. Hosea describes this Mothering God – God bending over Israel

[11] Ibid, introduction xli.

and saying 'When Israel was a child I loved him . . . I took him to my breast . . . I led him in leading reins,' (Hos 11:1ff).

Here is a picture of God, the Mother, desiring to hold the child Israel, to form and lead it into becoming the chosen people. Winnicott [12] expresses this thought for the human infant which, he says, 'cannot start to 'be' except under certain conditions . . . the inherited potential of an infant cannot become an infant unless linked to maternal care'. Winnicott's concept for the mother's provision at this stage of infant care is holding. Worship is the experience of being held by that which is greater than ourselves, which we call God.

As Winnicott recognizes three stages of dependence in the holding phase, we may recognize three stages in worship. First, Winnicott describes the stage of absolute dependence, in which the infant has no means of knowing about the maternal care but is simply held by it, gaining profit or suffering disturbance. So mankind is held in the prevenient grace of God, at times experiencing that holding as 'good' and sometimes as 'ill'. As Isaiah puts it:

> 'For the sake of Jacob my servant
> and Israel my chosen
> I have called you by name
> and given you your title, though
> you have not known me.
> I am the Lord, there is no other;
> there is no god beside me.
> I will strengthen you though you
> have not known me,
> so that men from the rising and the
> setting sun
> may know that there is none
> but I:
> I am the Lord, there is no other;
> I make the light, I create darkness,
> author alike of prosperity and
> trouble.
> I, the Lord, do all these things.'   (Is 44:4-7)

Winnicott's second stage is that of relative dependence

---

[12] Ibid, introduction xxxviii.

where the infant can become aware of the need for the details of maternal care, and can to a growing extent relate them to personal impulse. It is this stage which is seen to lead to the possibility of relating to the analyst as parent in psychoanalytic treatment. It is this 'transference' which can then be used to help the client to a new and better understanding of themselves. Similarly, in worship, dependence on a sense of God may be mainly comprised of the earlier experiencing of parents, which can be reinterpreted and revalued through the understanding of the worshiping community of God. Whether this reinterpretation will help in maturity or prove to be dysfunctional will depend on the institutionalized ideas of the worshiping community itself. Bruce Reed in his *Dynamics of Religion* usefully expands this notion of functional and dysfunctional religion.[13] It is into this stage of relative dependence that the pastoral carer can help the person to move in worship.

In the third stage, the infant develops means for doing without actual care. Memories of care build up self confidence. The experience of care becomes internalized, and a greater confidence develops in the environment.[14] With this there are all the implications of intellectual understanding. It is possible to see here the practice of the presence of God, the experience of the 'Peace of Christ ruling in the heart' (Phil 4:7).

Acts of worship are the movements by which we link the world outside and the inner world. At times when life seems to overwhelm, at moments of great suffering and loss, there is the possibility of entering into worship where suffering and loss are symbolized in bread and wine, yet where the symbols, and all that they stand for, carry the person beyond impotence and hopelessness to a new confidence and sense of resurrection. From this act of worship comes the ability to go out into the world with new strength and courage. The need to offer the self in worship for renewal is brought out by St Paul when he encourages the Romans to 'go on offering yourselves to God for the renewing of your minds . . . think your way through to a

13 Bruce Reed, *The Dynamics of Religion*. (Darton, Longman and Todd, London [1978])
14 Winnicott, op. cit., p. 129.

sober estimate of yourselves' (Rom 12:1ff).

We must always be discovering and re-discovering the way in which the world around us fits and makes sense for ourselves and of ourselves. Winnicott writes of a 'limiting membrane',[15] through which the experiences of our outer world are filtered before they are linked to our 'inner world'. This membrane is the world of symbols stored in our imagination. John Beer[16] defines imagination as 'a creative act of perception which attempts seriously to impose some form of unity upon things in the world'. He quotes Coleridge, for whom imagination brought 'the whole soul of man into activity, with the subordination of its faculties to each other, according to their relative worth and dignity'. A reminder, here, of Jimmie R.

Imagination is seen as 'that by which we interpret sense experience, in accordance with the ordinary presuppositions we need and use in everyday life'. It is that faculty by which we give particular significance to things in the world. Here is that 'limiting membrane' through which we may pass the experience of the world around us in our worship: 'imagination defined . . . as creative, perceptive, 'spiritual', searching with that inner eye for reality as it is intuited to be'. Beer has a cautionary word for the pastoral carer when he says that if we fail to show much imagination in the sense of 'recognizing continuities in language, tradition and experience; that innate capacity for sensing what is going on, when people who are essentially different attempt to communicate with and understand one another; that willingness to invest time and emotion in the process of 'hearing' what another human being is trying to say', then we might quite literally misunderstand, and fail them.'

The great need is for the symbols of our imaginative world to be fitting, lively, resonant with both the outer reality and our own inner needs. Beer quotes Nineham: 'Men find it hard to believe in God because they do not have available to them any lively imaginative picture of the way a god, and the world as they know it, are related. What they need most is a story, a

---

[15] Ibid, p 219ff.
[16] John Beer, 'Imagination in Christology', *Theology*, March 1985 (SCM Press).

picture, a myth, which will capture their imagination, while meshing in with the rest of their sensibility'.[17]

Through our inner representation we name and receive the outer experiences. Beginning with mother and all the meaning that grows up around her ordering gestures, our area of 'illusion' is used to negotiate the partially satisfying care we receive with the never completely satisfied inner needs. The symbols, or inner pictures we use, derive in part from the world outside, partly from phantasies of our own need; but in themselves they carry us beyond both, pointing always beyond themselves to a greater and more complete satisfaction which is 'full, perfect and sufficient'.[18]

These symbols, or 'transitional objects', provide the meeting place for worship: the place where the things that happen around us in the world, our sense of ourselves, our own inner needs, can meet in symbols which point to a reality and meaning beyond ourselves, the world around us, and even the very symbols themselves, for their function is always to be pointing to that which is greater and beyond. In this way worship brings us to the point at which our theologies, our doctrines, our faith concepts, our very use of the word God, in itself a symbol for God, are all handmaidens to the act of dependence in worship itself. Because of this we need to be constantly ready to enlarge and renew our symbolic and imaginative inner world since it is the provider of our personal tradition and identity. Here lies the great task for the pastoral carer, in enabling the growth of personality through worship.

Worship is that which contains and moulds the inarticulate human process. It is the way in which God, the holy, the altogether other than ourselves, is met in the everyday experiences of life, is met in the symbol 'Christ', the One who is made in all things like unto us (Heb 4:15) and yet in whom all thing hold together (Col 1:13ff), for He is the fullness of the Godhead bodily (Col 2:9).

As he describes normal development, Winnicott describes

---

[17] Ibid, quoting Dennis Nineham, 'Epilogue', in J. Hick (ed), *The Myth of God Incarnate* (SCM Press [1977]).

[18] *The Book of Common Prayer*, from the Prayer of Consecration.

our need for worship, for he sees development as a movement from our everyday work world into those times when we need to regress to dependence, so that 'gaining inner strength and poise we may progress to independence and so to working with others again in inter-dependence'.

All human beings act from time to time in ways which restore their sense of inhabiting a world of meanings rather than being objects at the mercy of other objects.

As pastoral carers we are given the possibility, responsibility and joy of being with people at difficult and dangerous, empty and meaningless, fruitful and enlarging moments of their lives and helping them to find expression of these times in a worship experience. This will mean that they 'come apart and rest awhile' (Mk 6:31) and value their experience, being valued in it themselves, so that with minds renewed they may go out with God's peace ruling in their hearts to be fellow workers with God (1 Cor 3:9) and one another in the world.

General Index

Index of Biblical Quotations

OLD TESTAMENT

NEW TESTAMENT